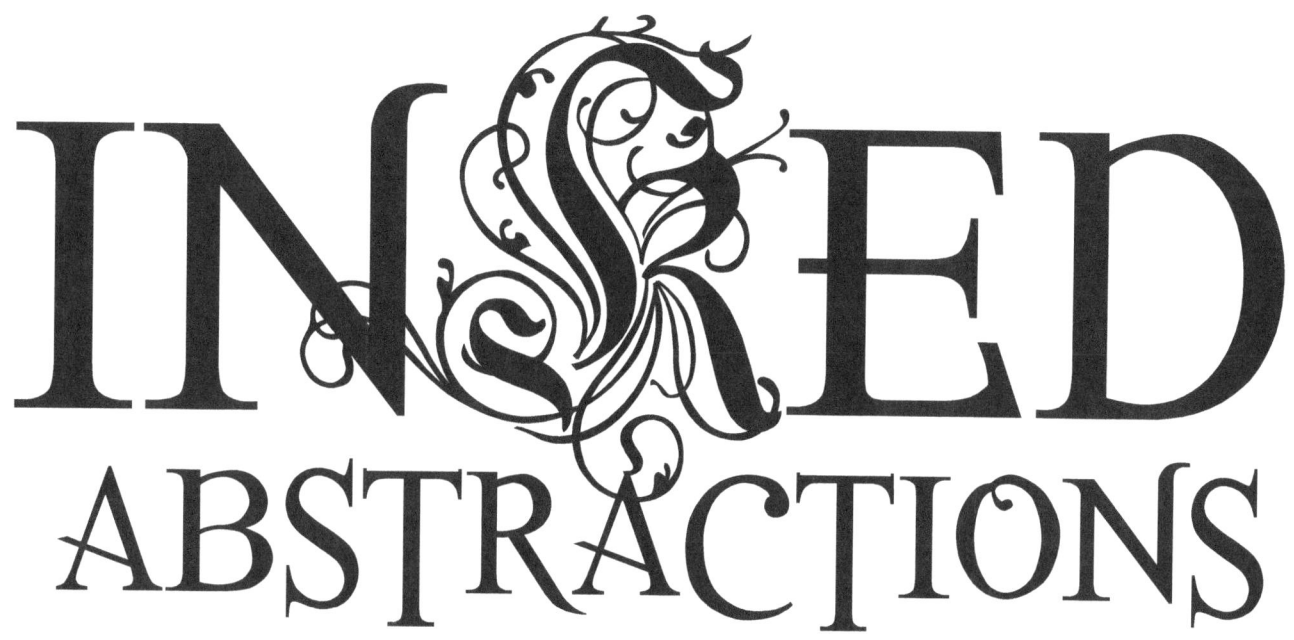

INTRODUCTION

This is a collection of my designs over the last few years. I hope you enjoy coloring them as much as I did designing them.

This book is dedicated to my clientele who have inspired me over the years.

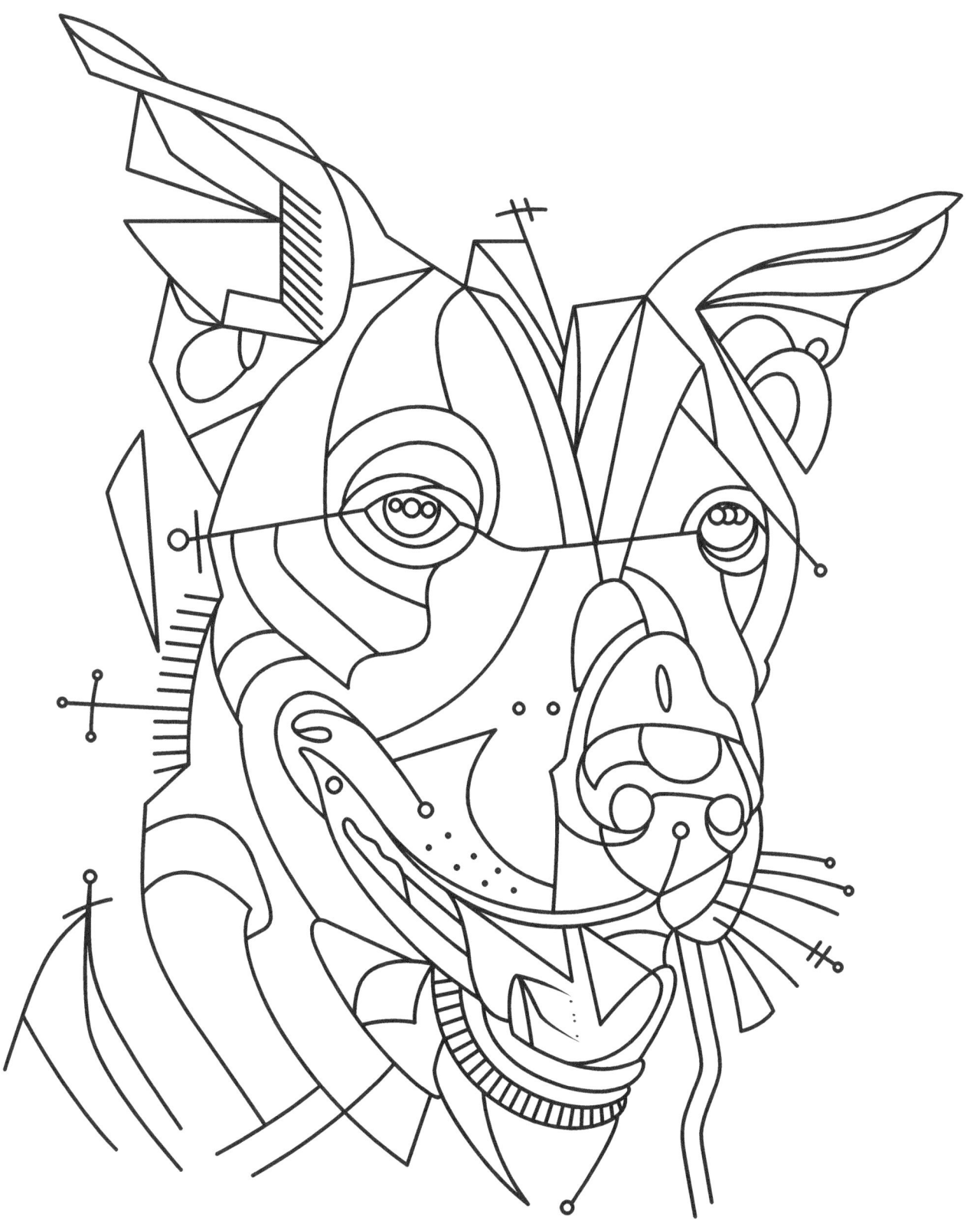

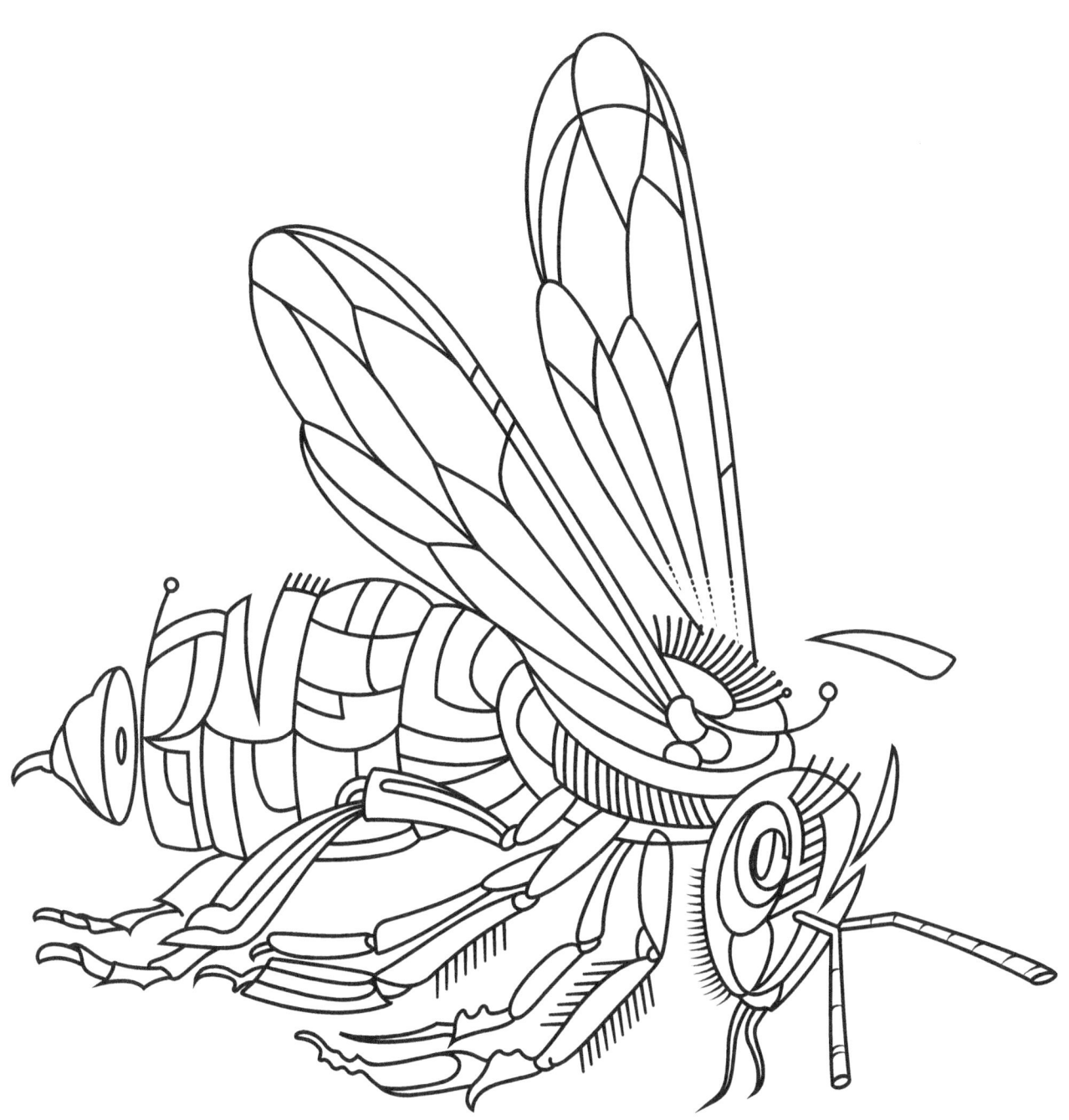

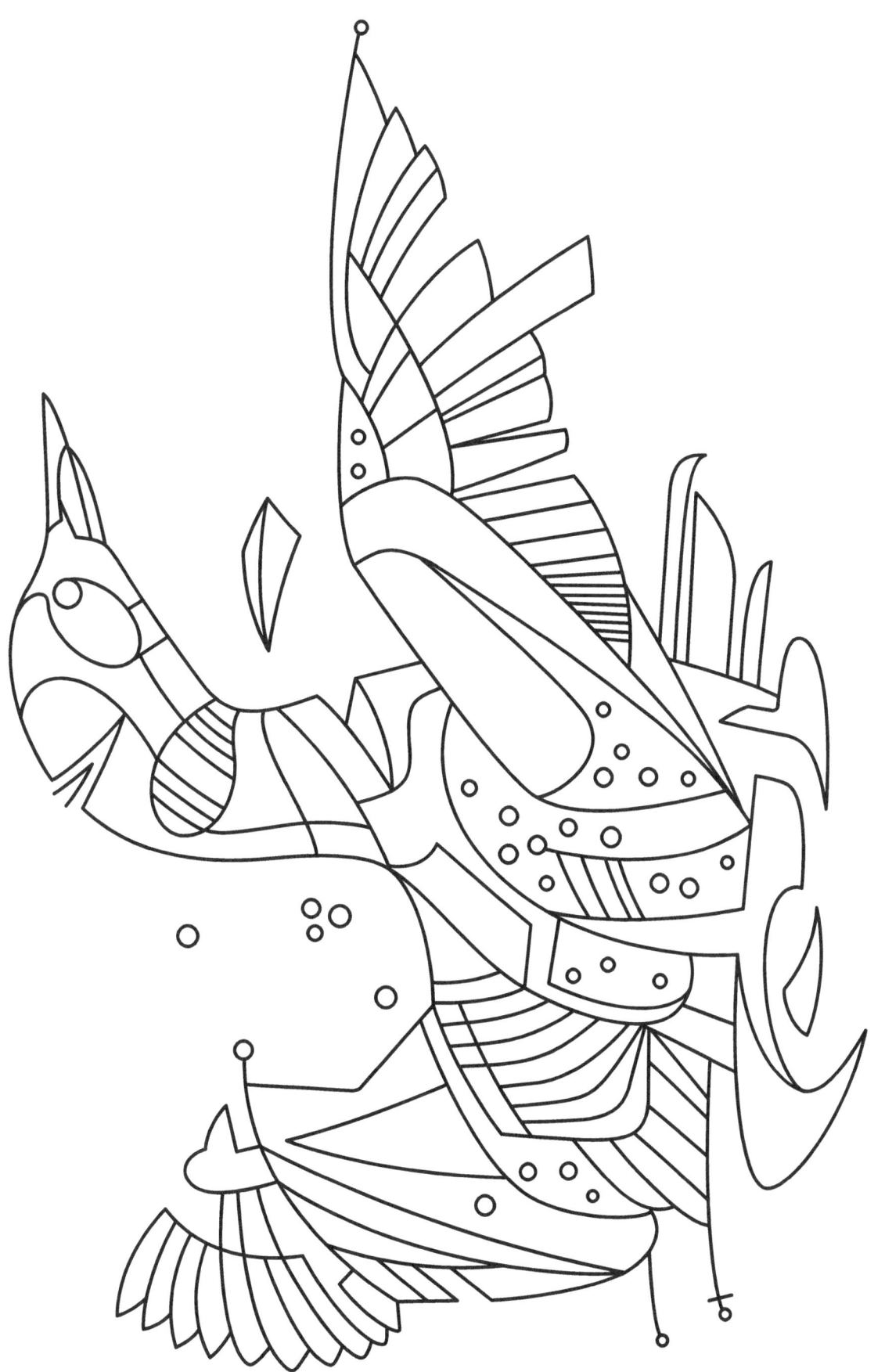

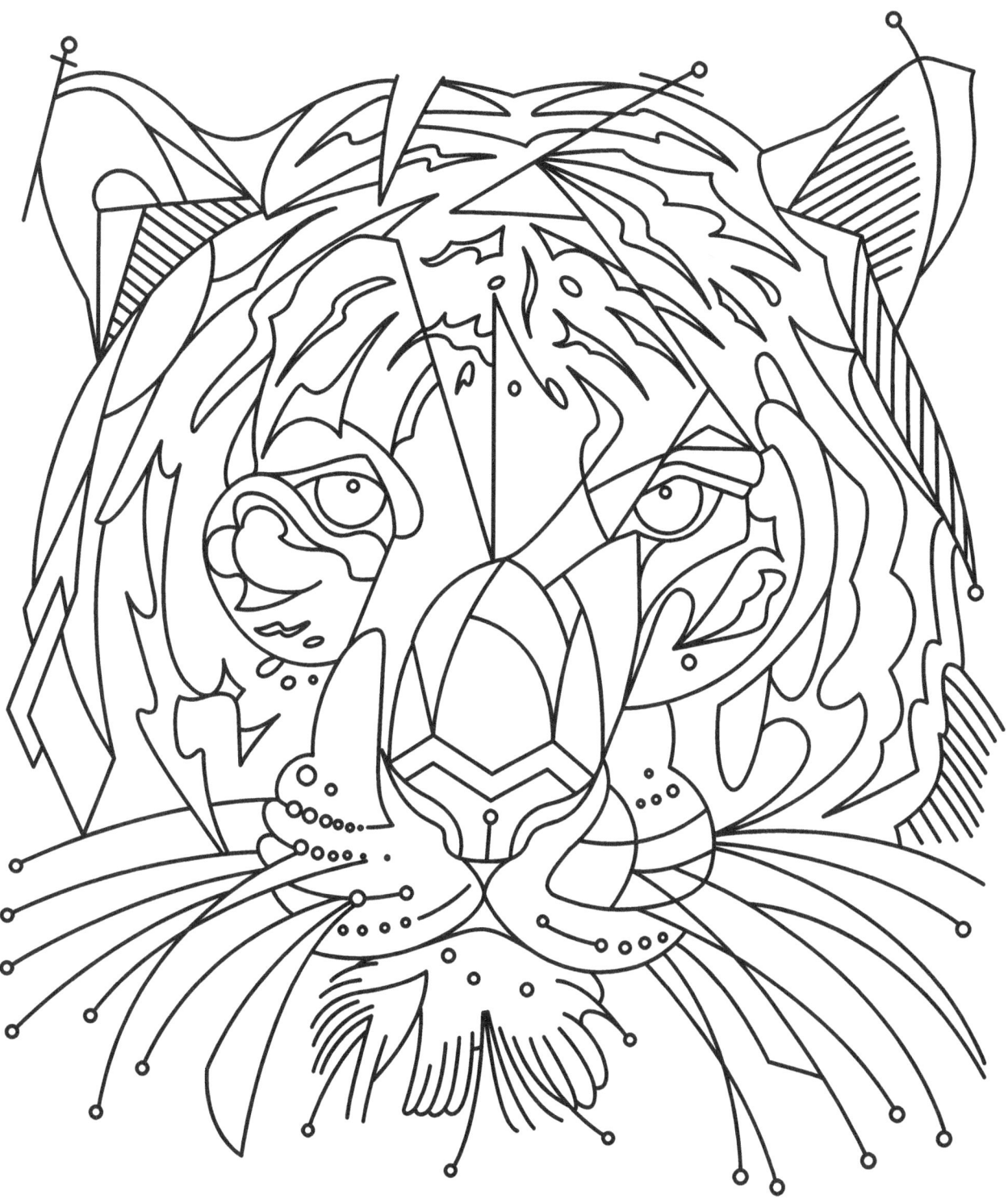

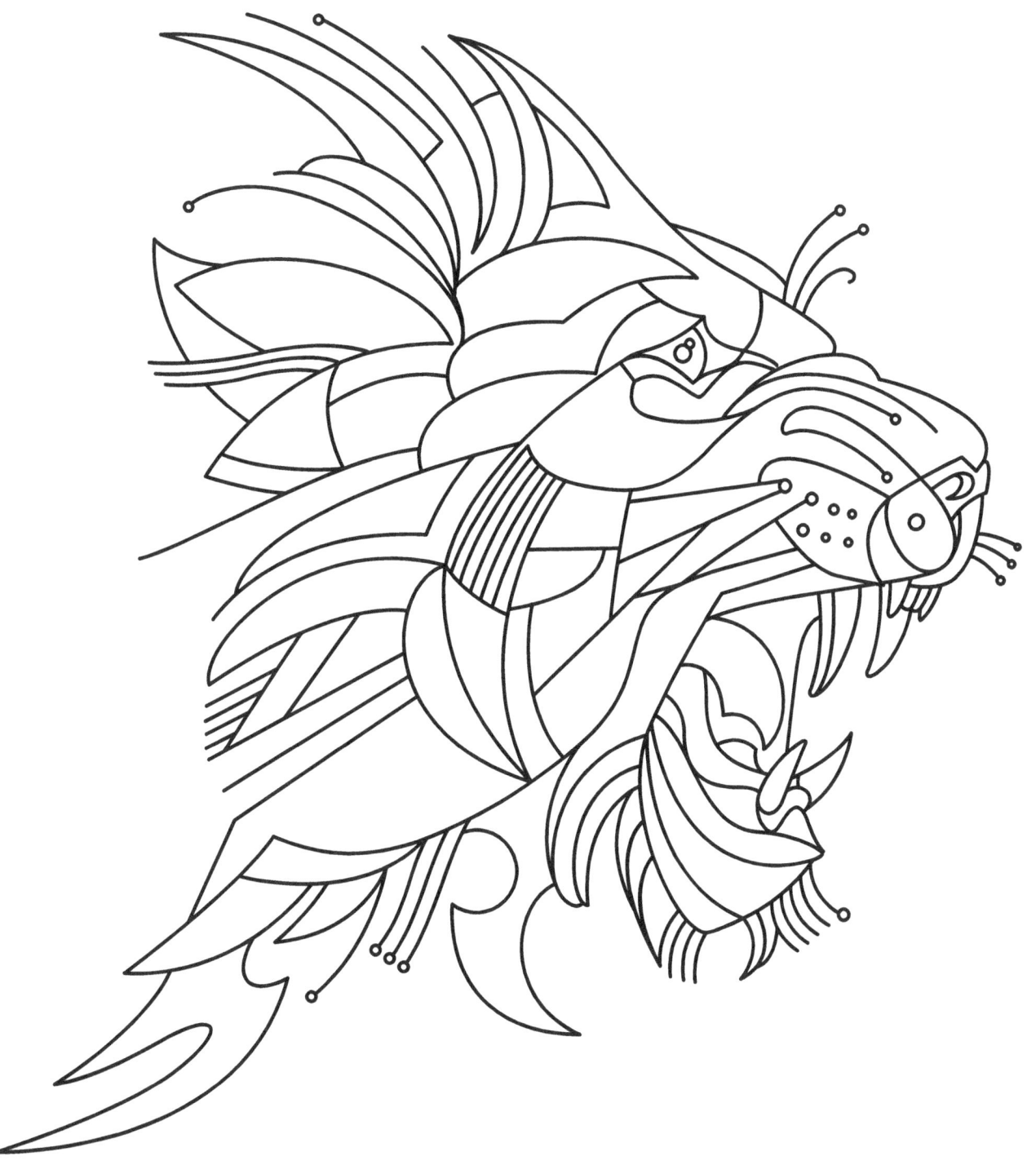

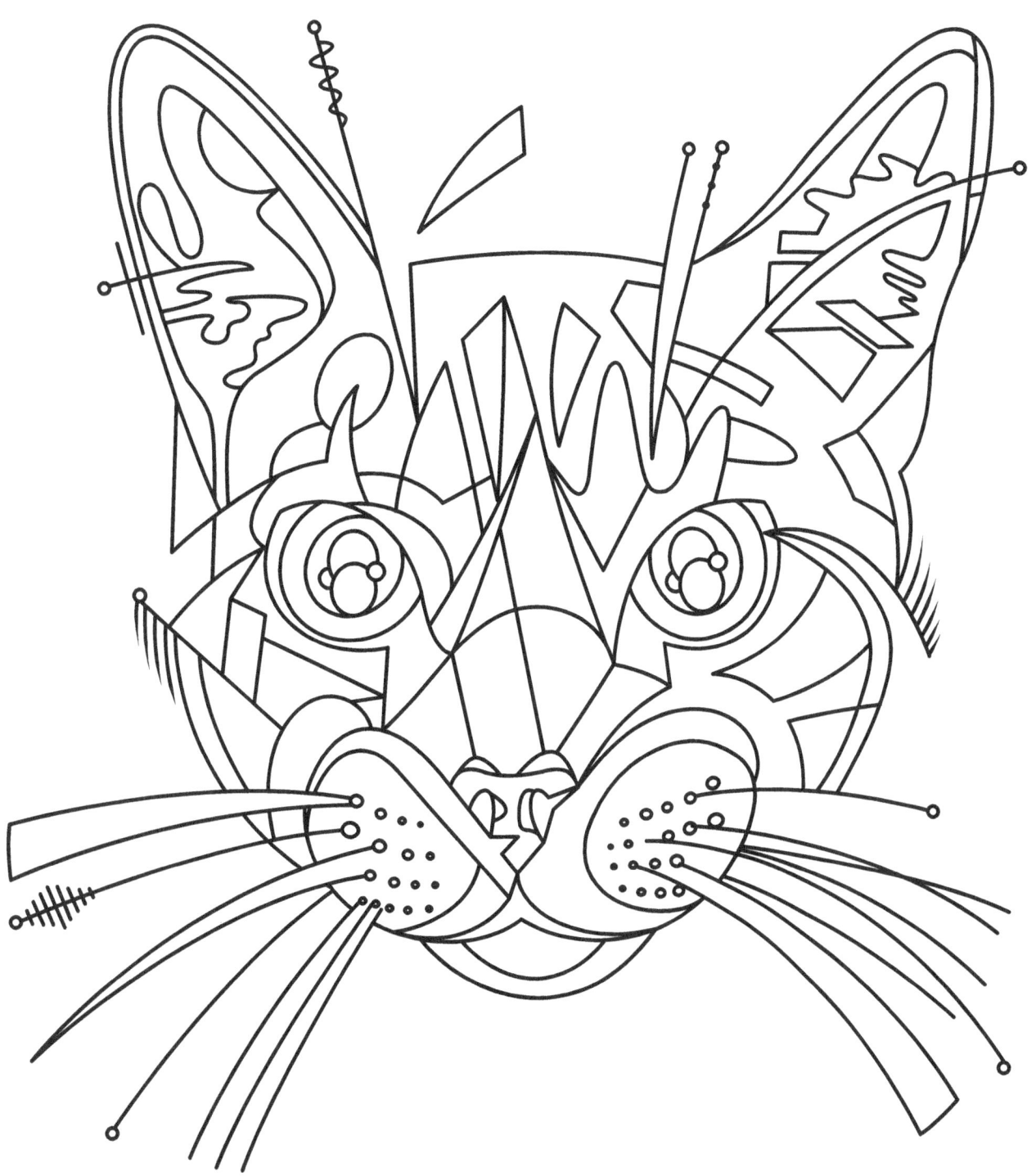

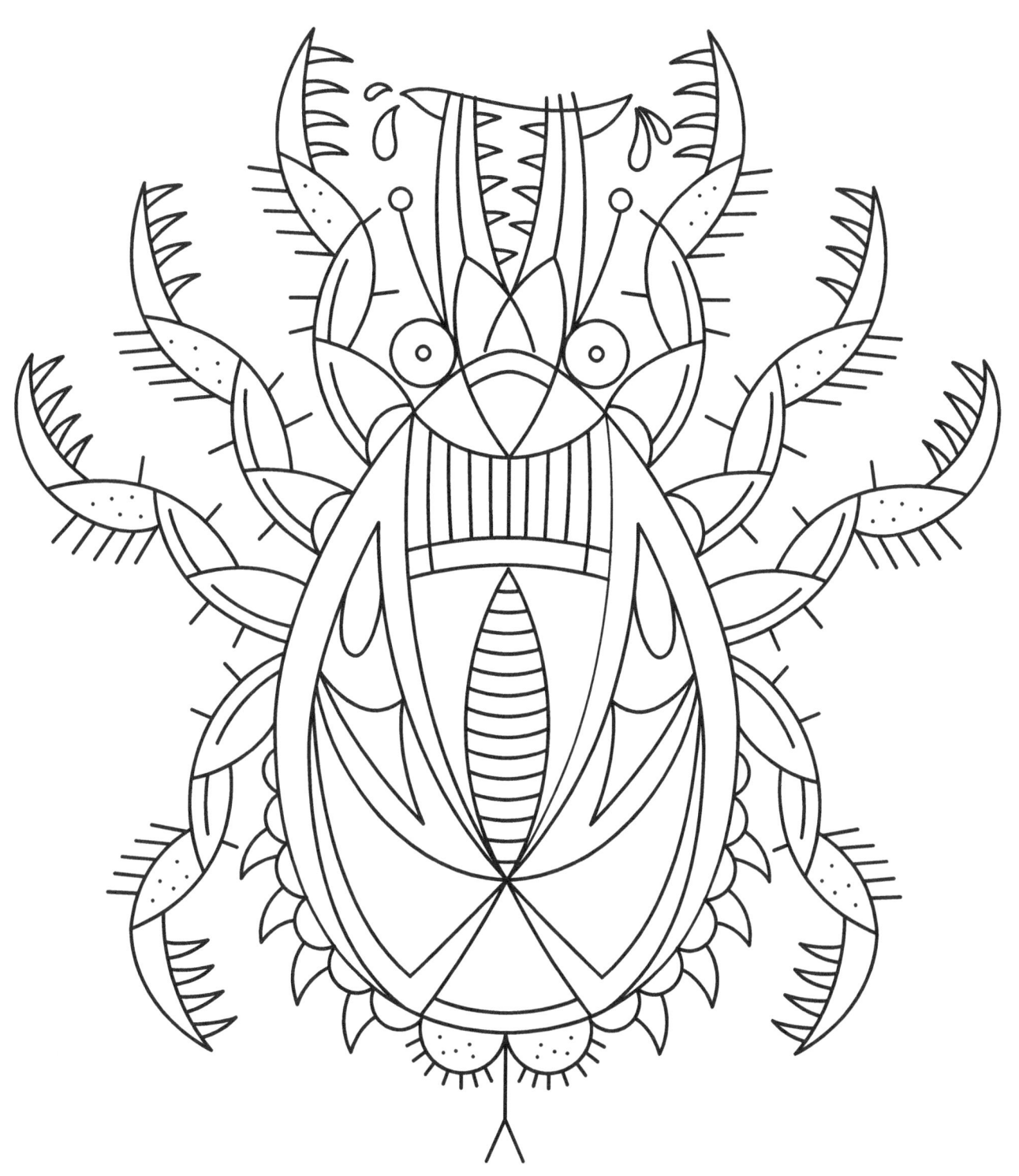

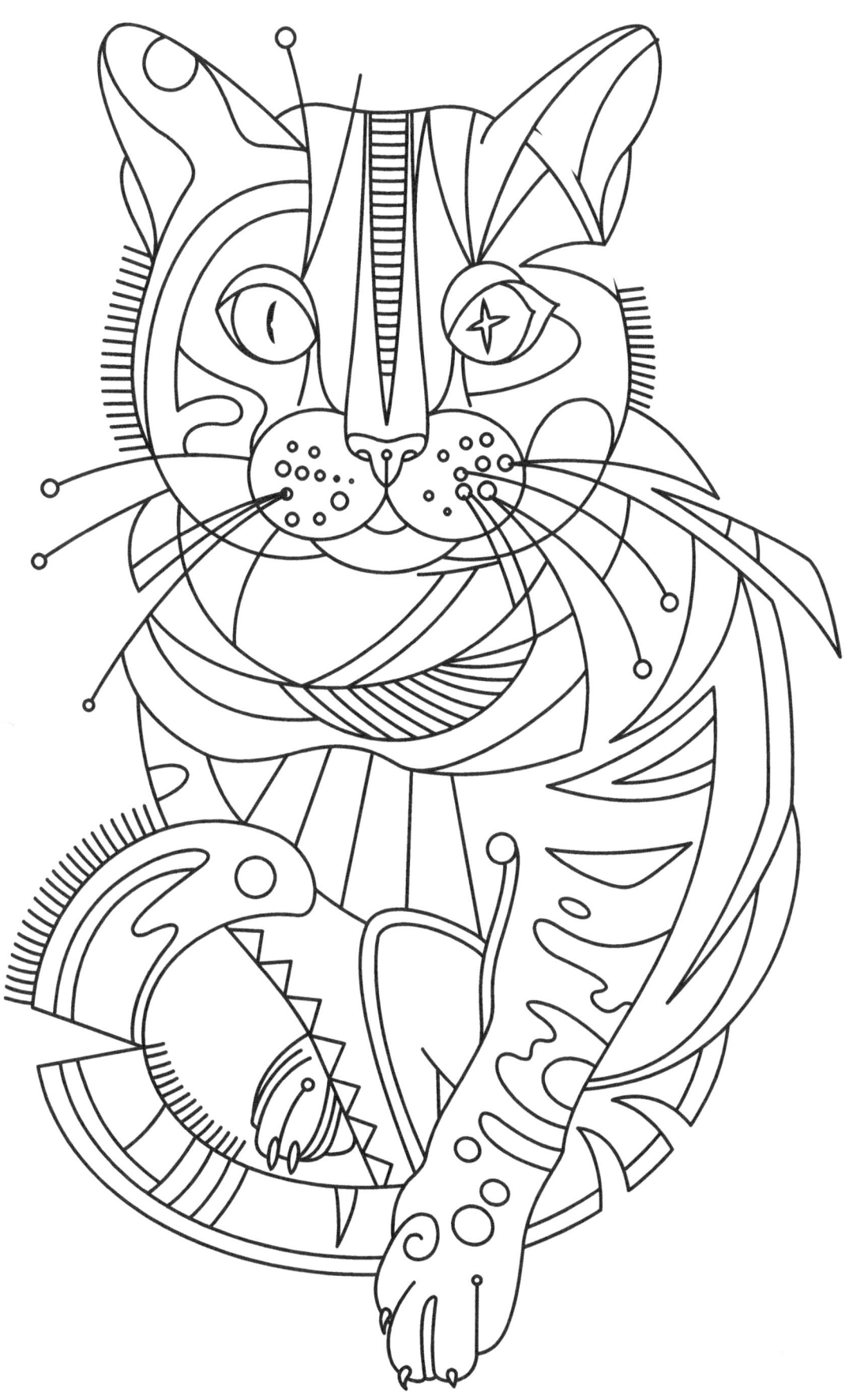

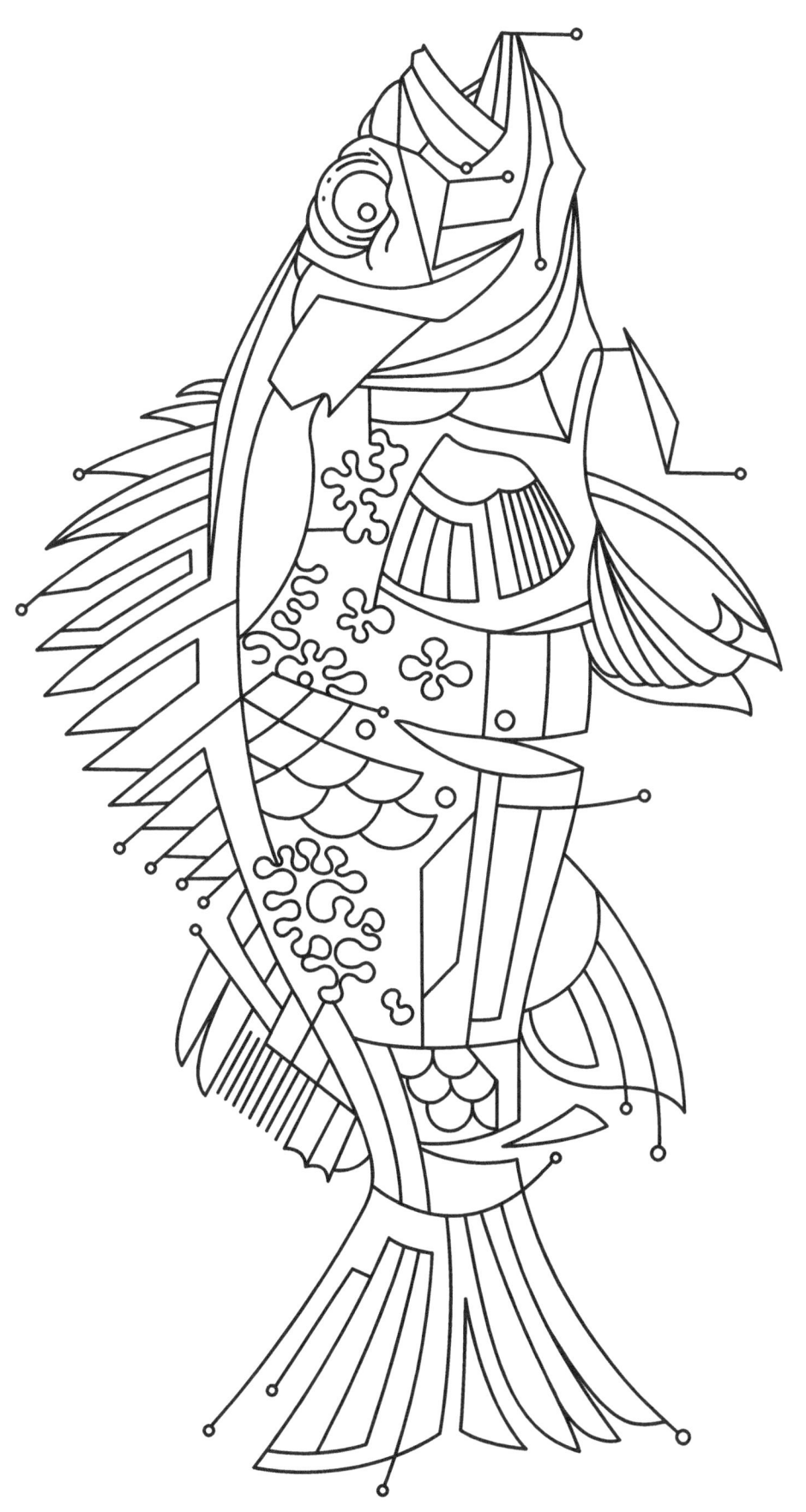

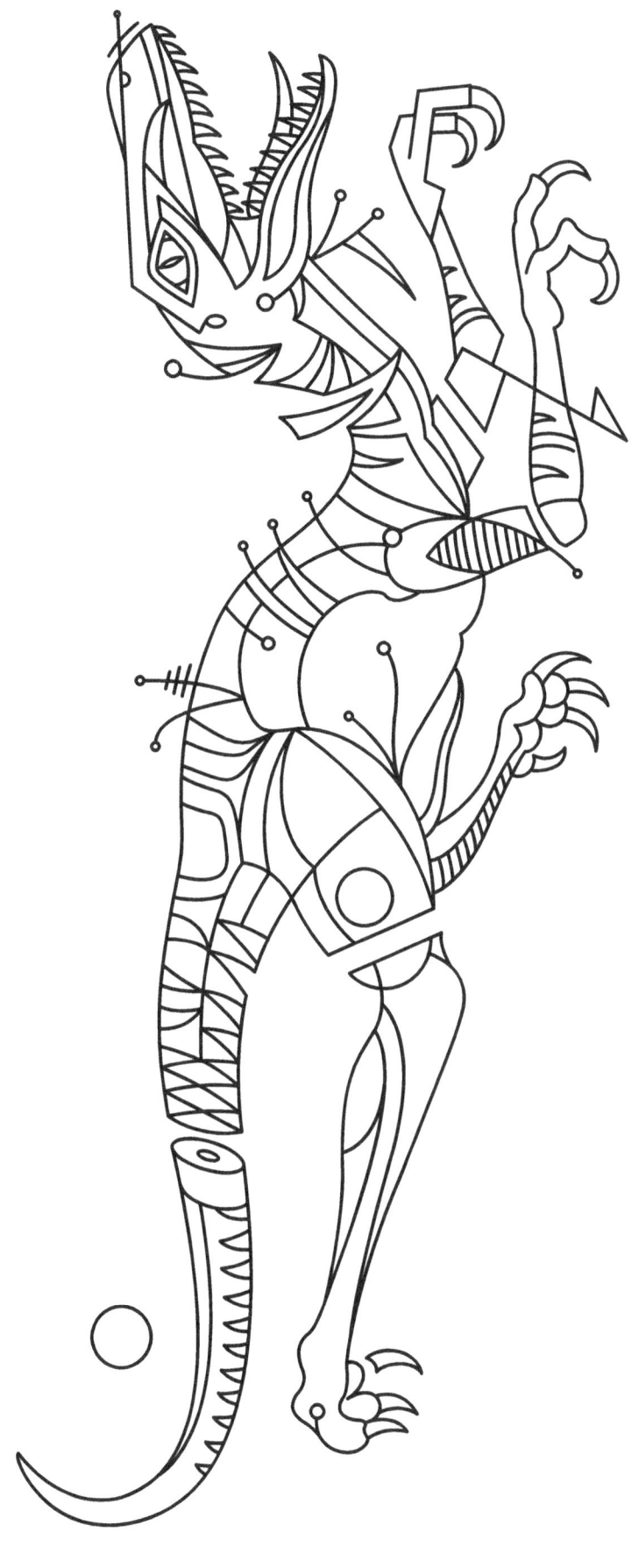

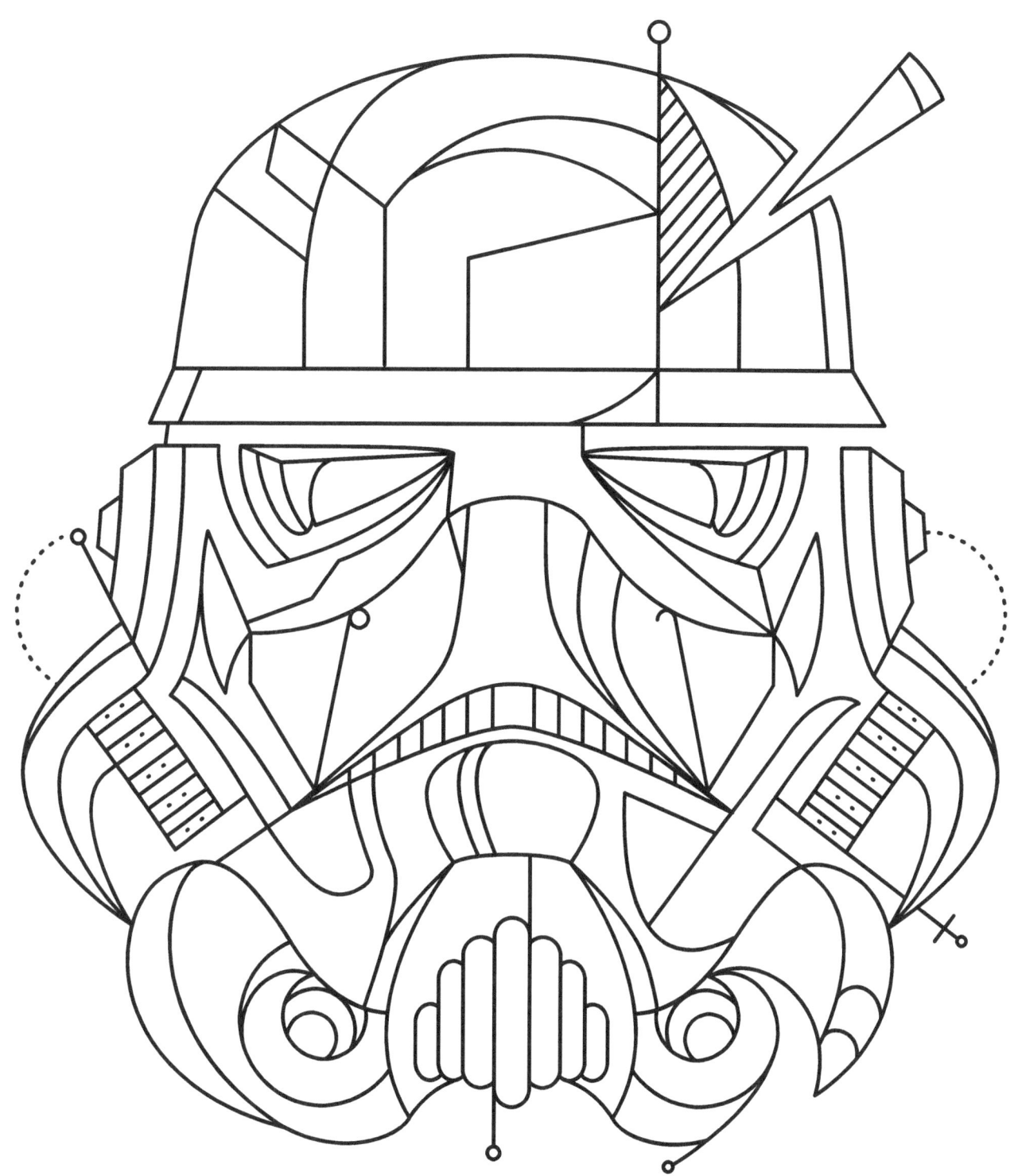

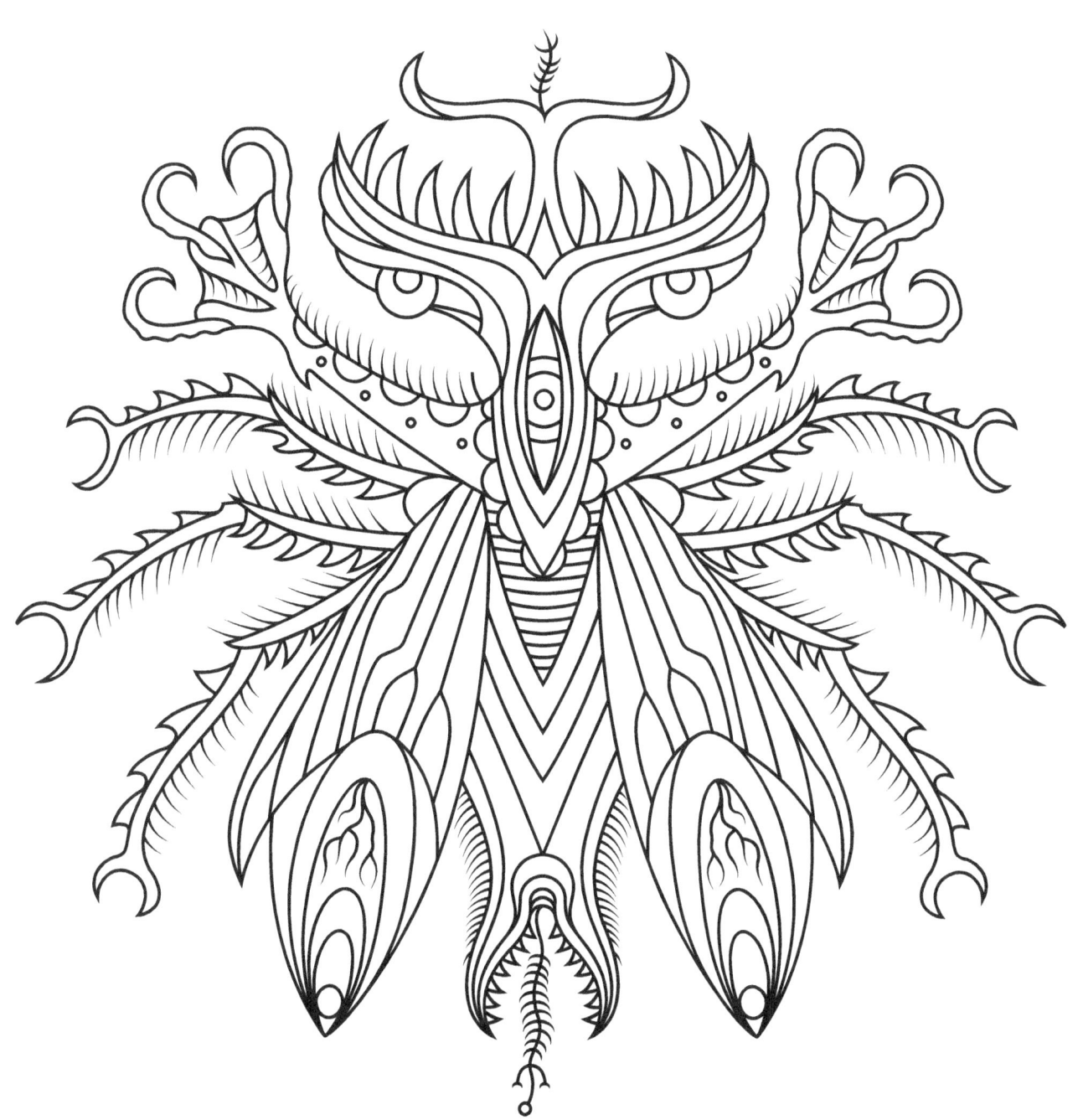

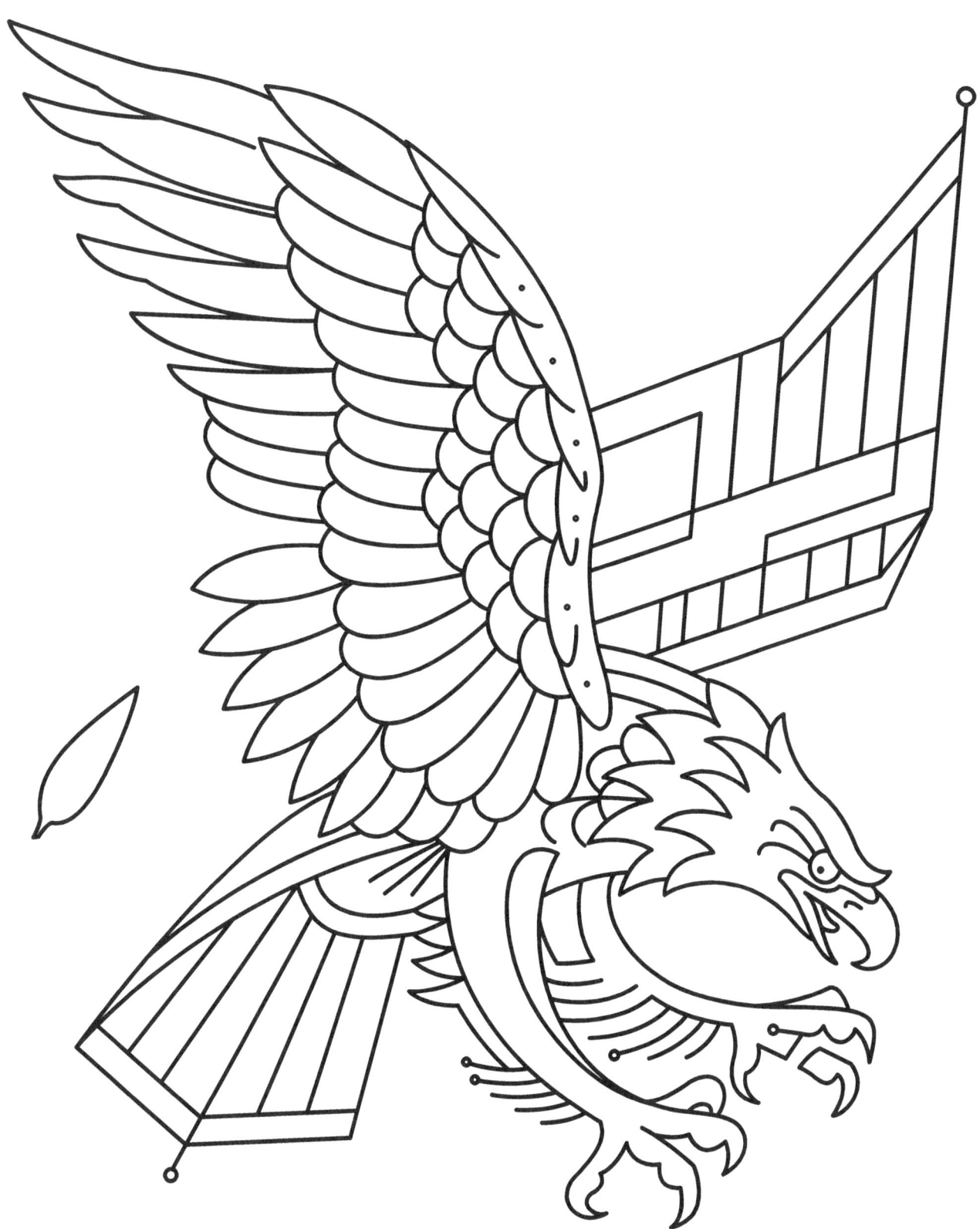

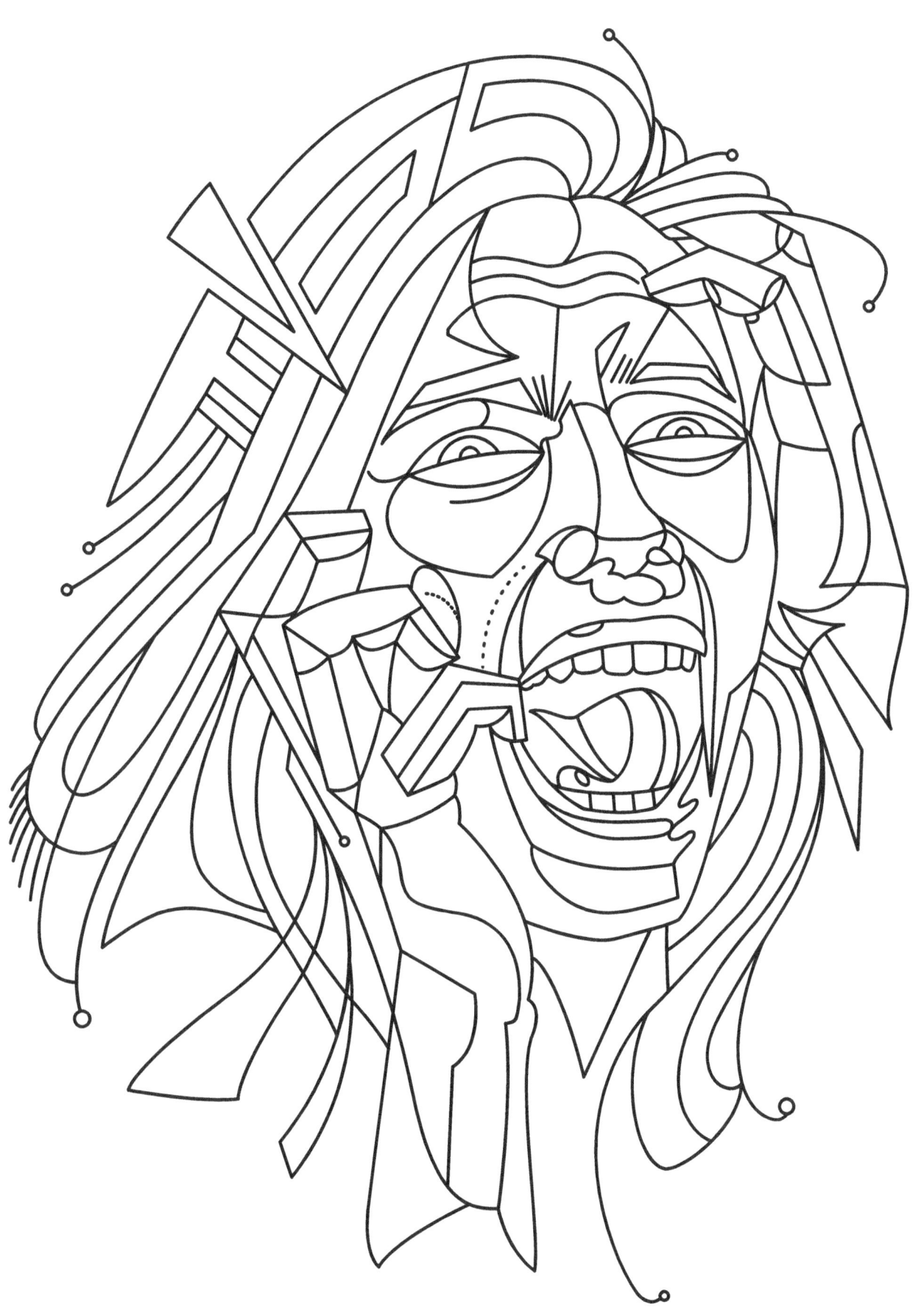

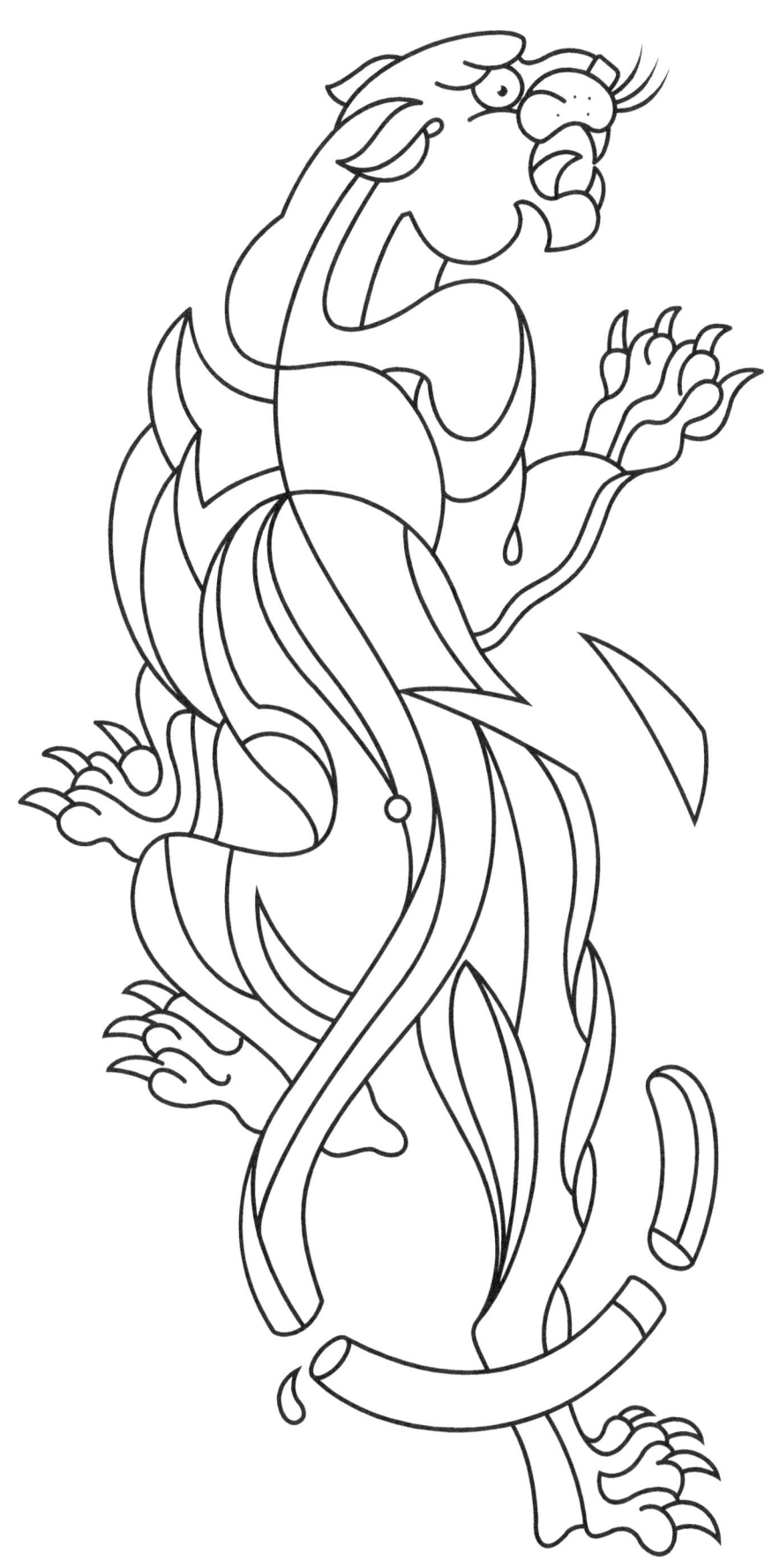

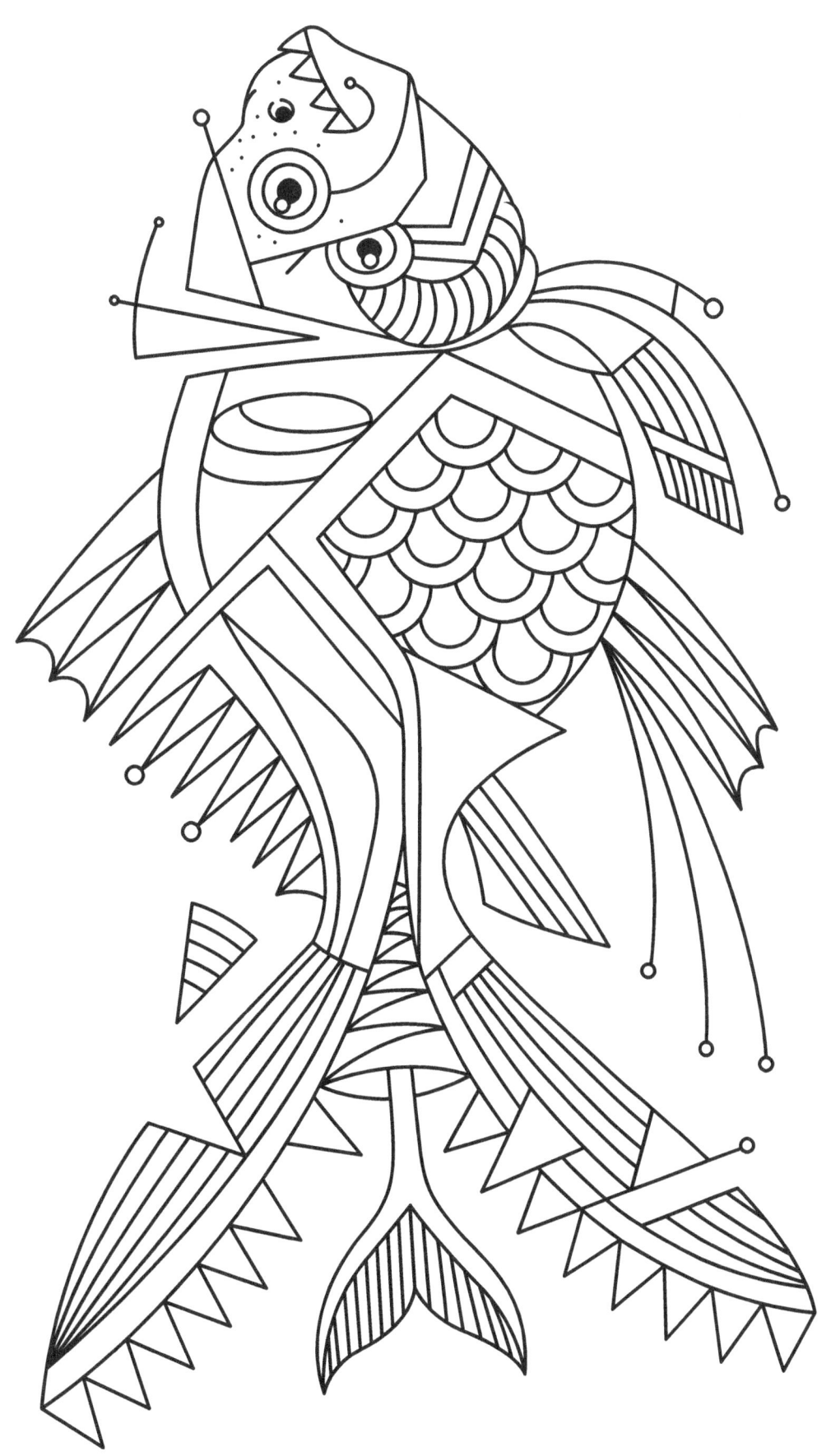

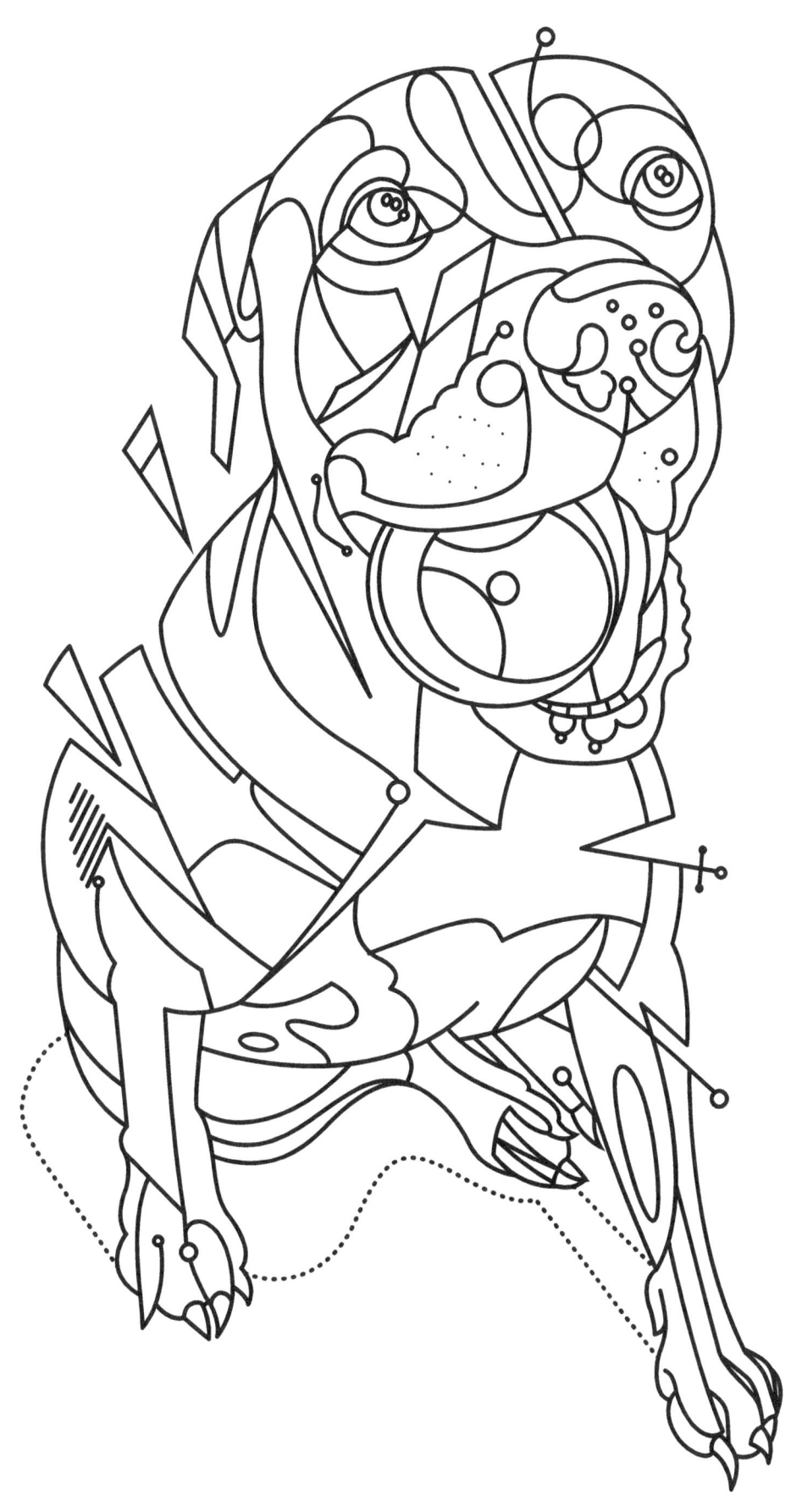

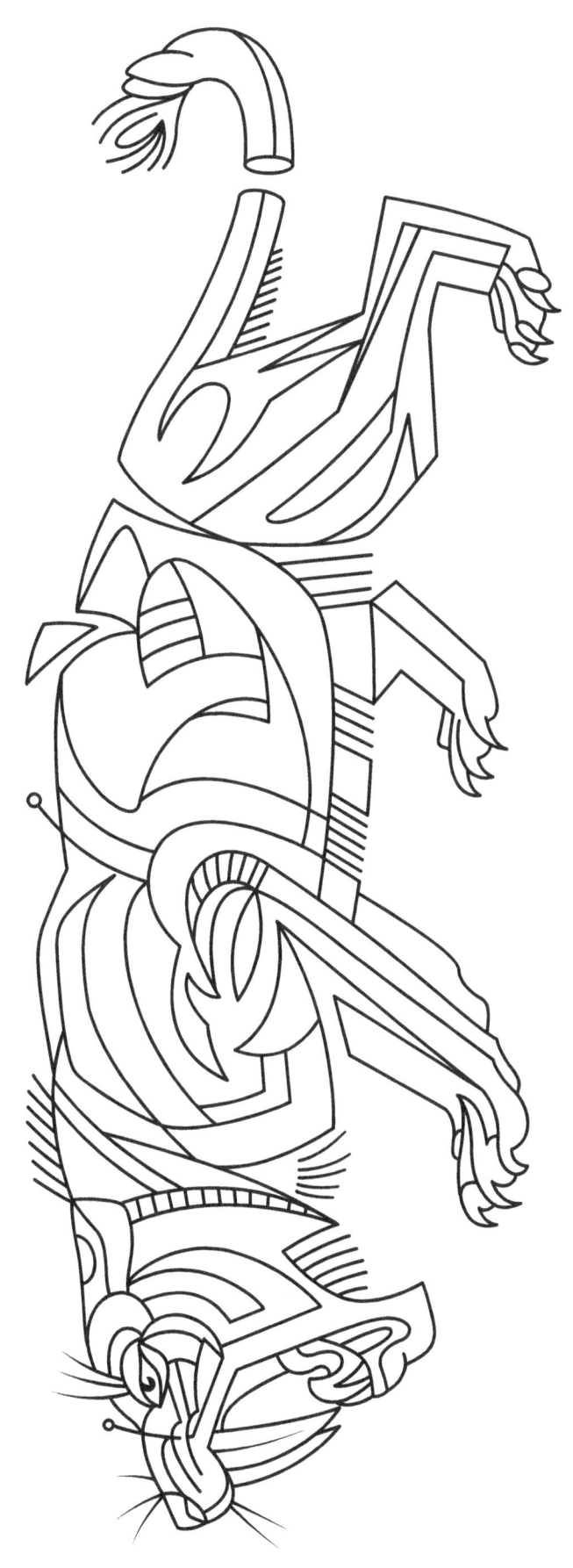

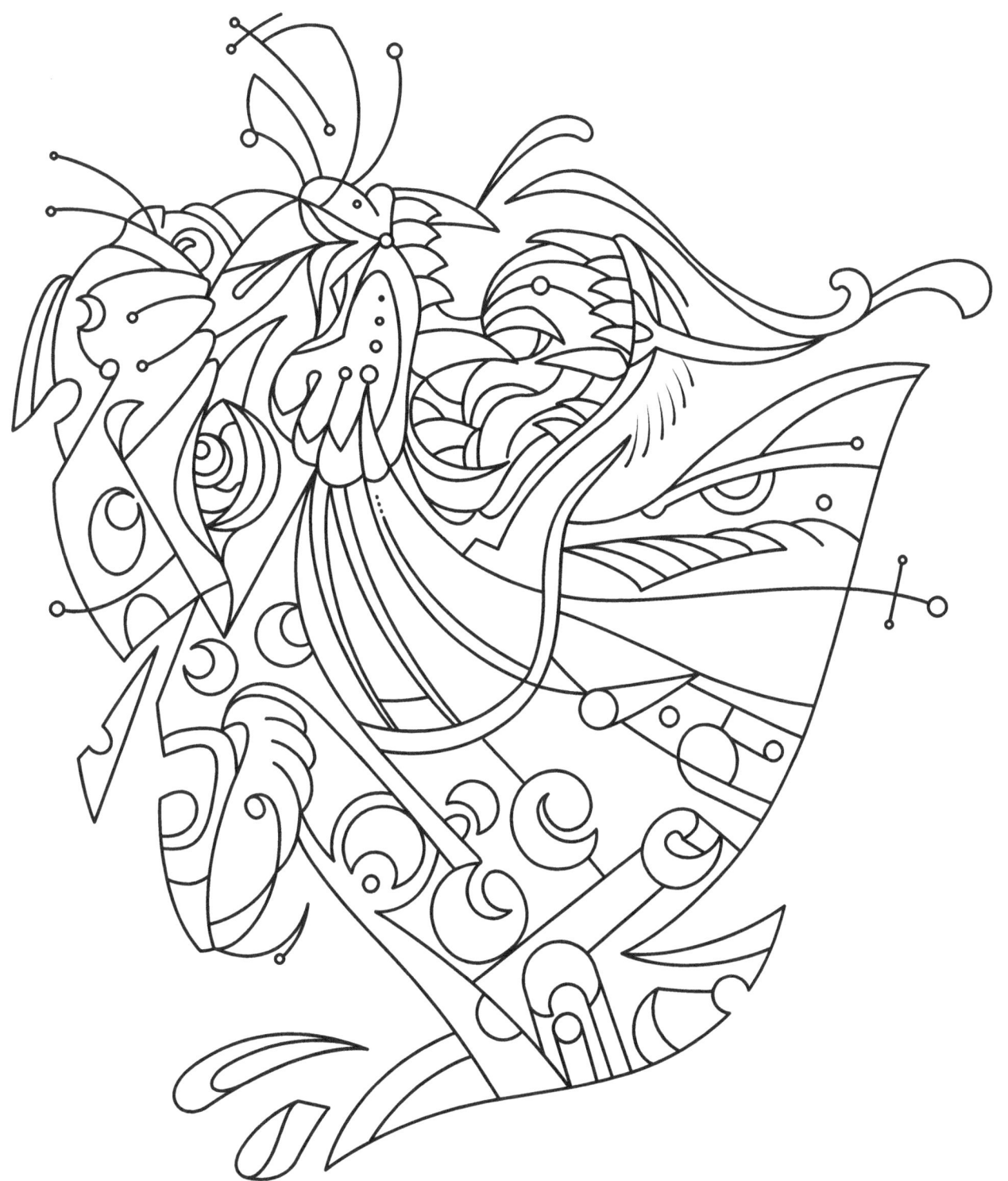

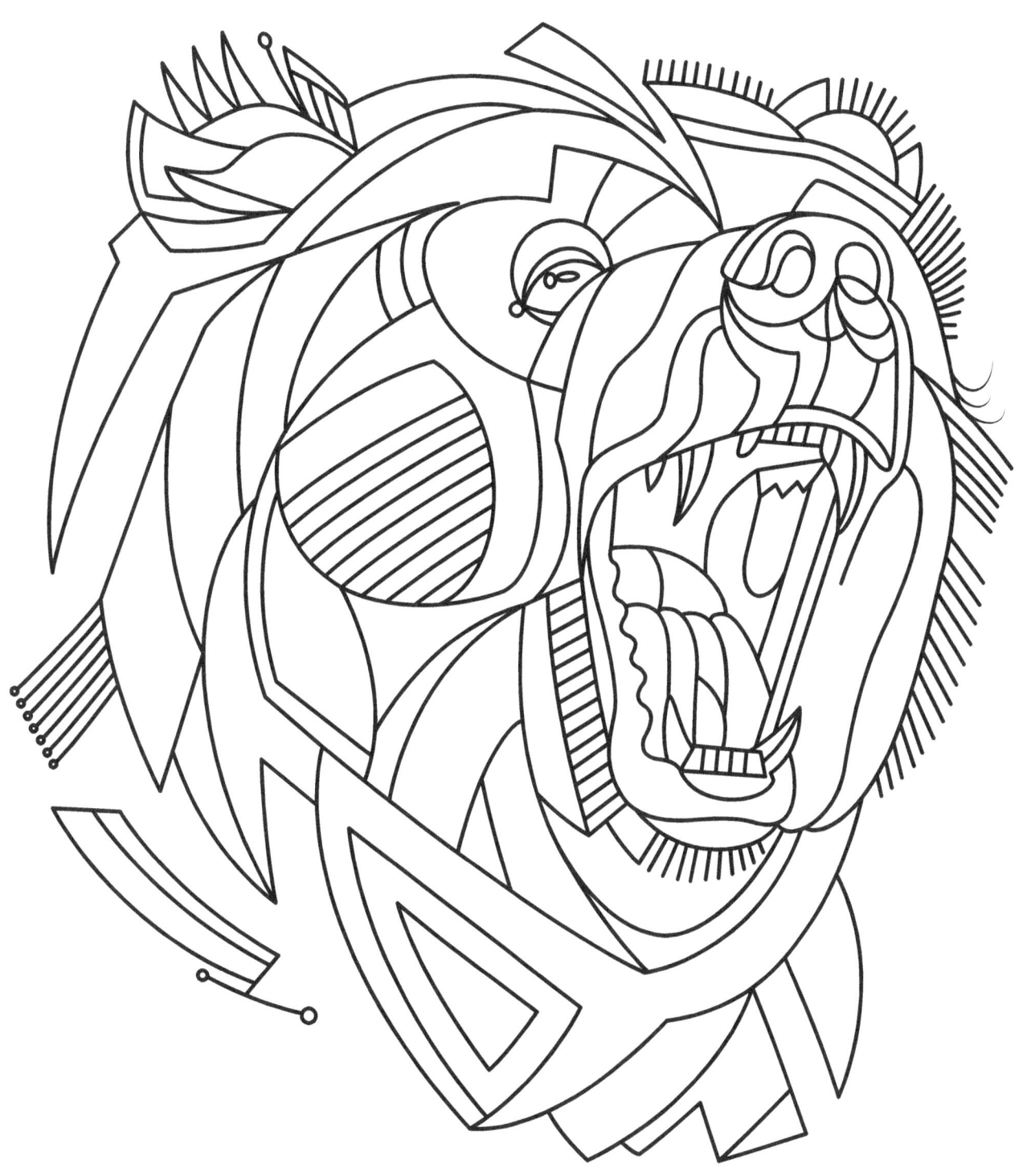

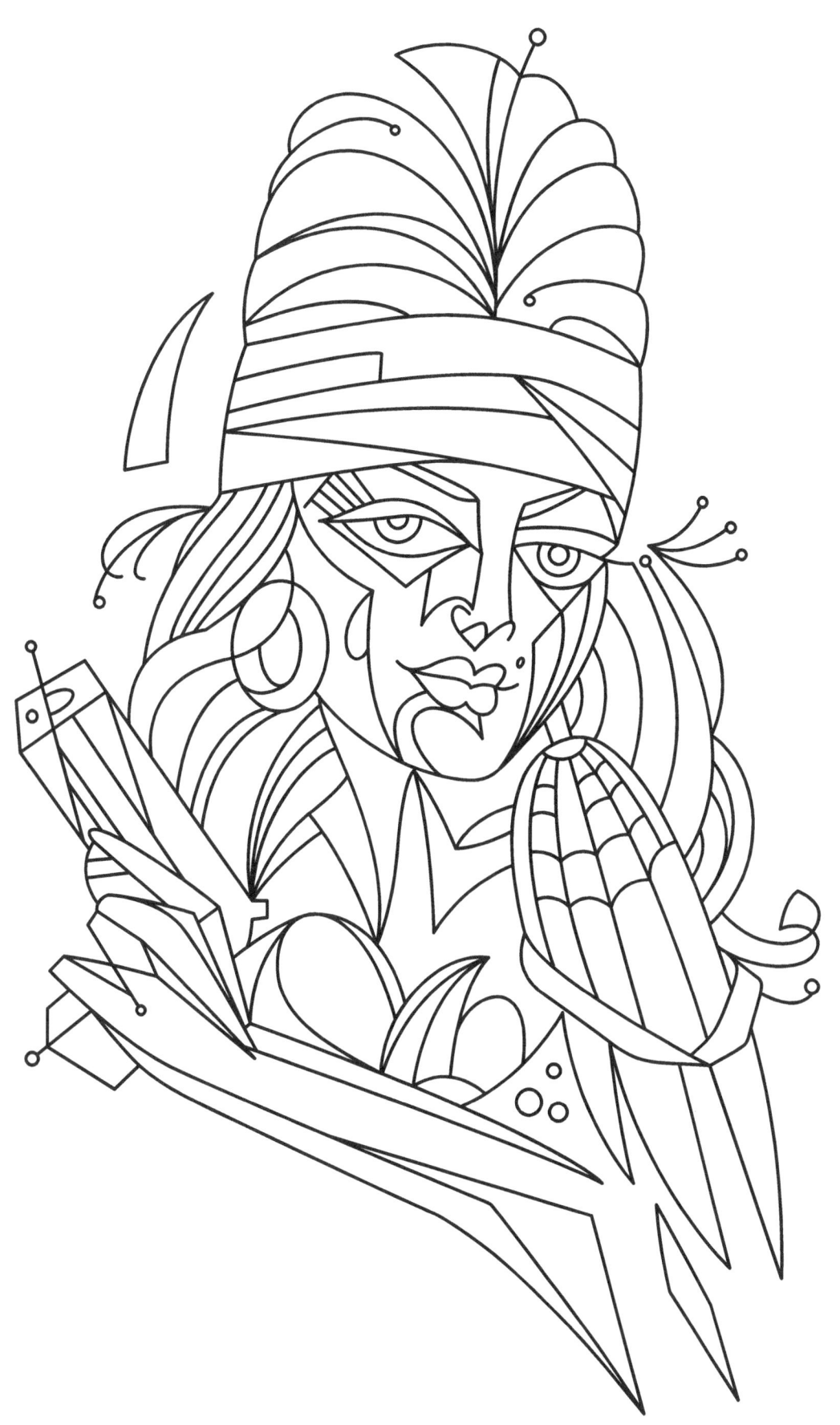

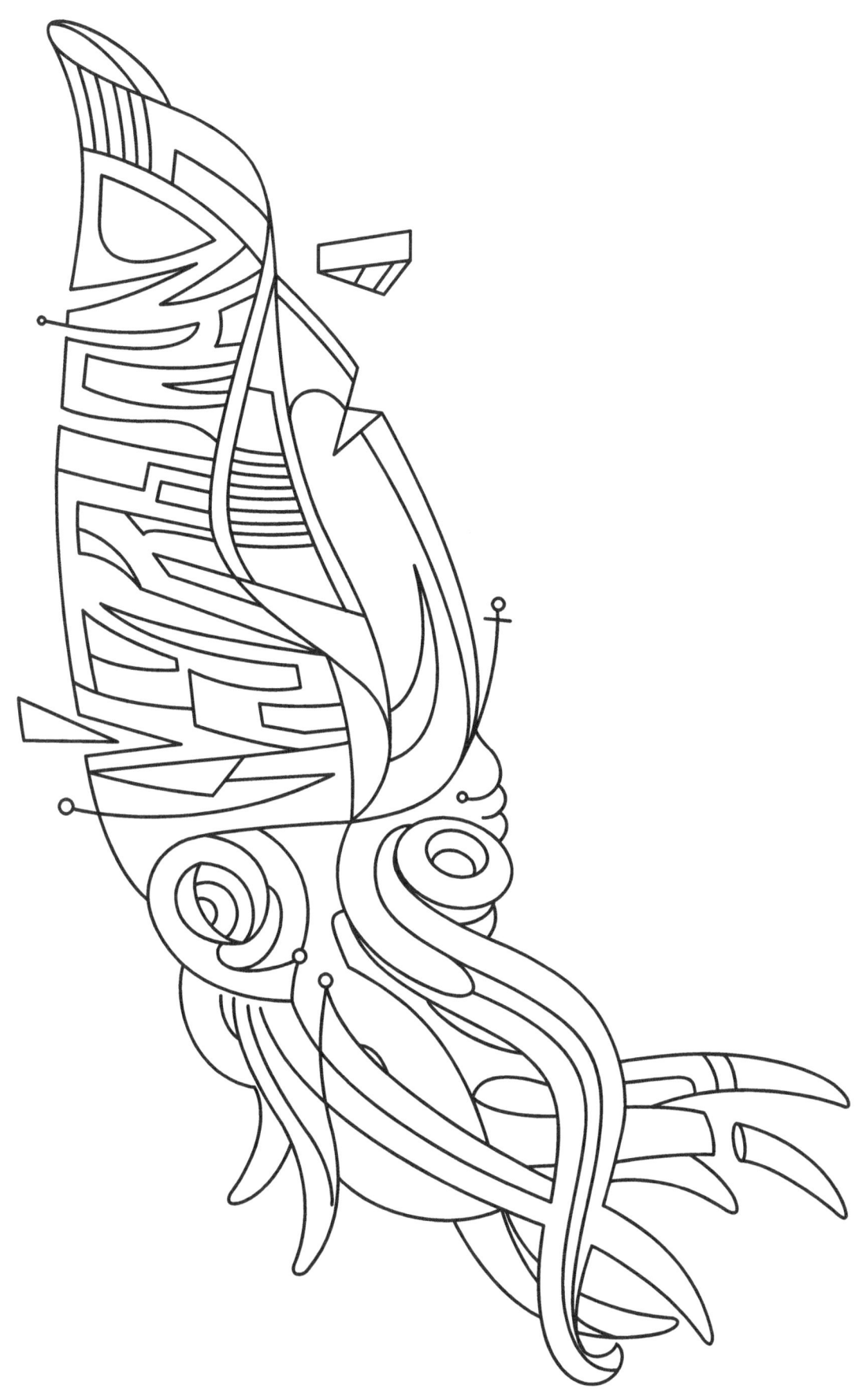

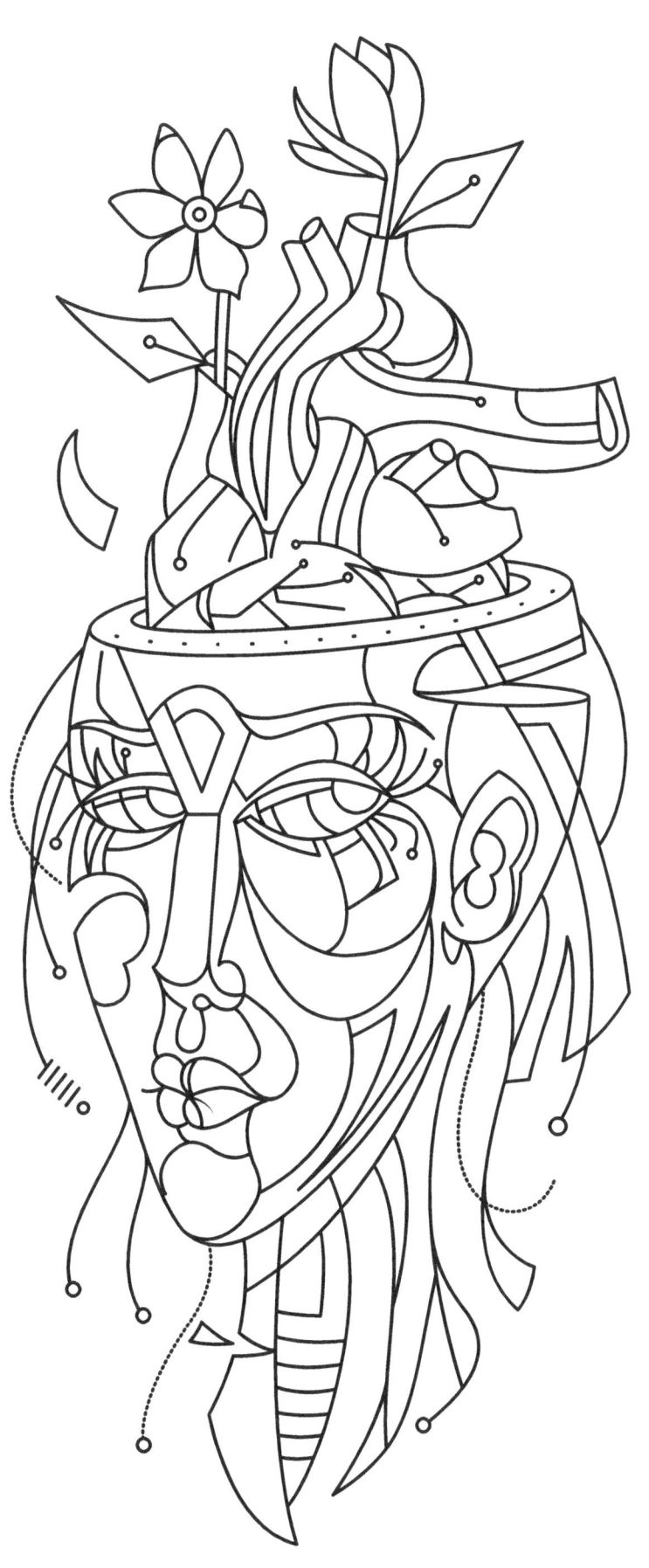

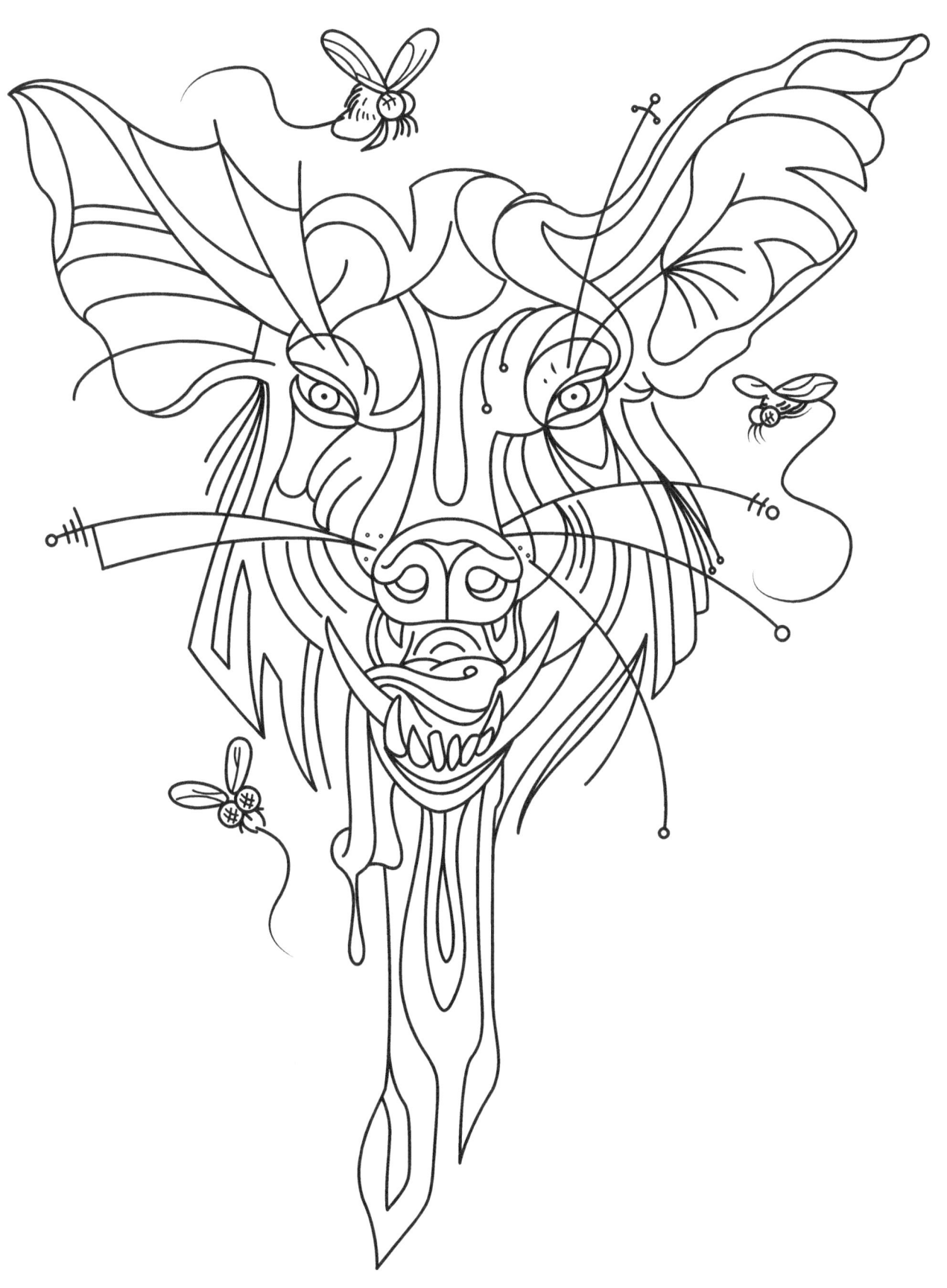

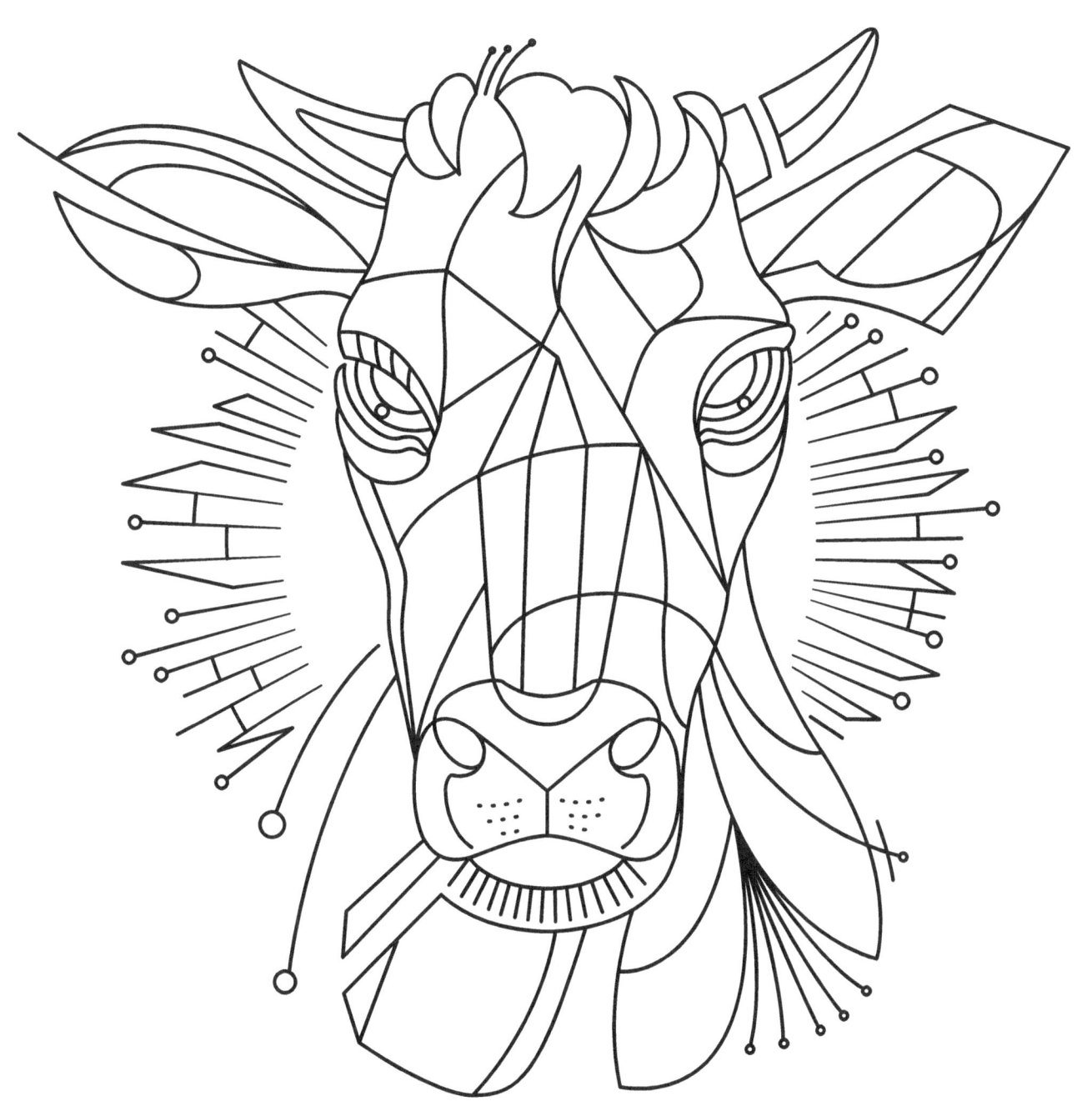

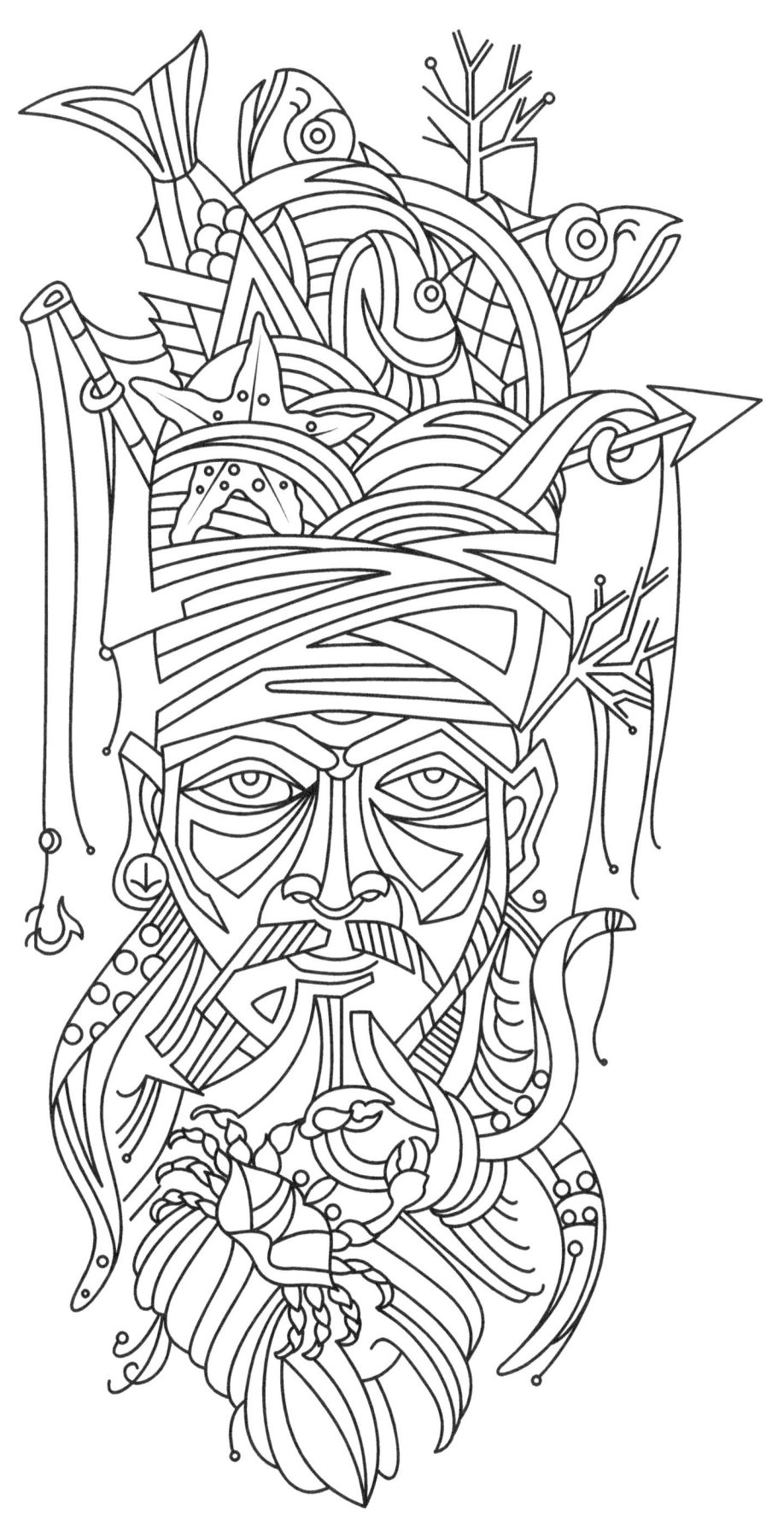

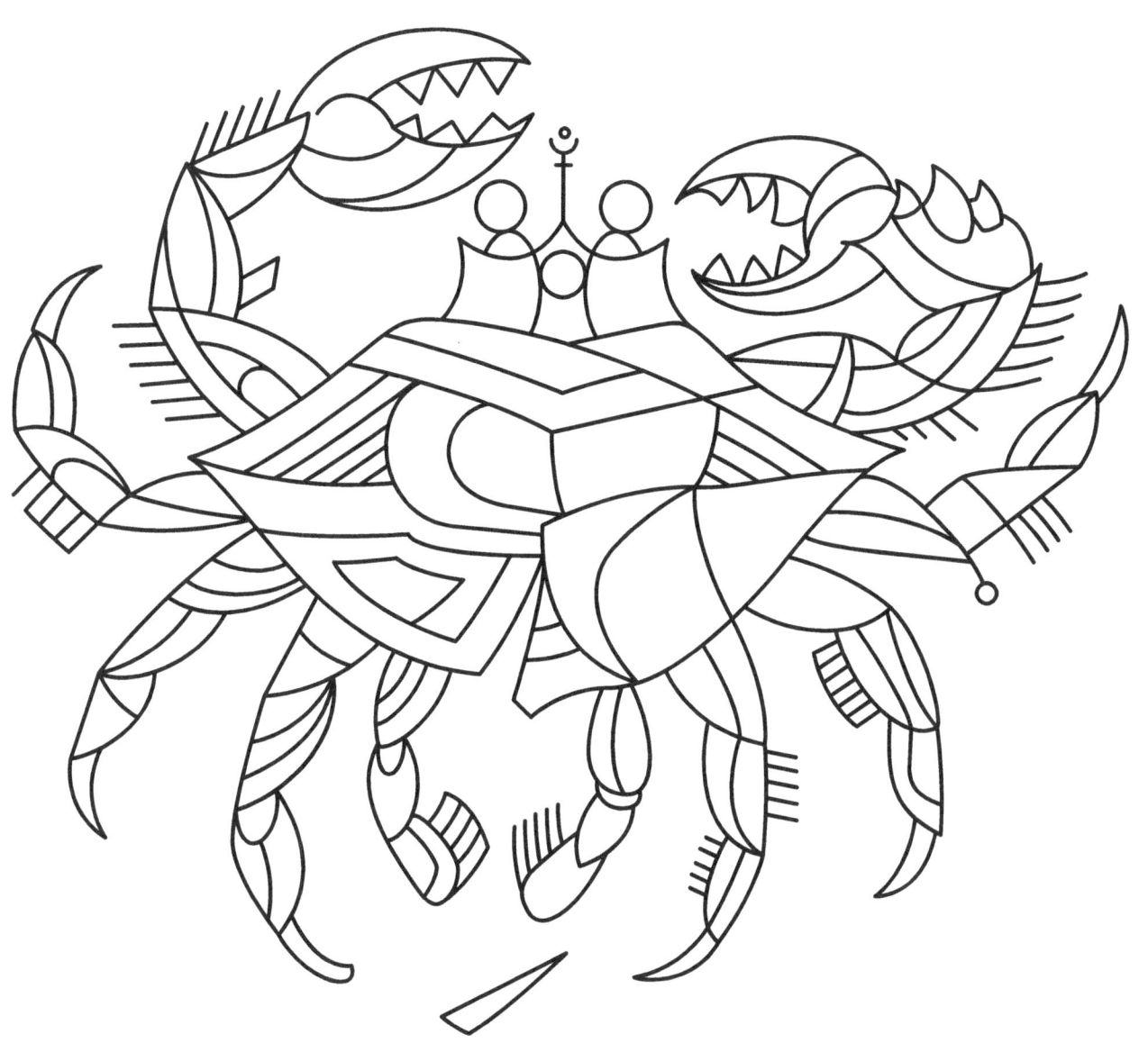

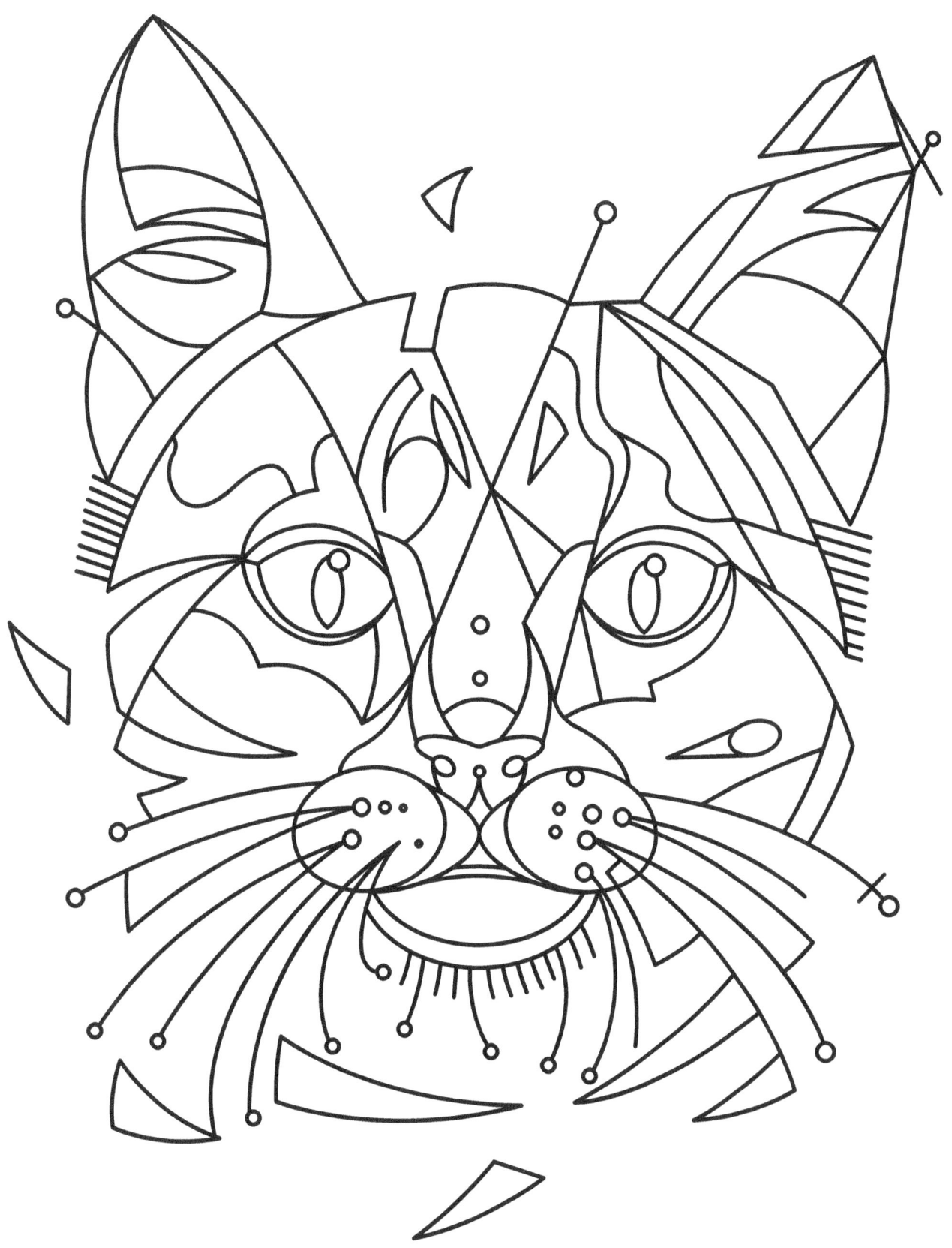

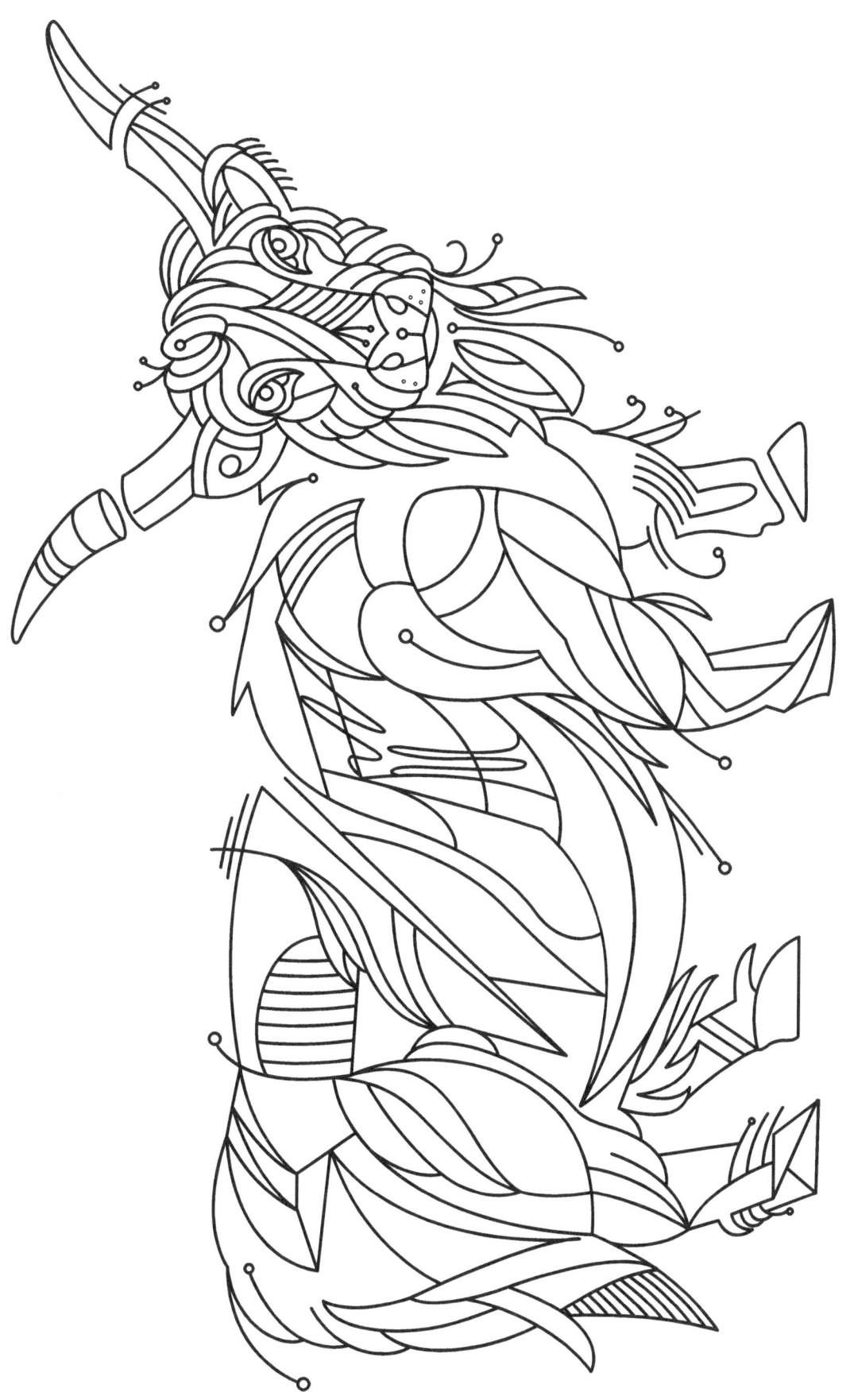

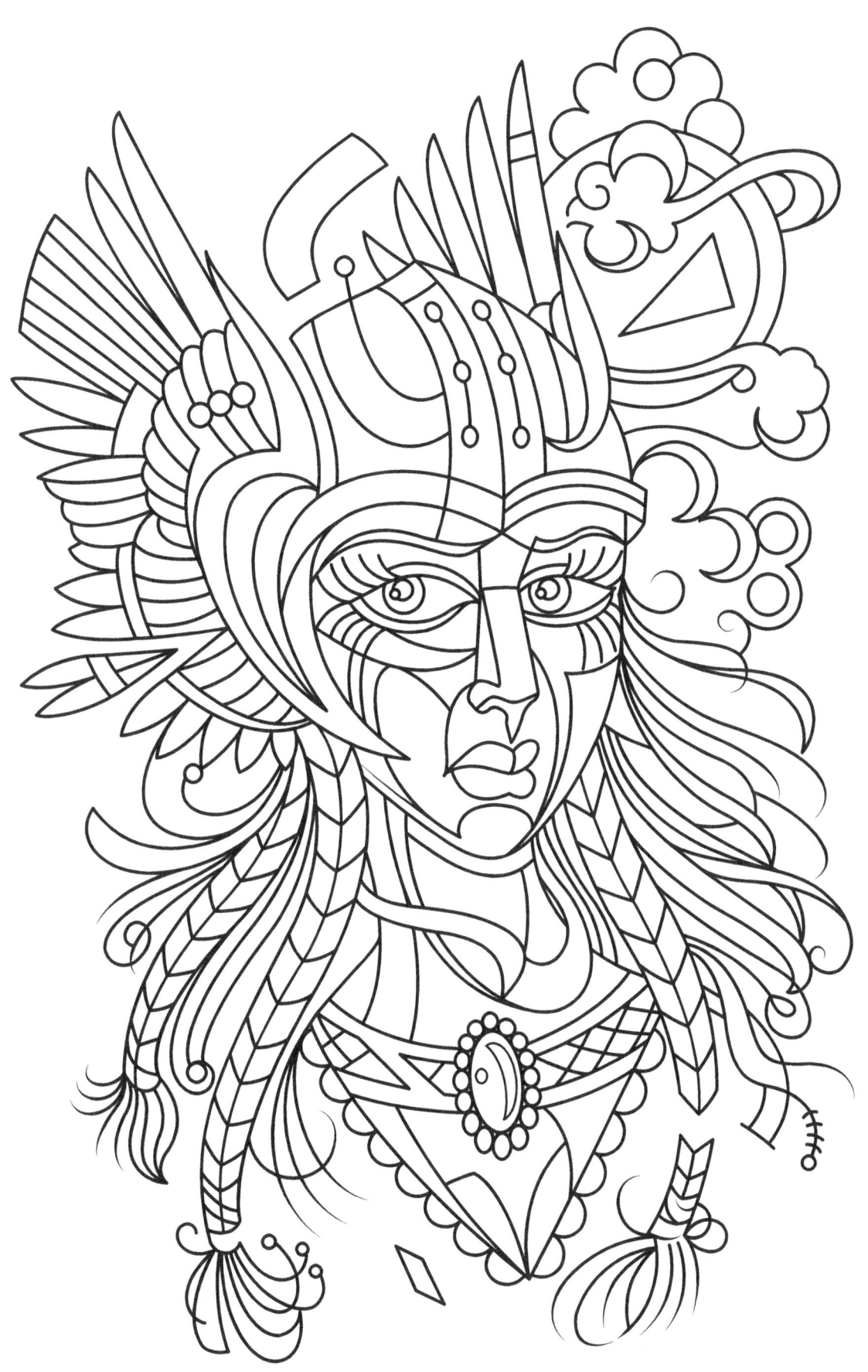

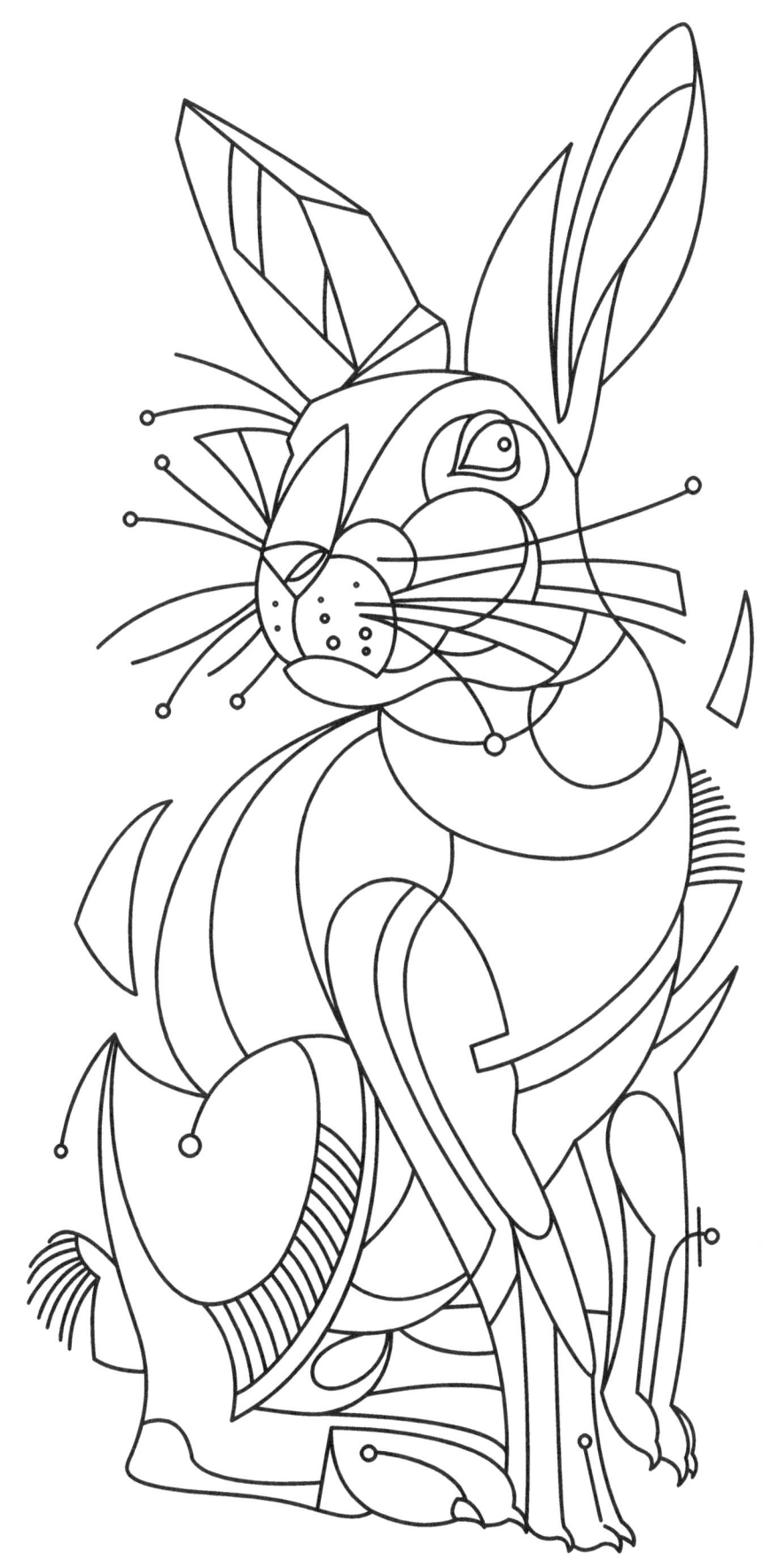

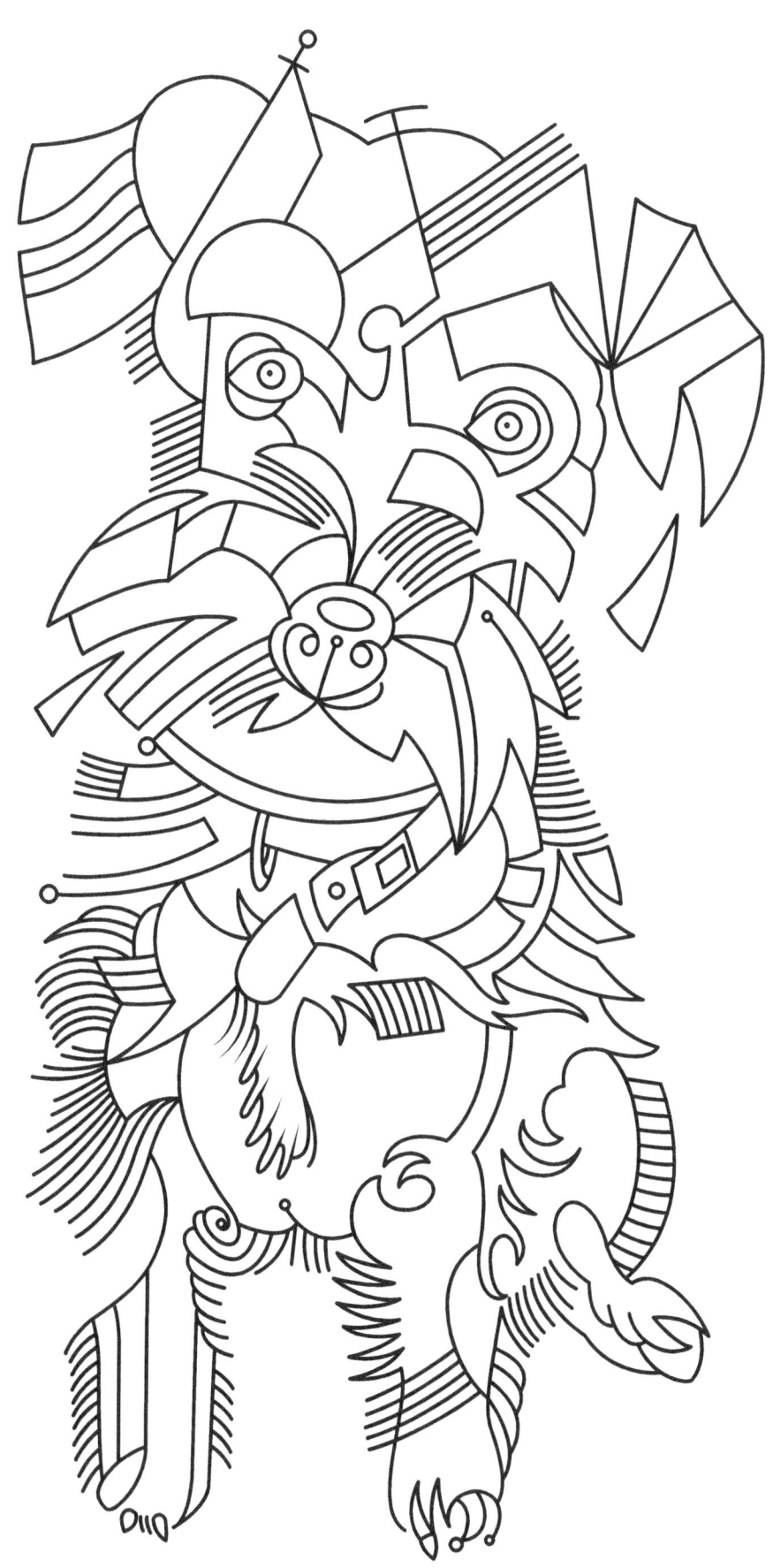

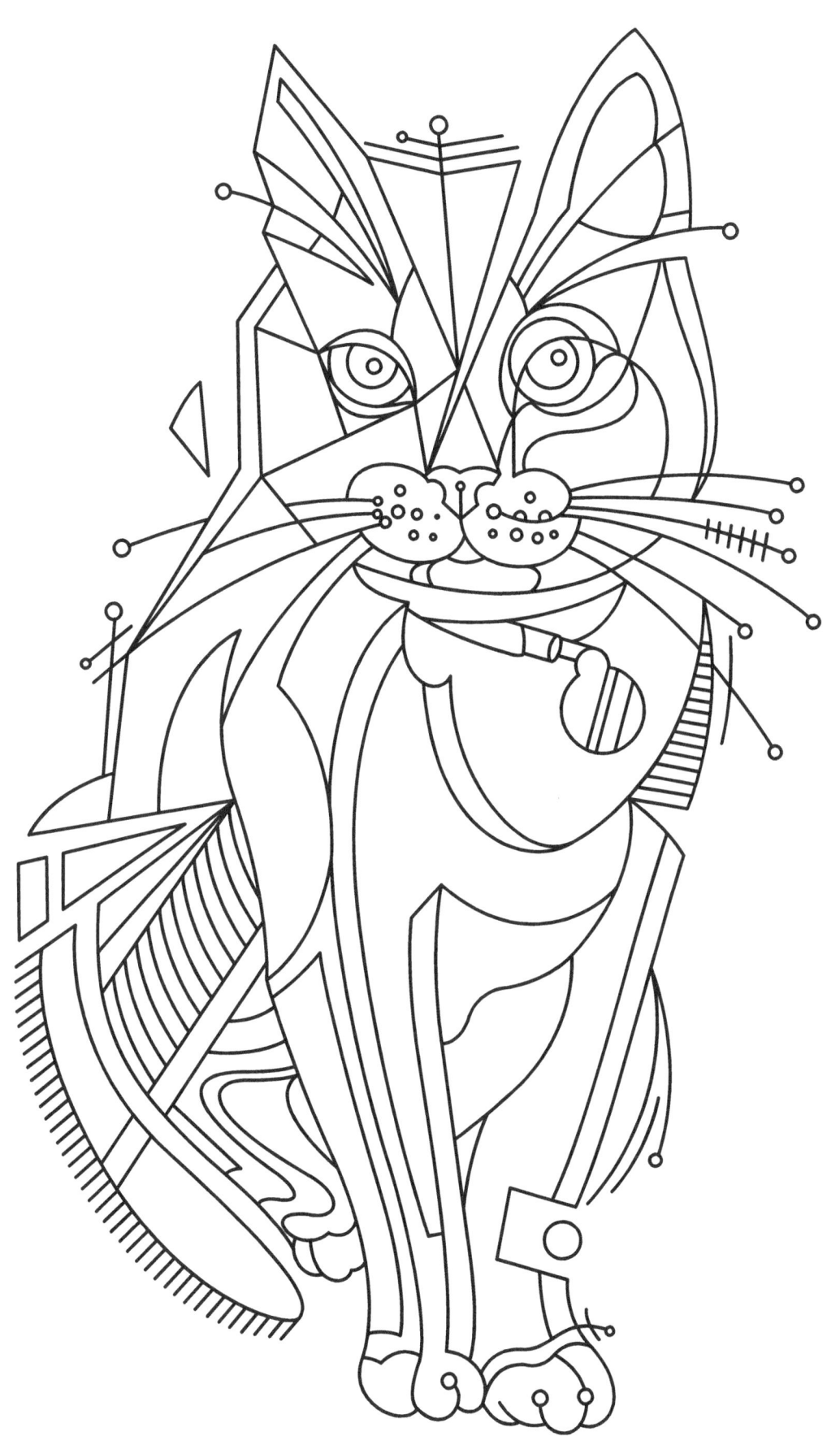

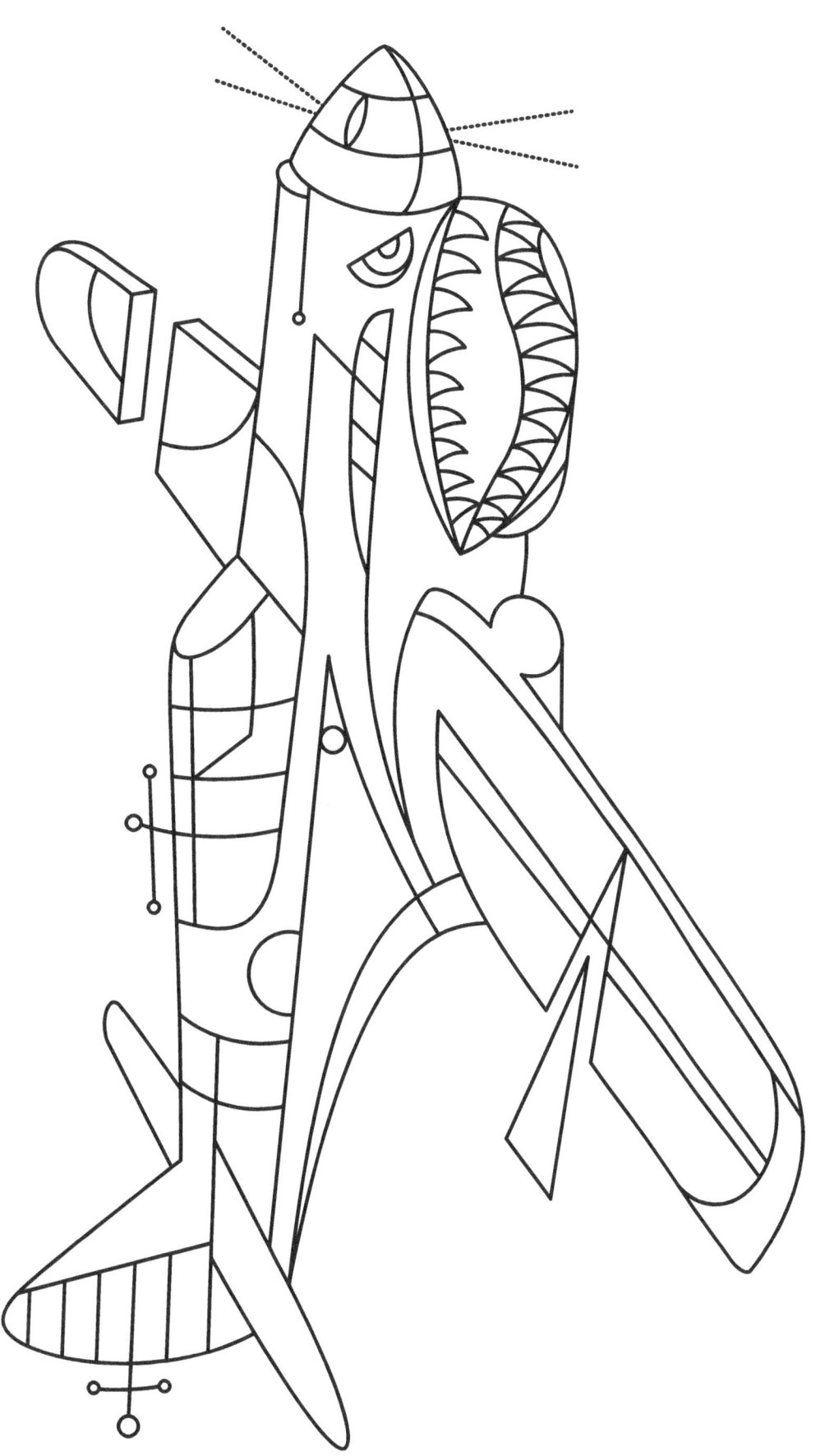

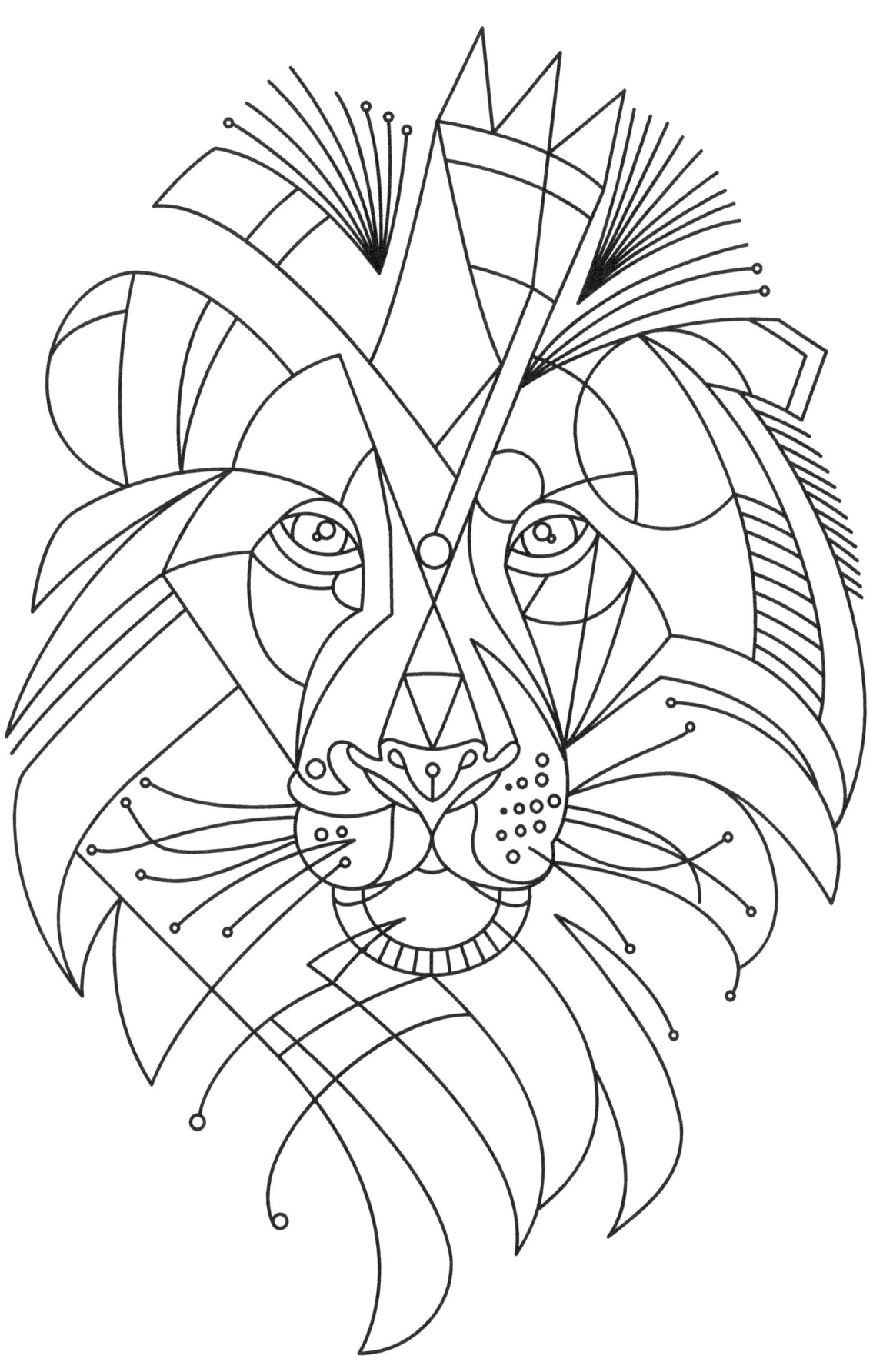

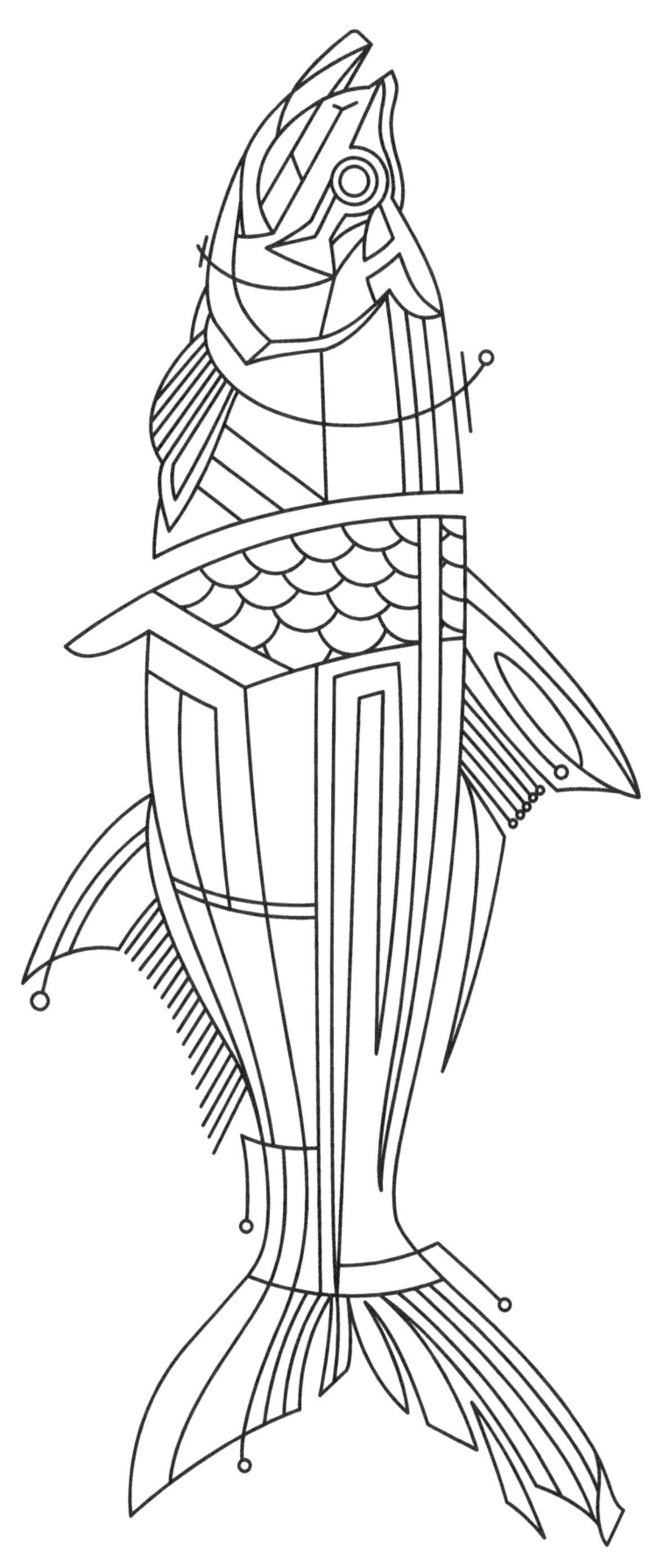

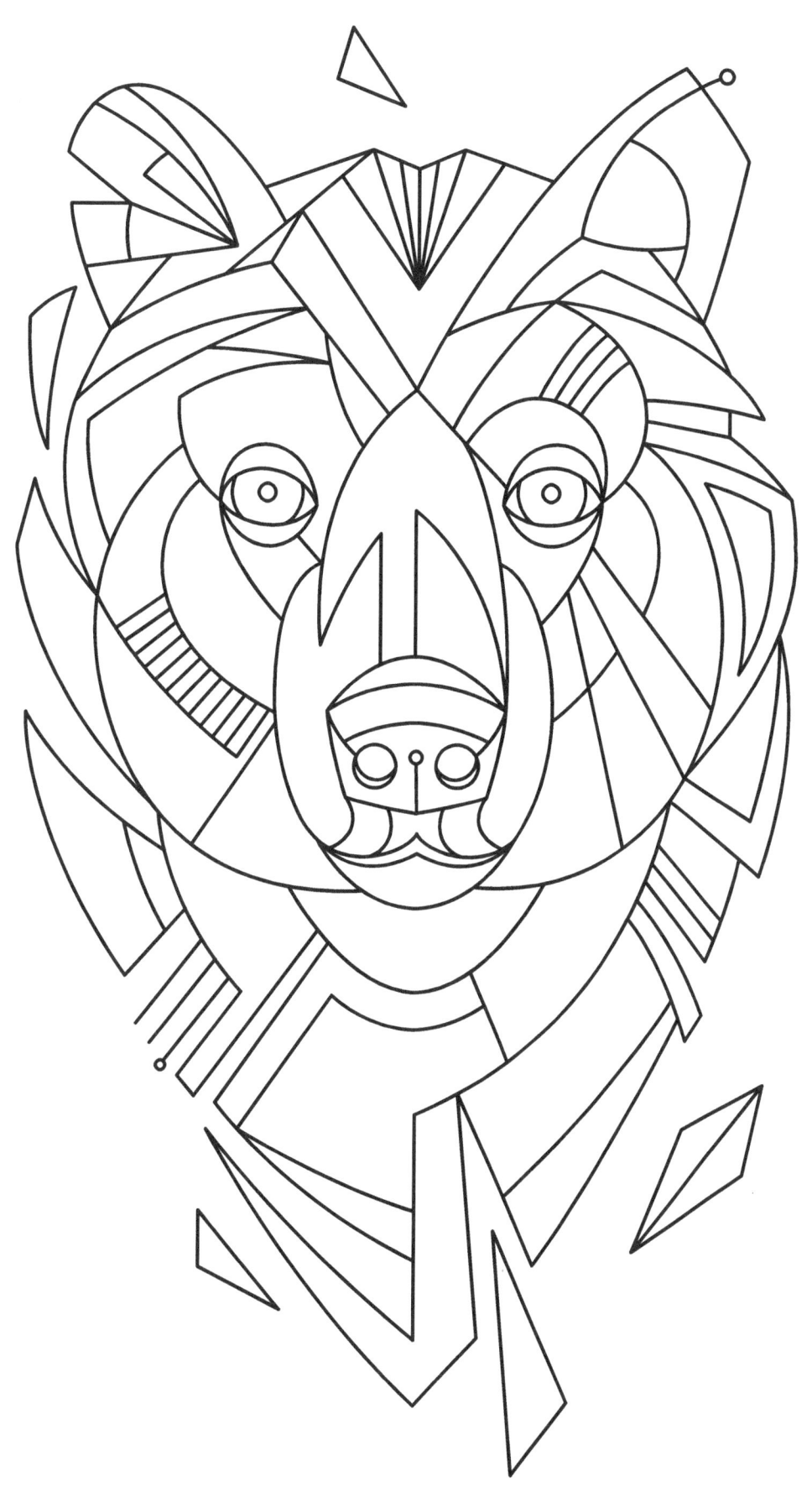

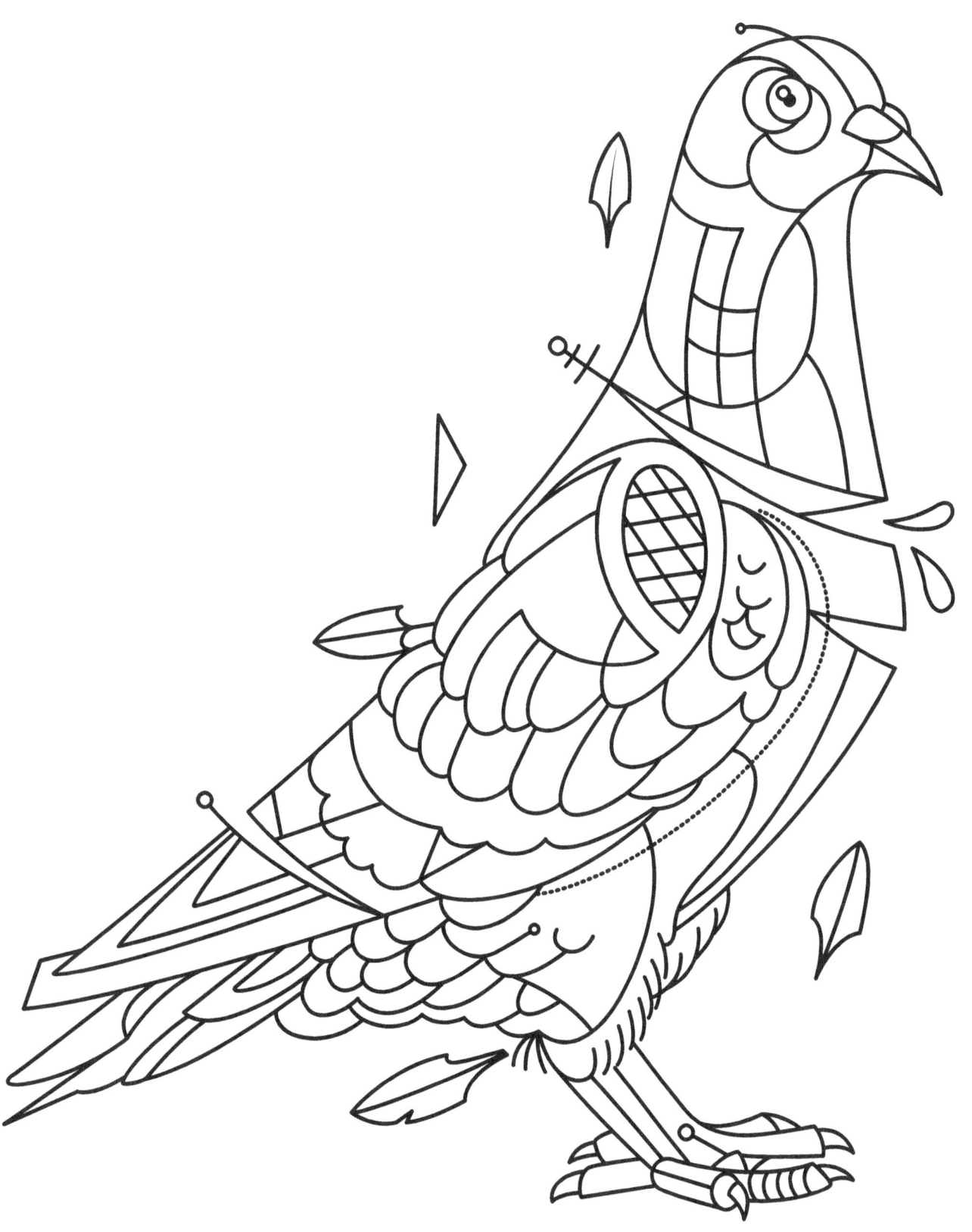

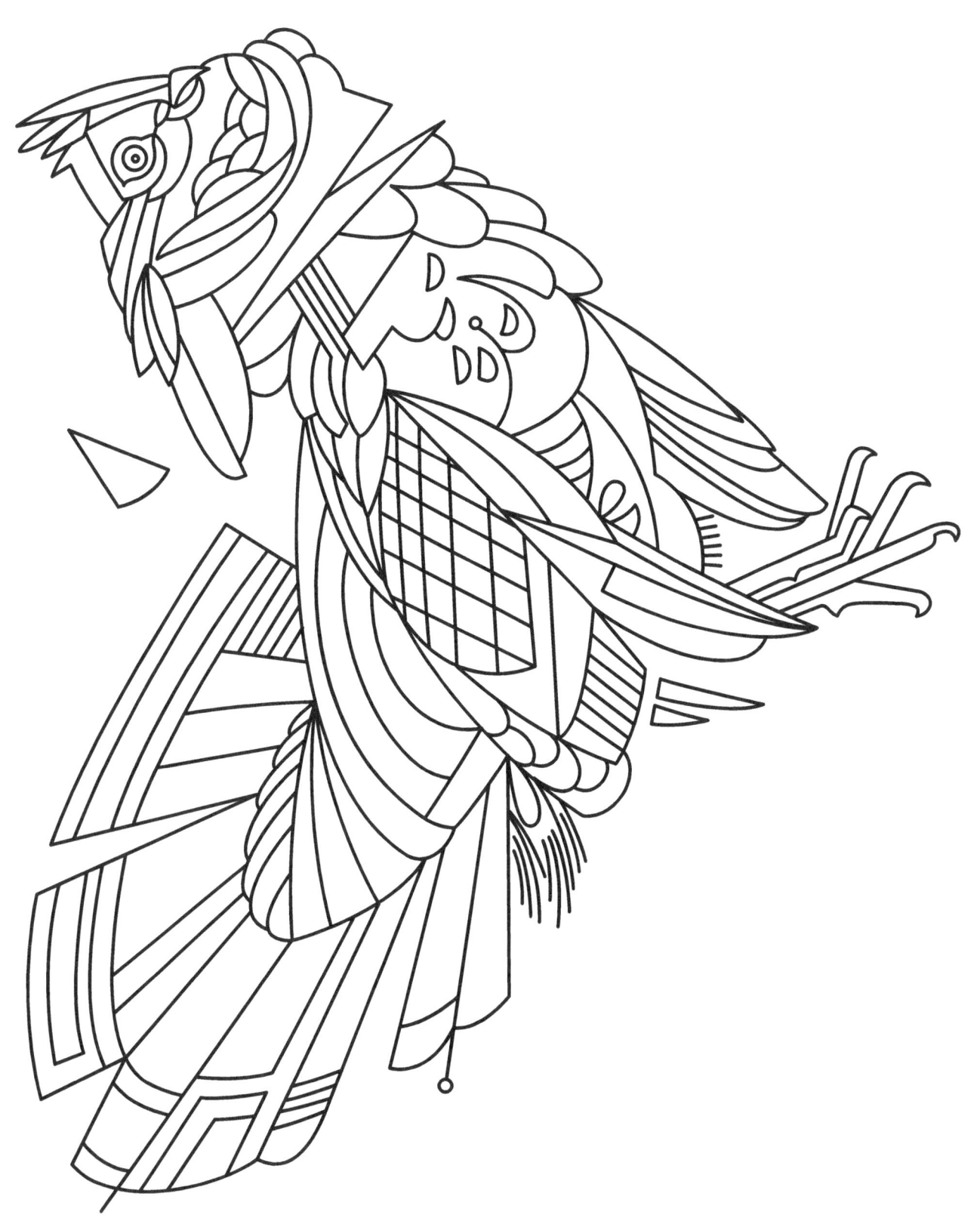

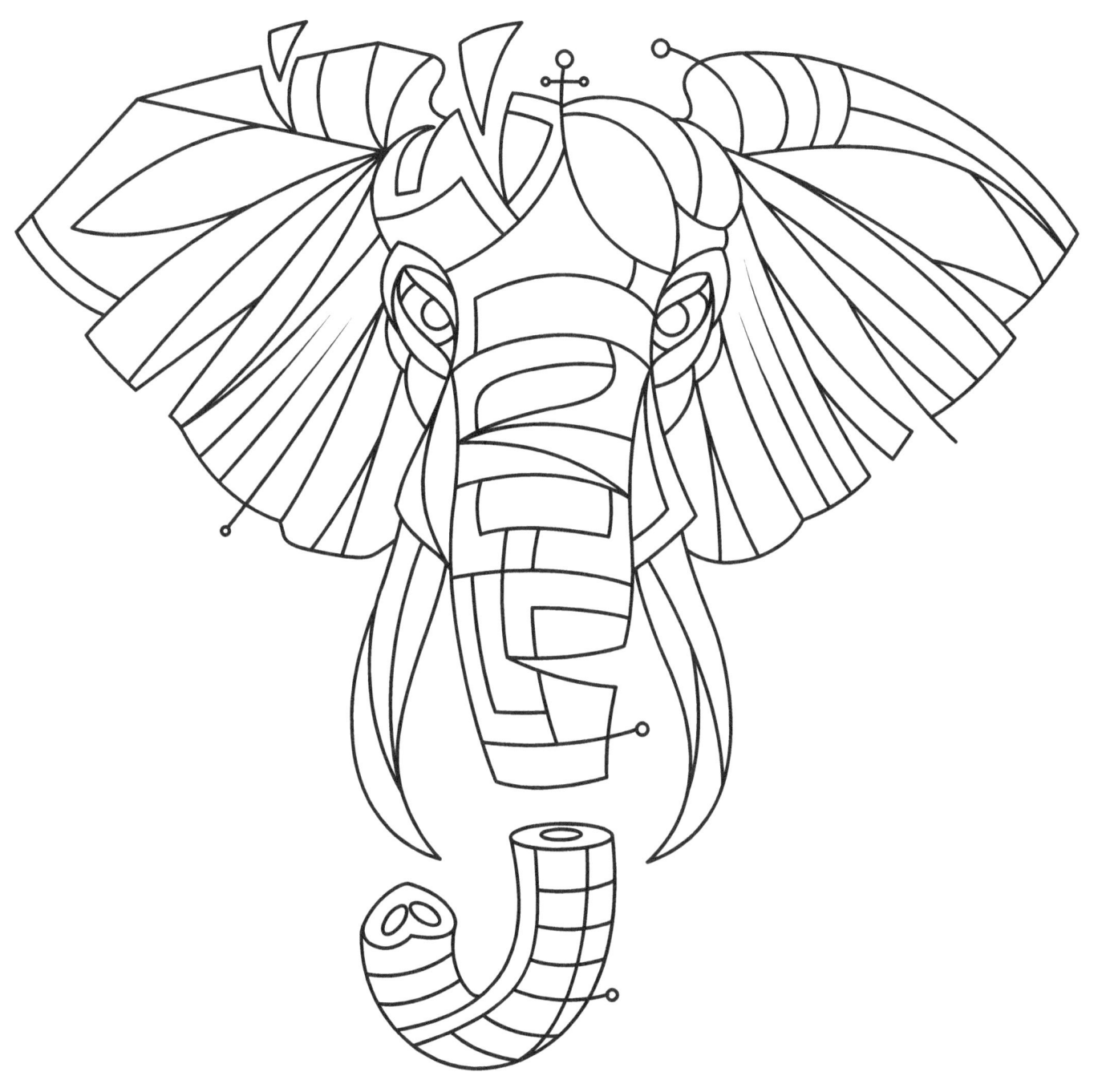

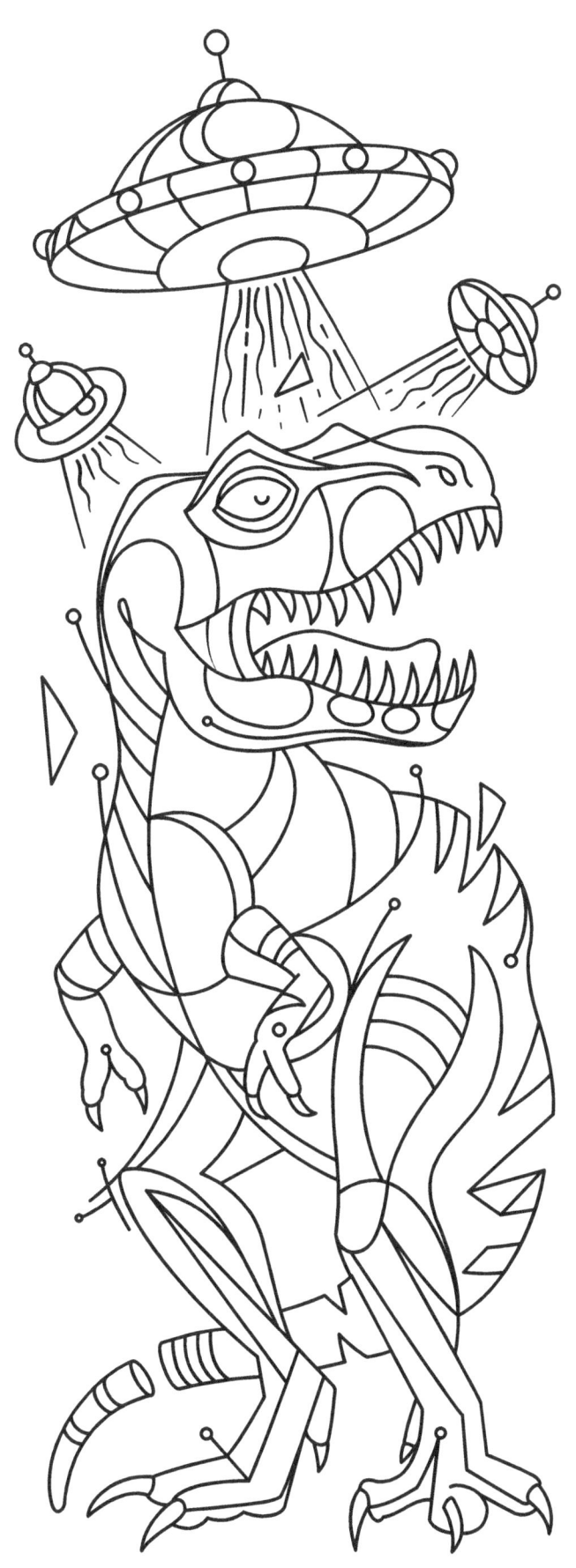

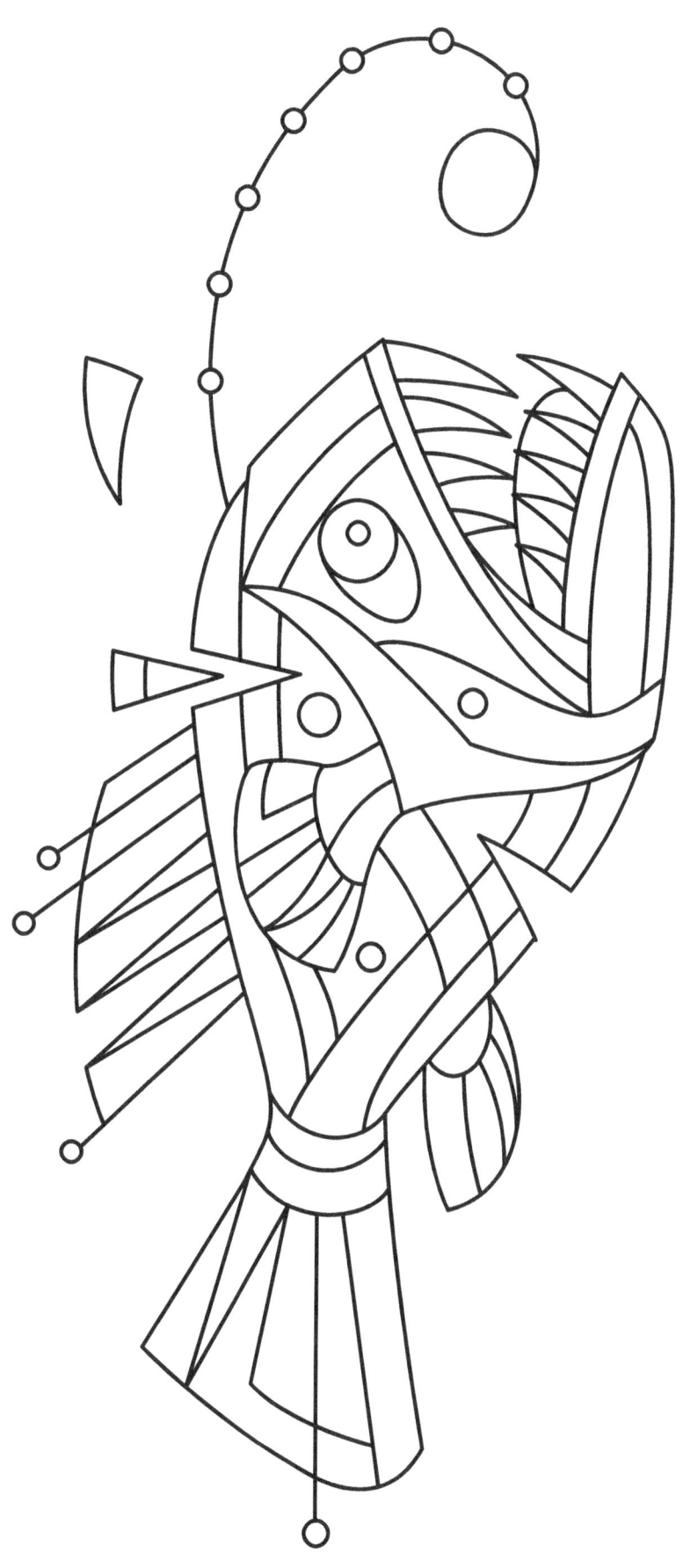

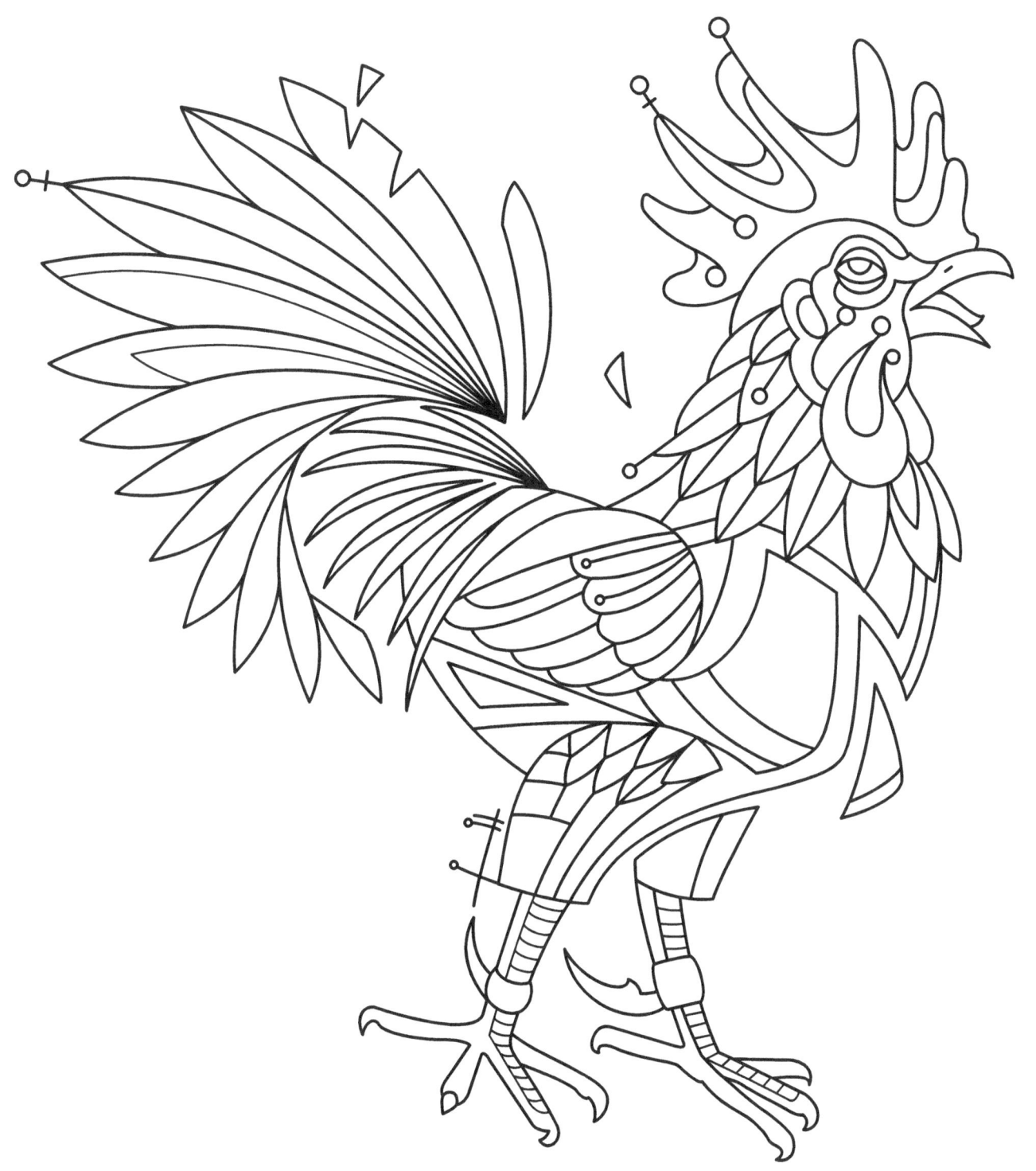

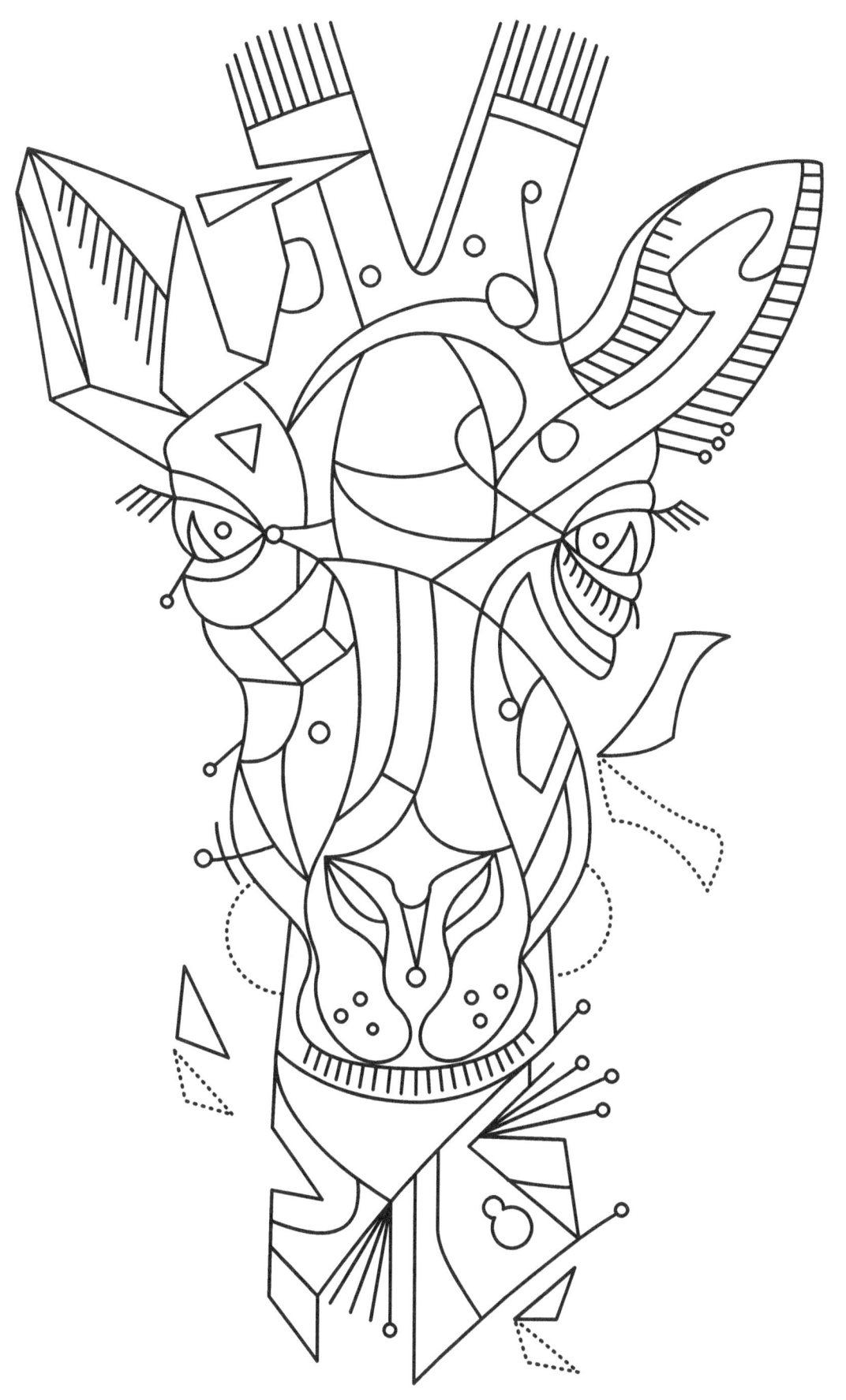

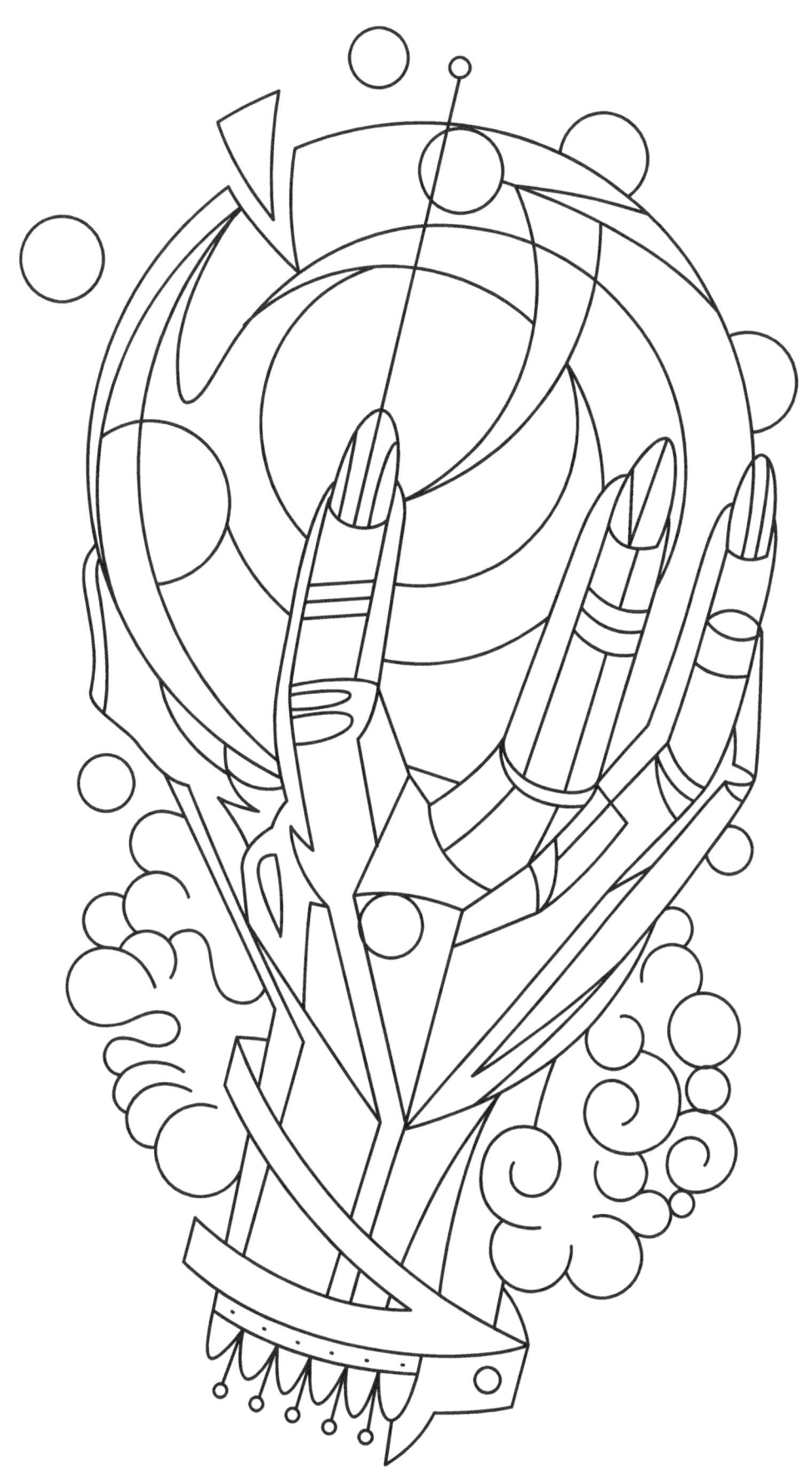

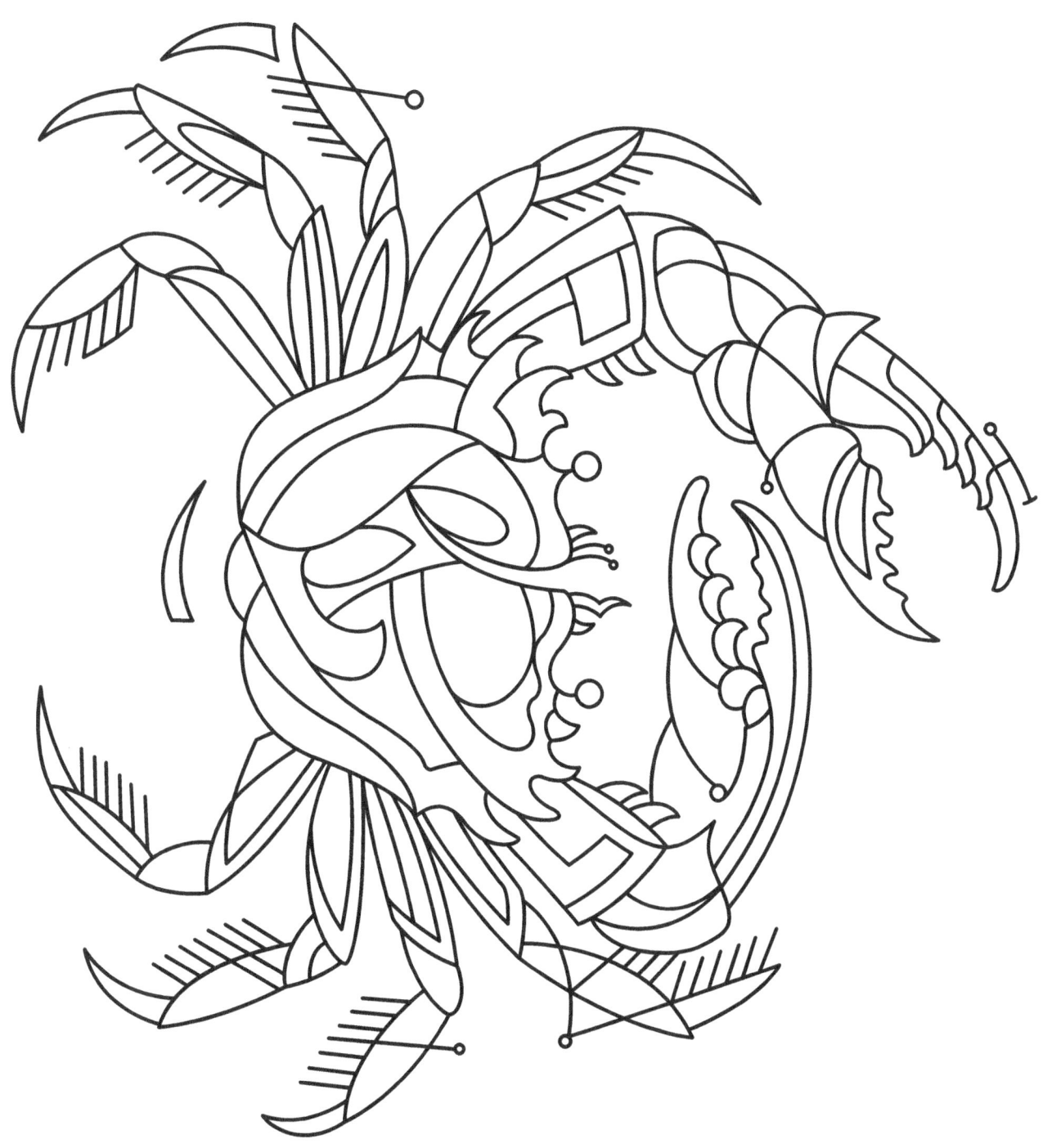

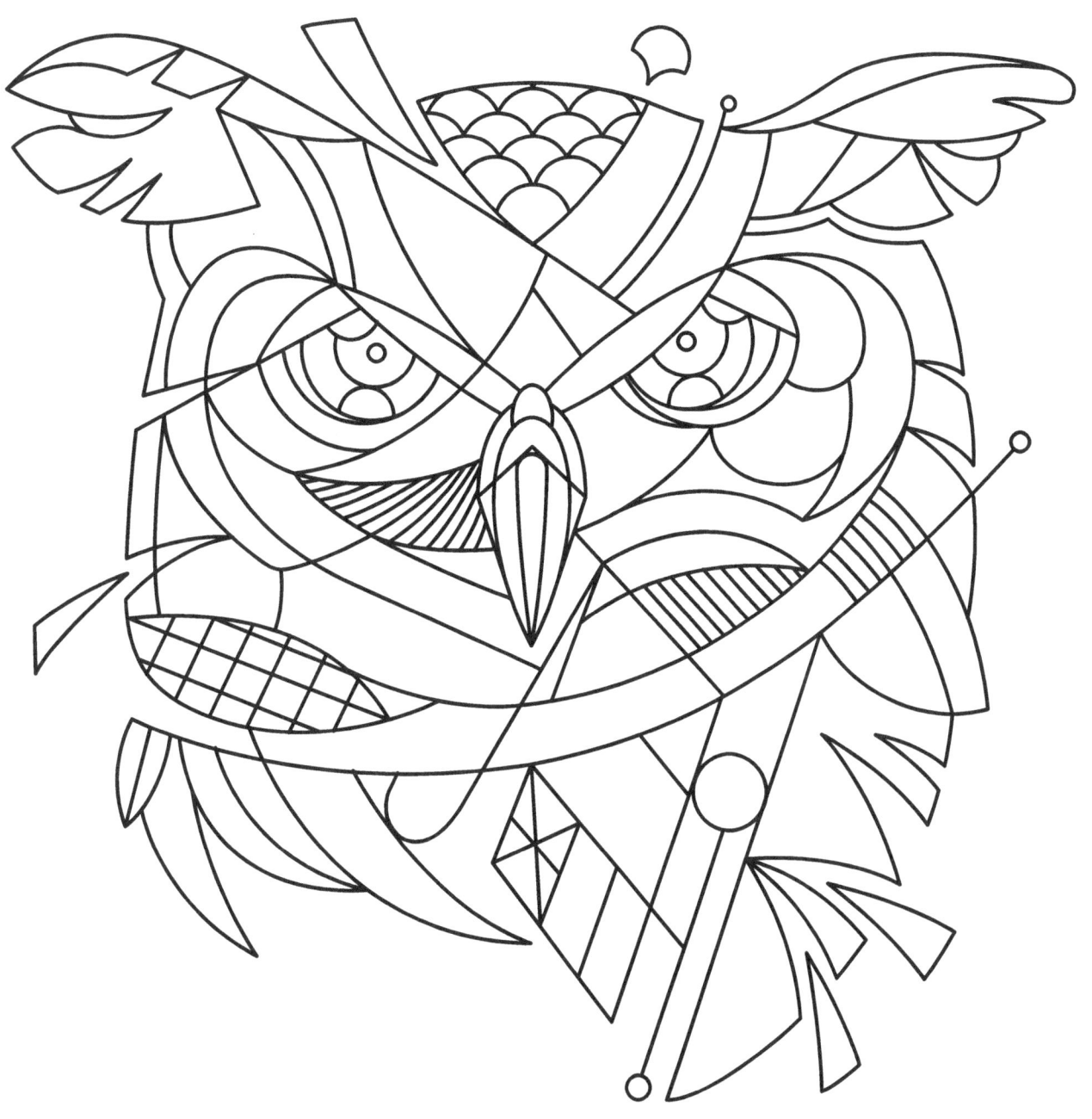

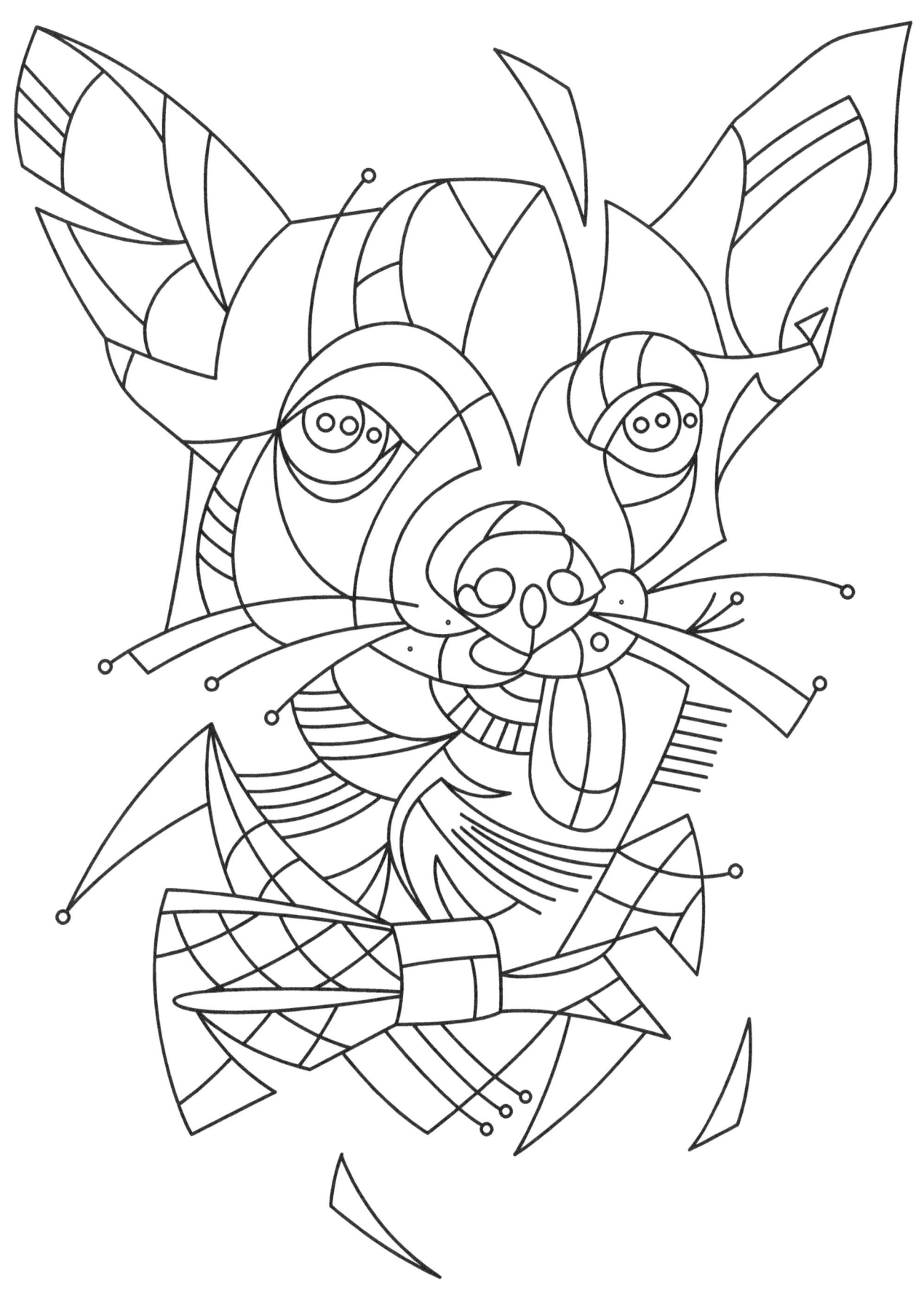

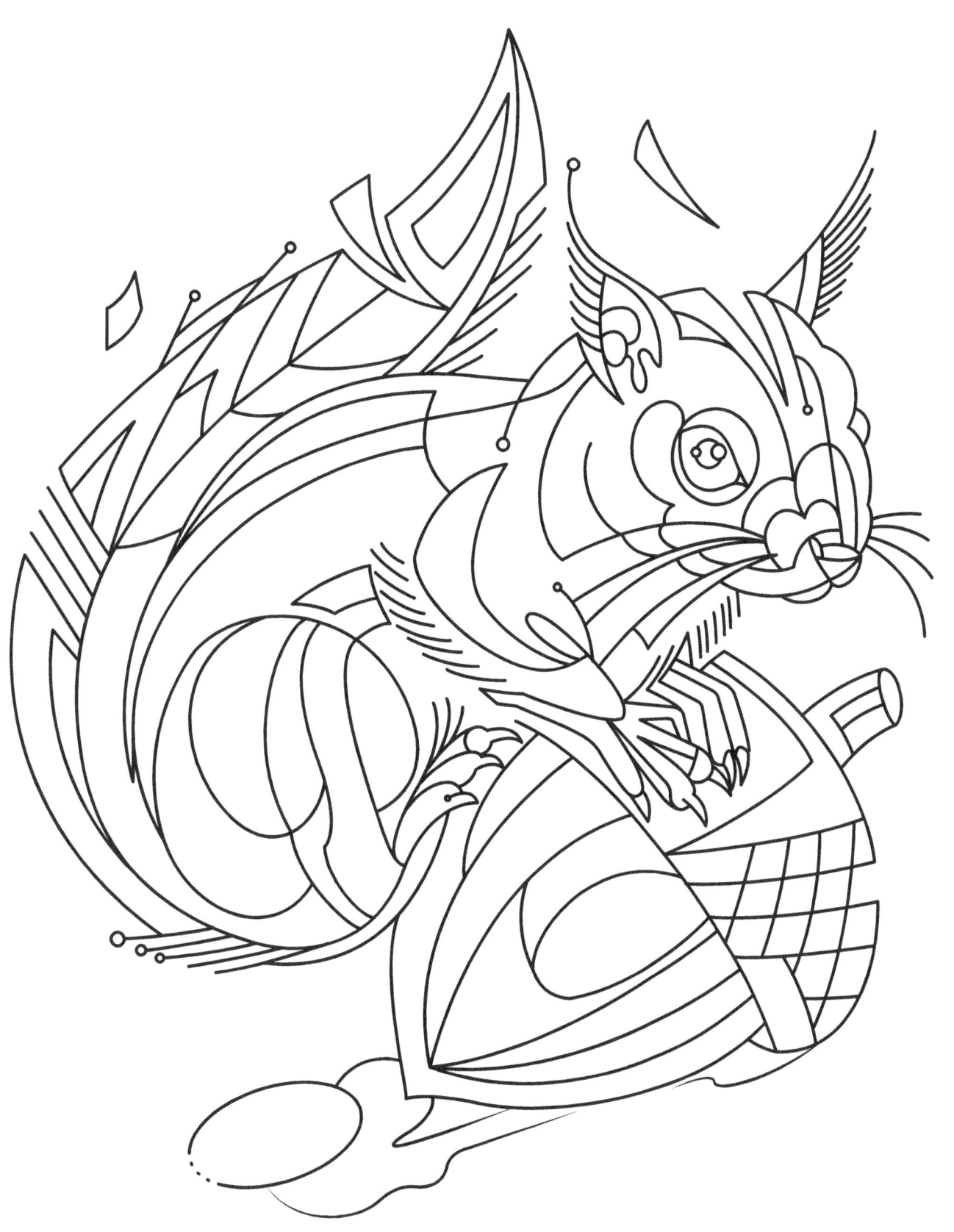

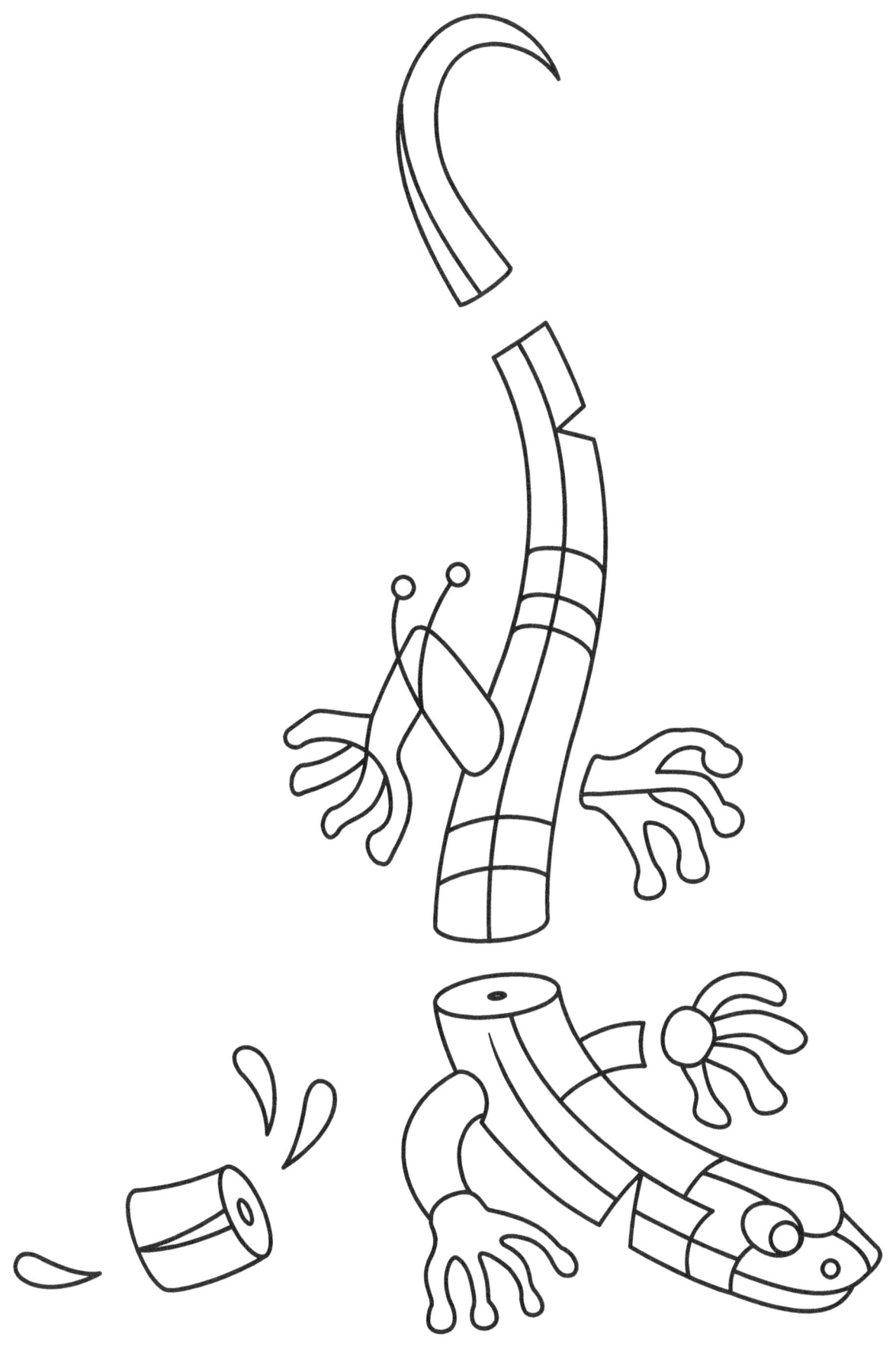

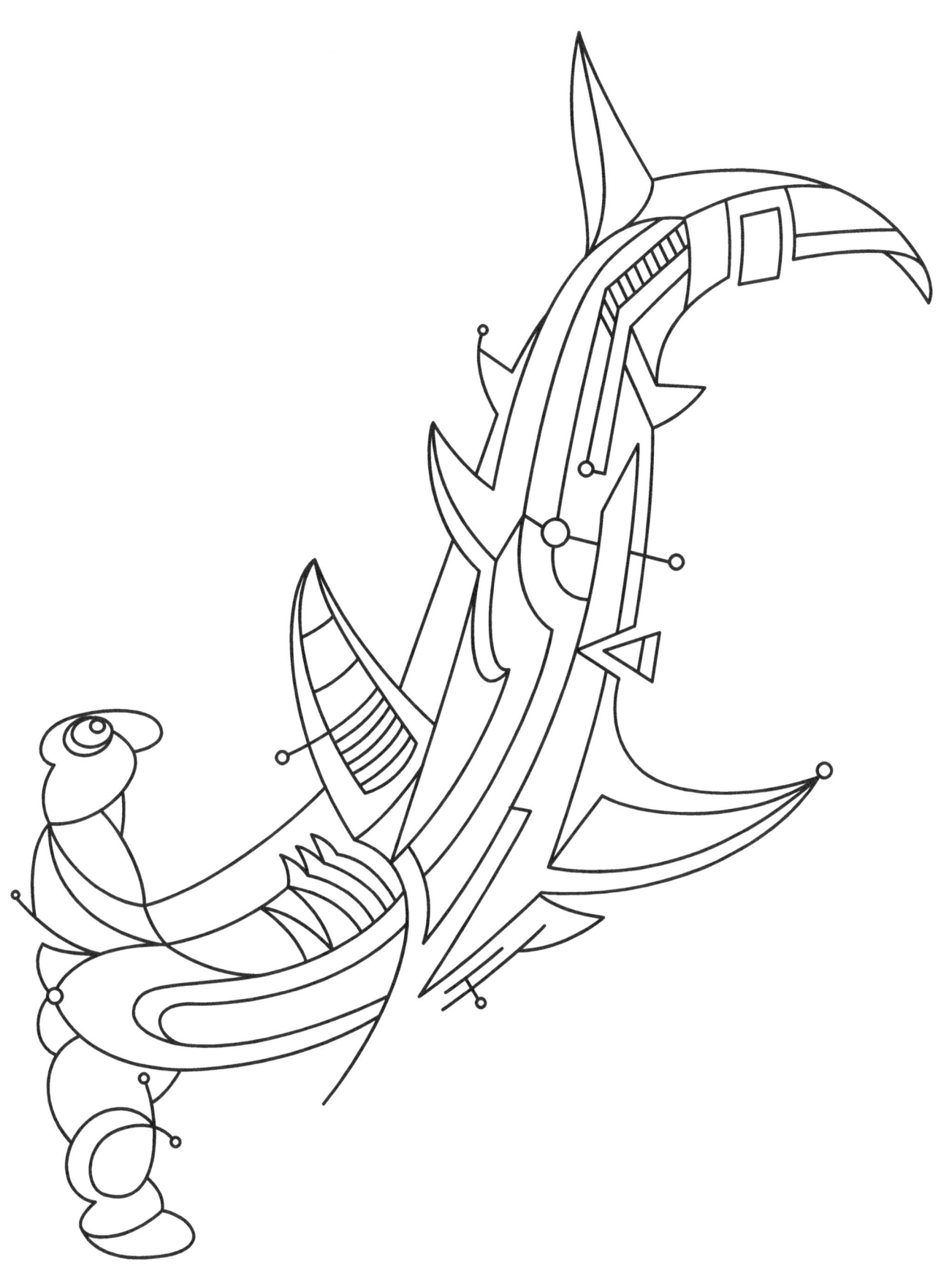

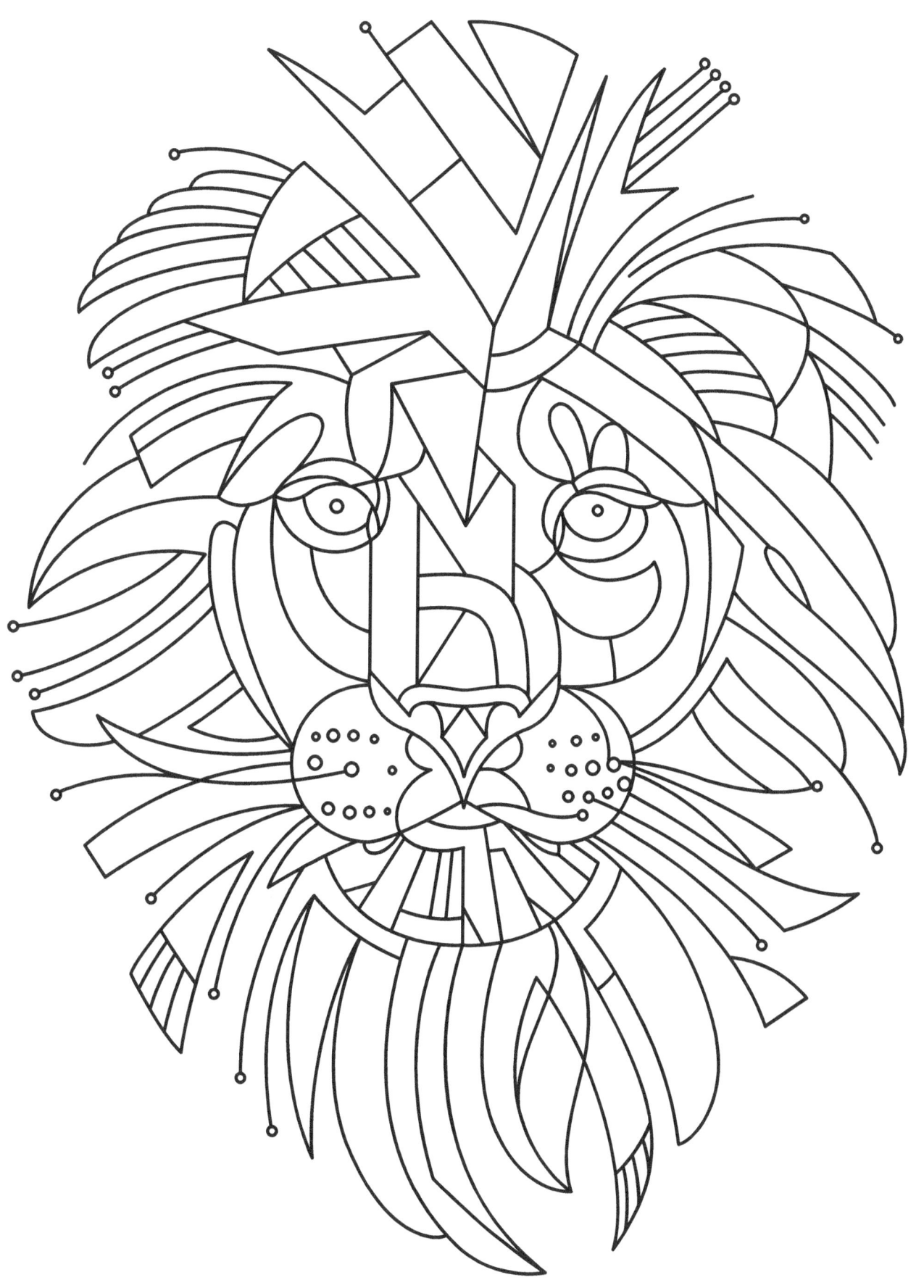

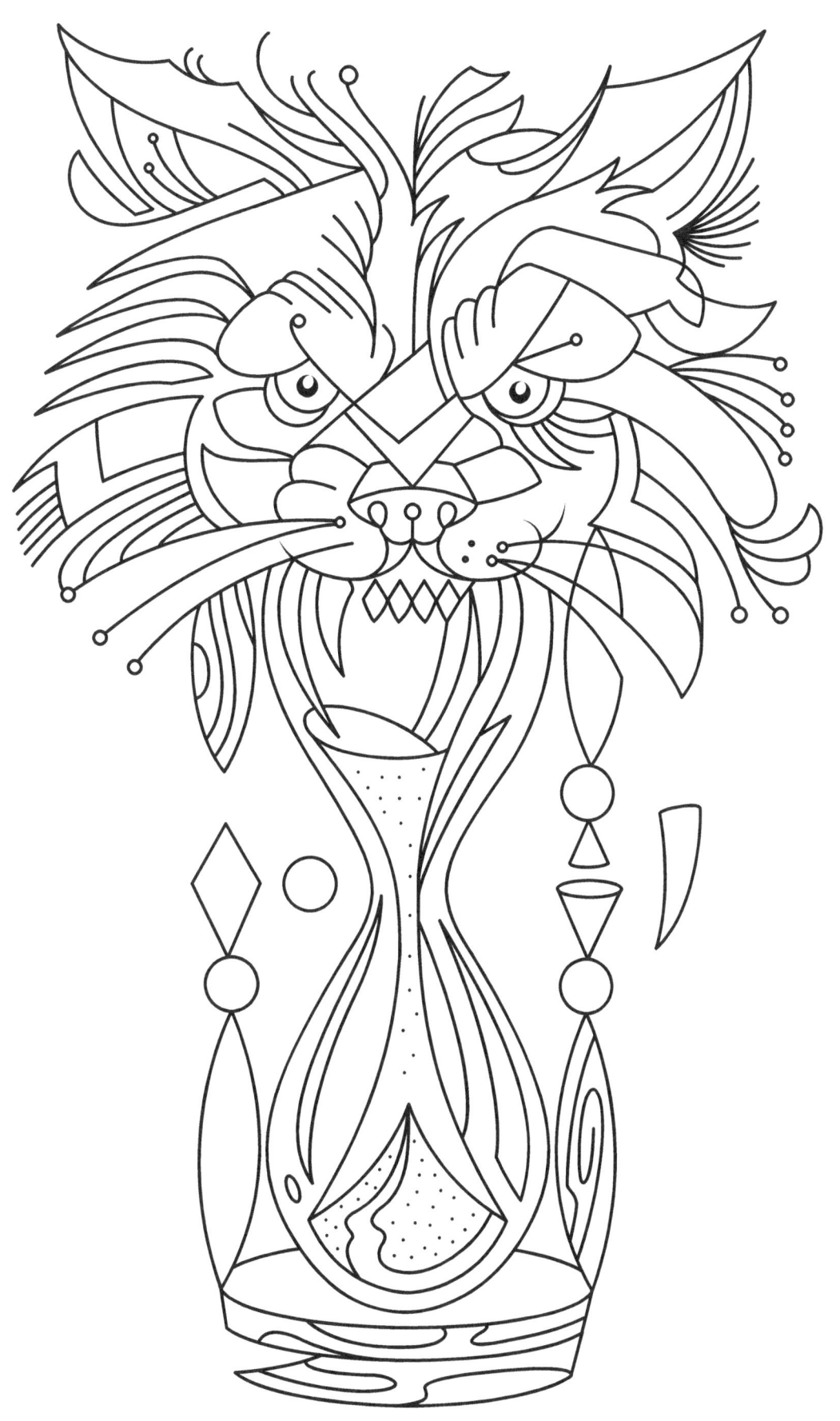

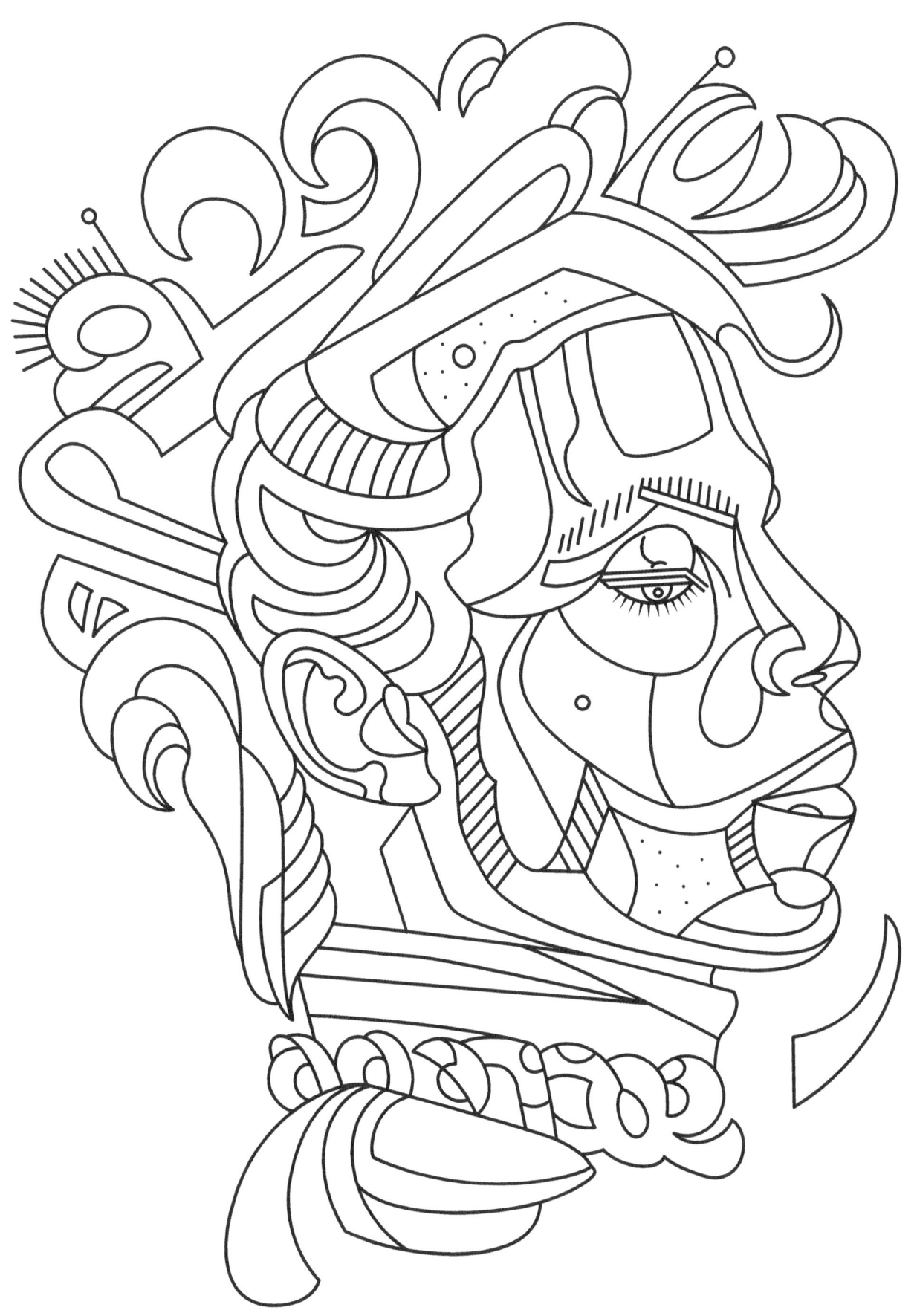

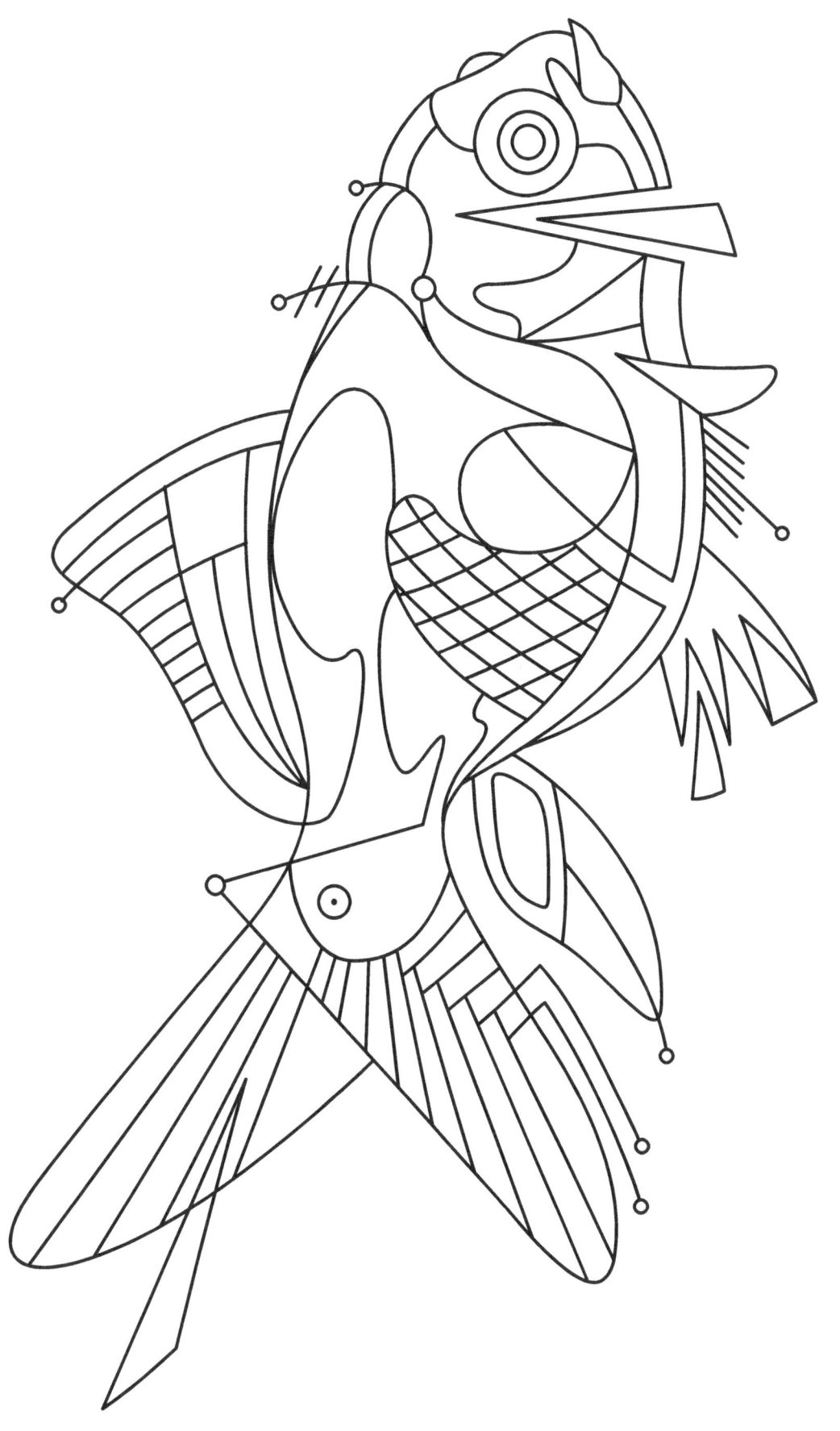

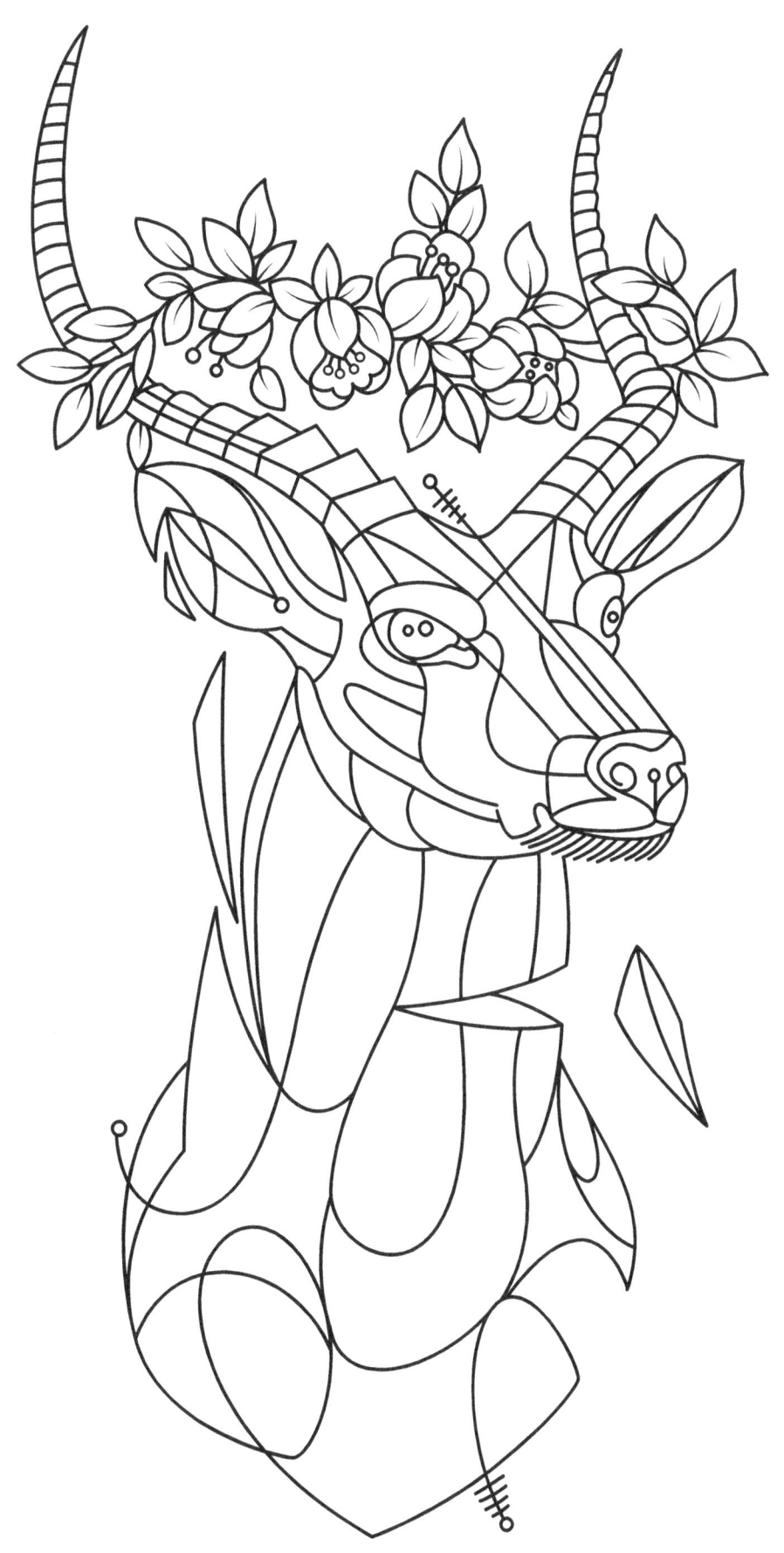

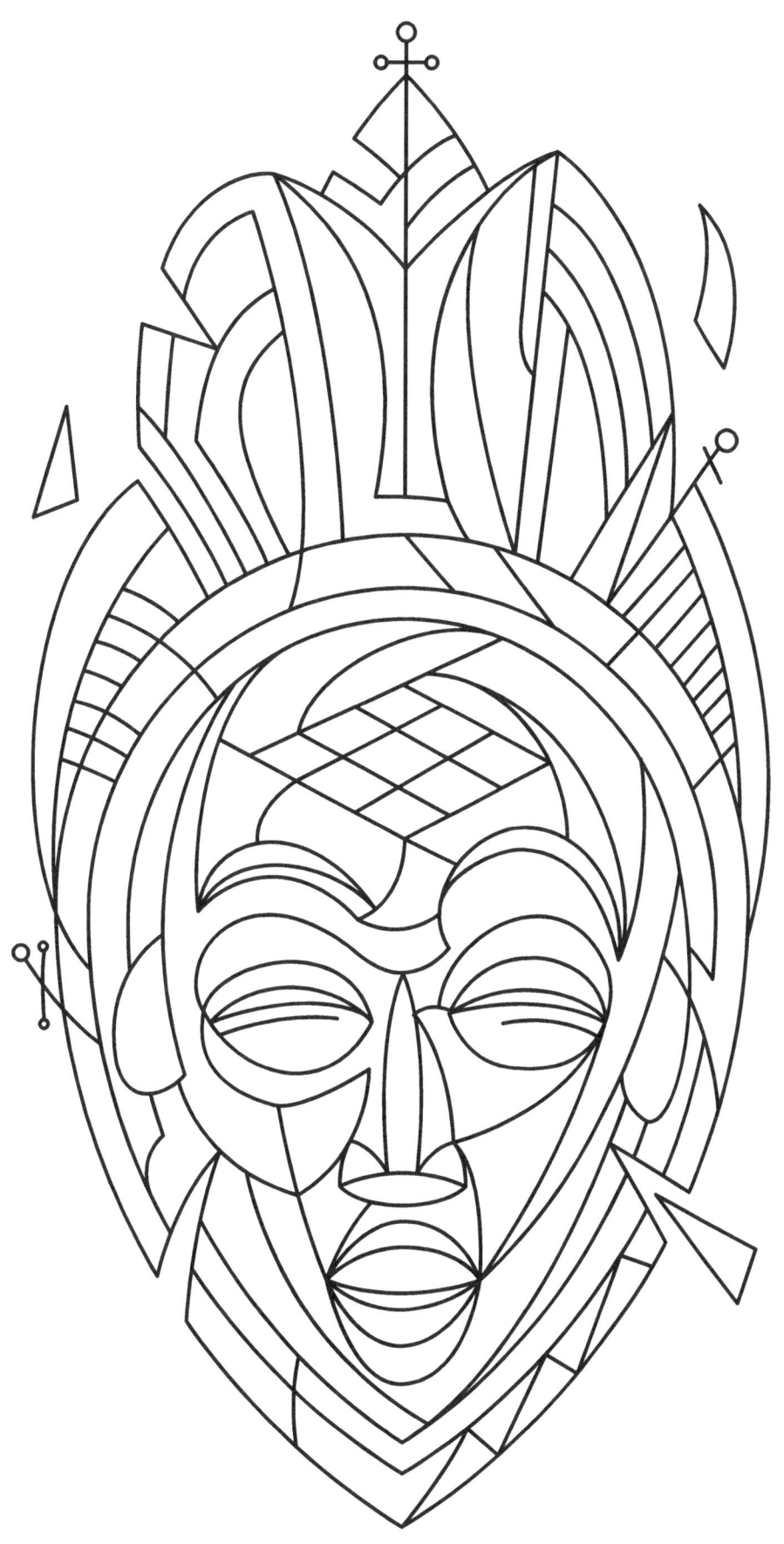

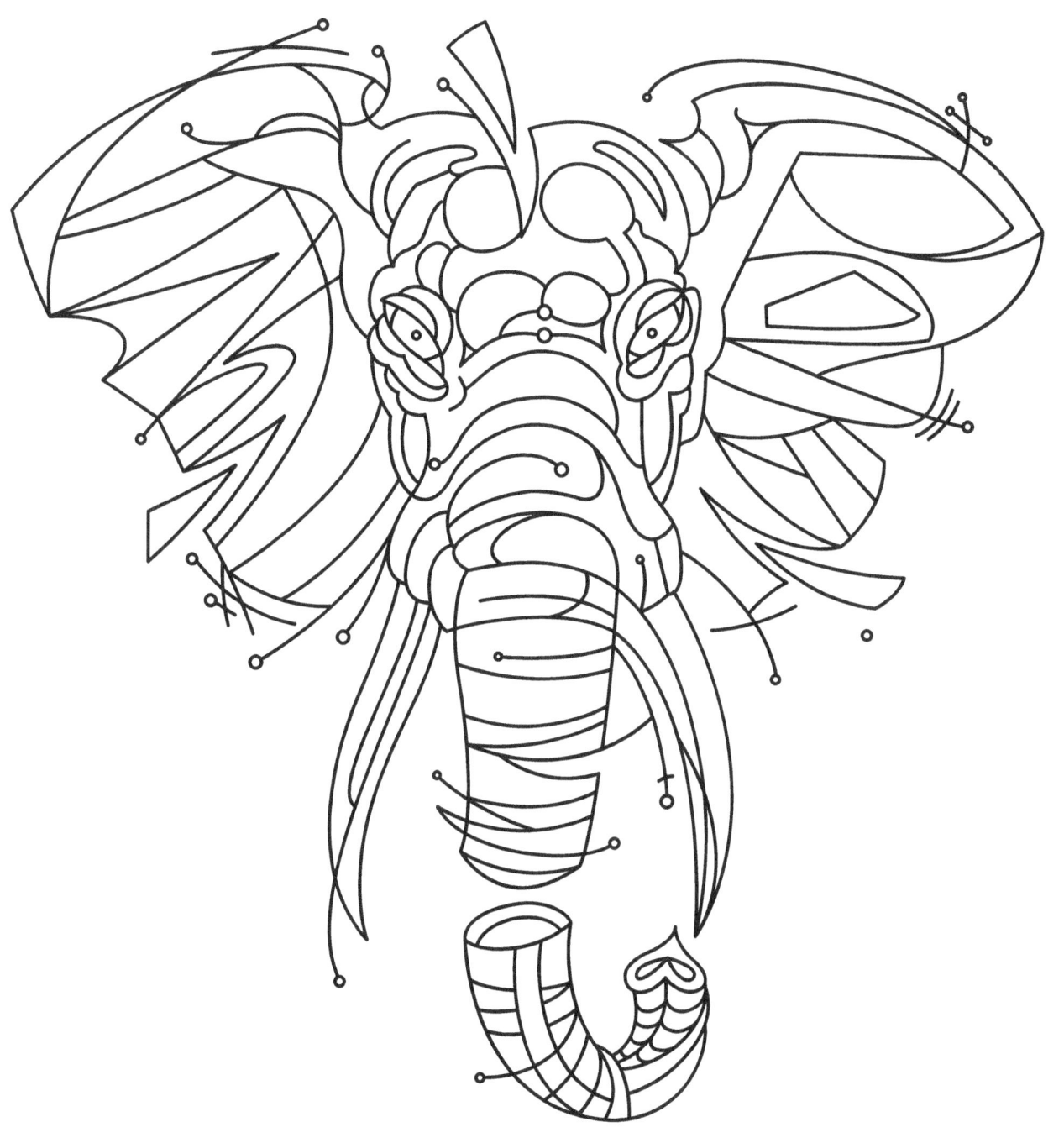

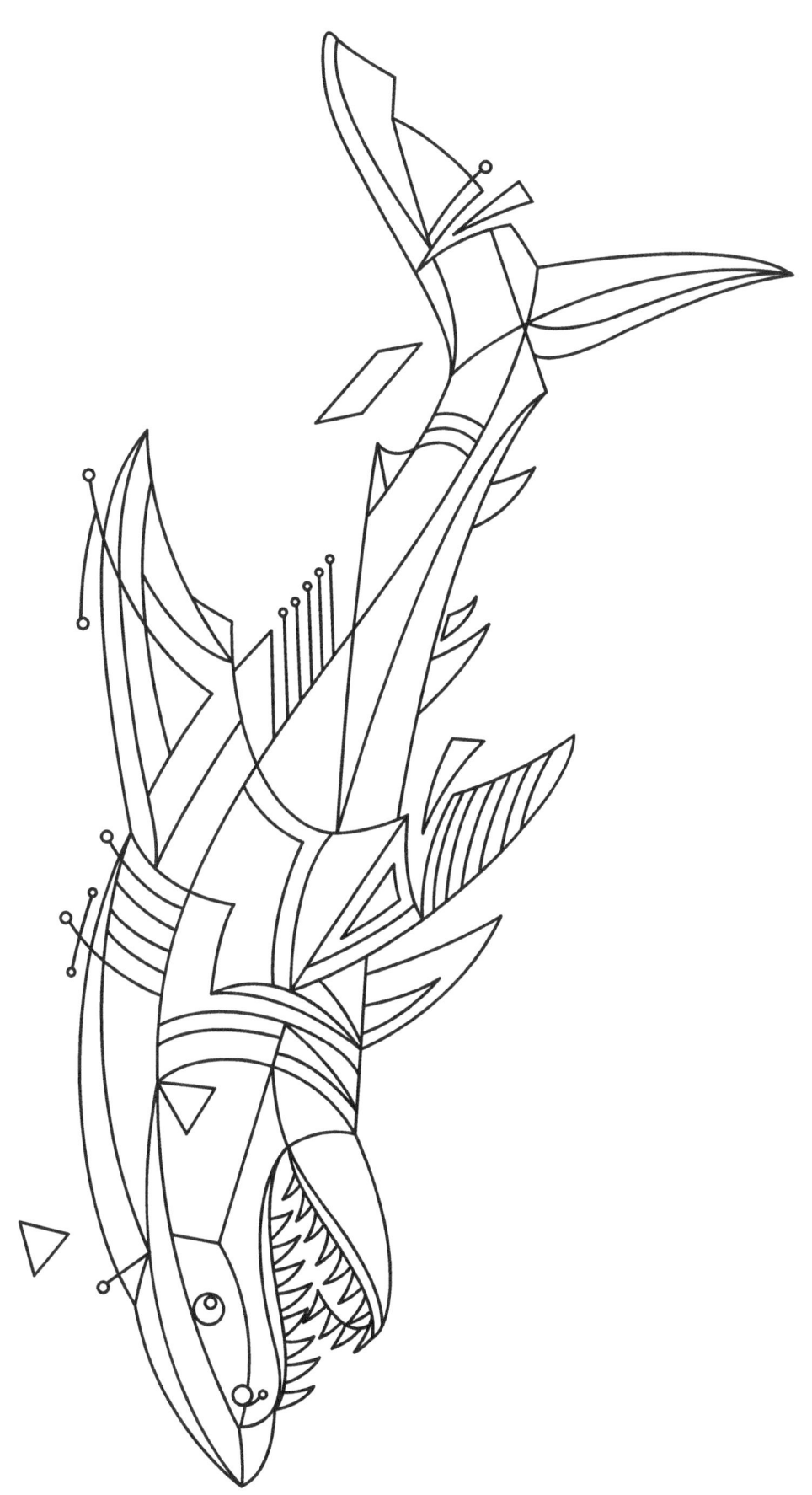

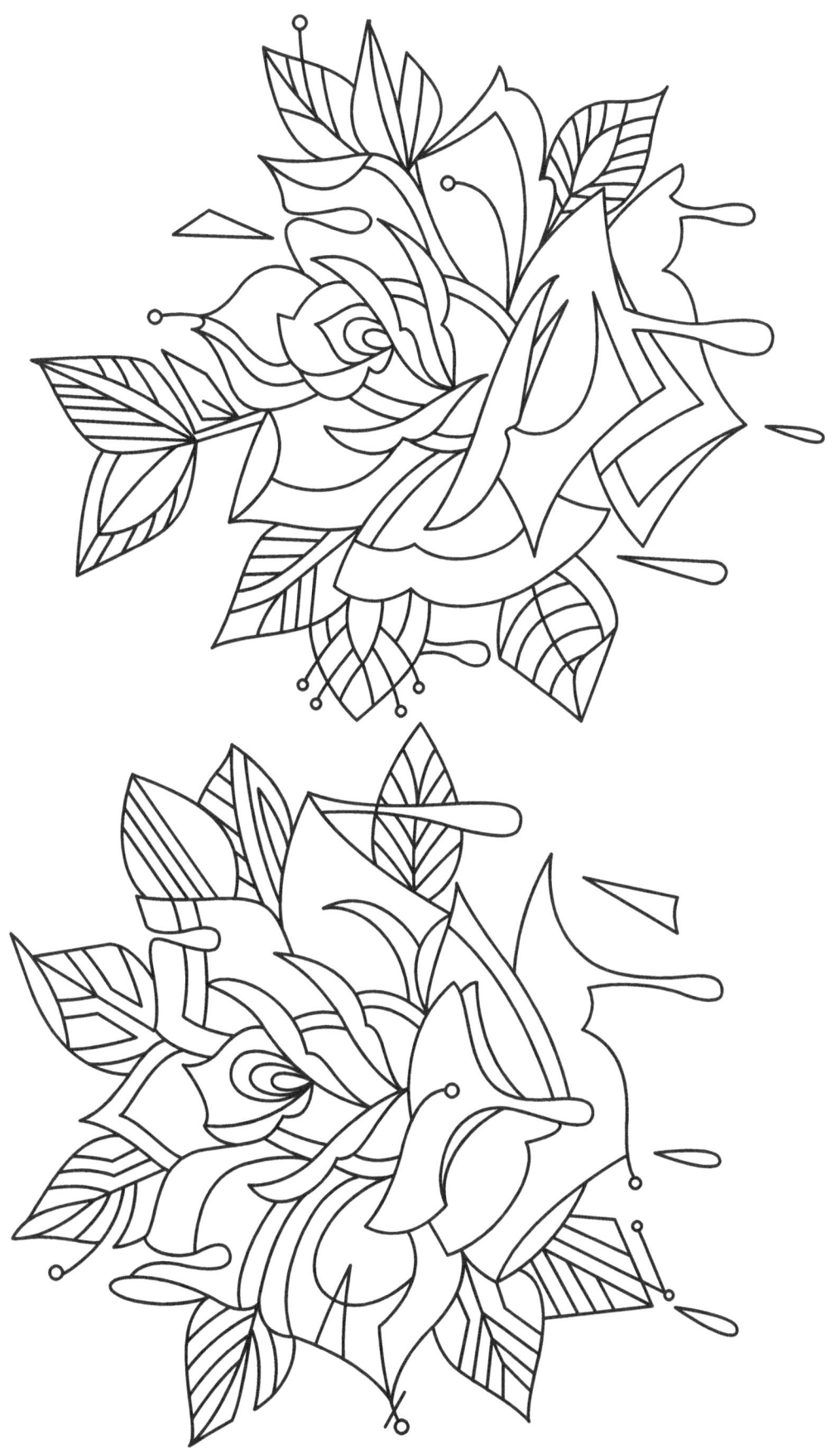

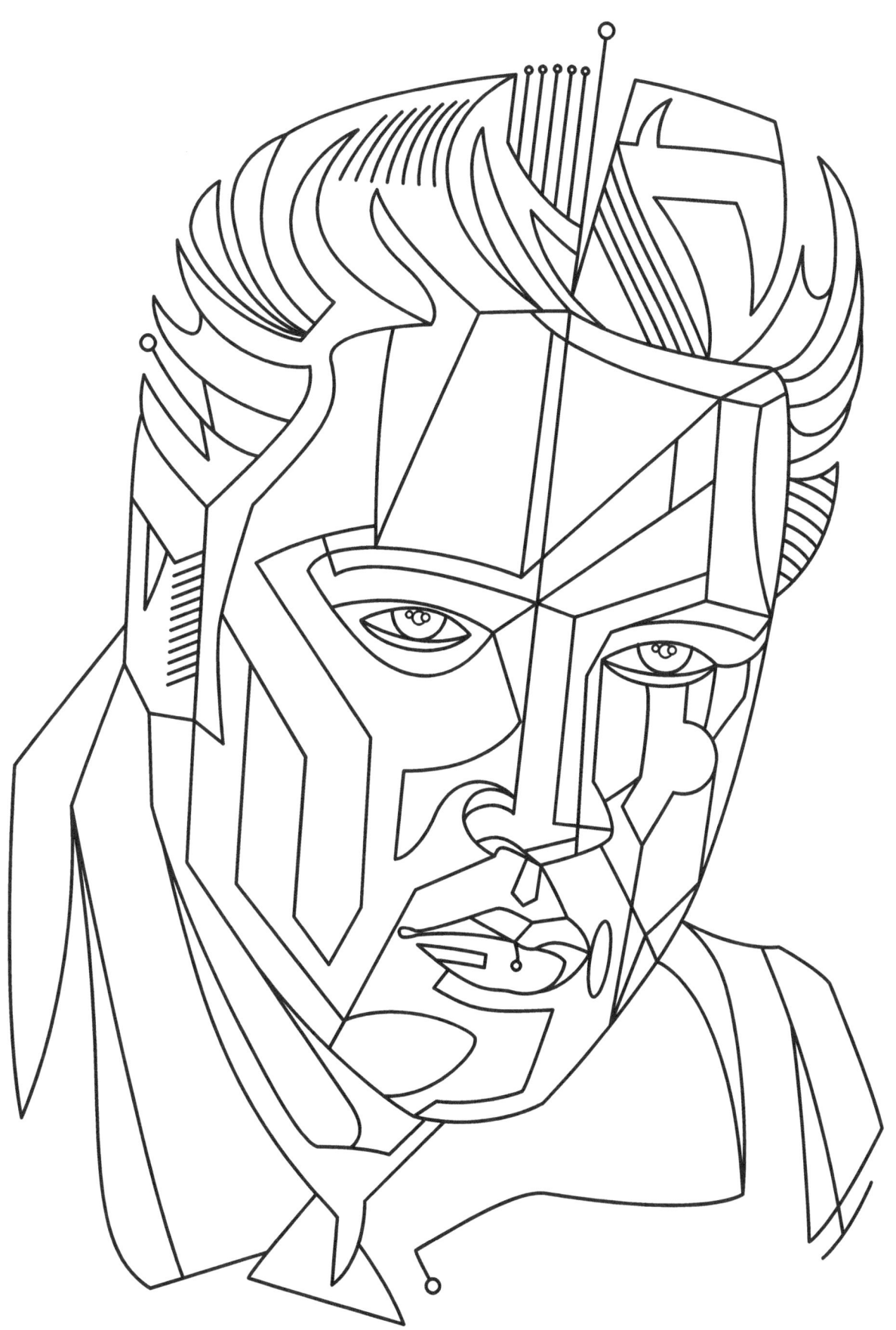

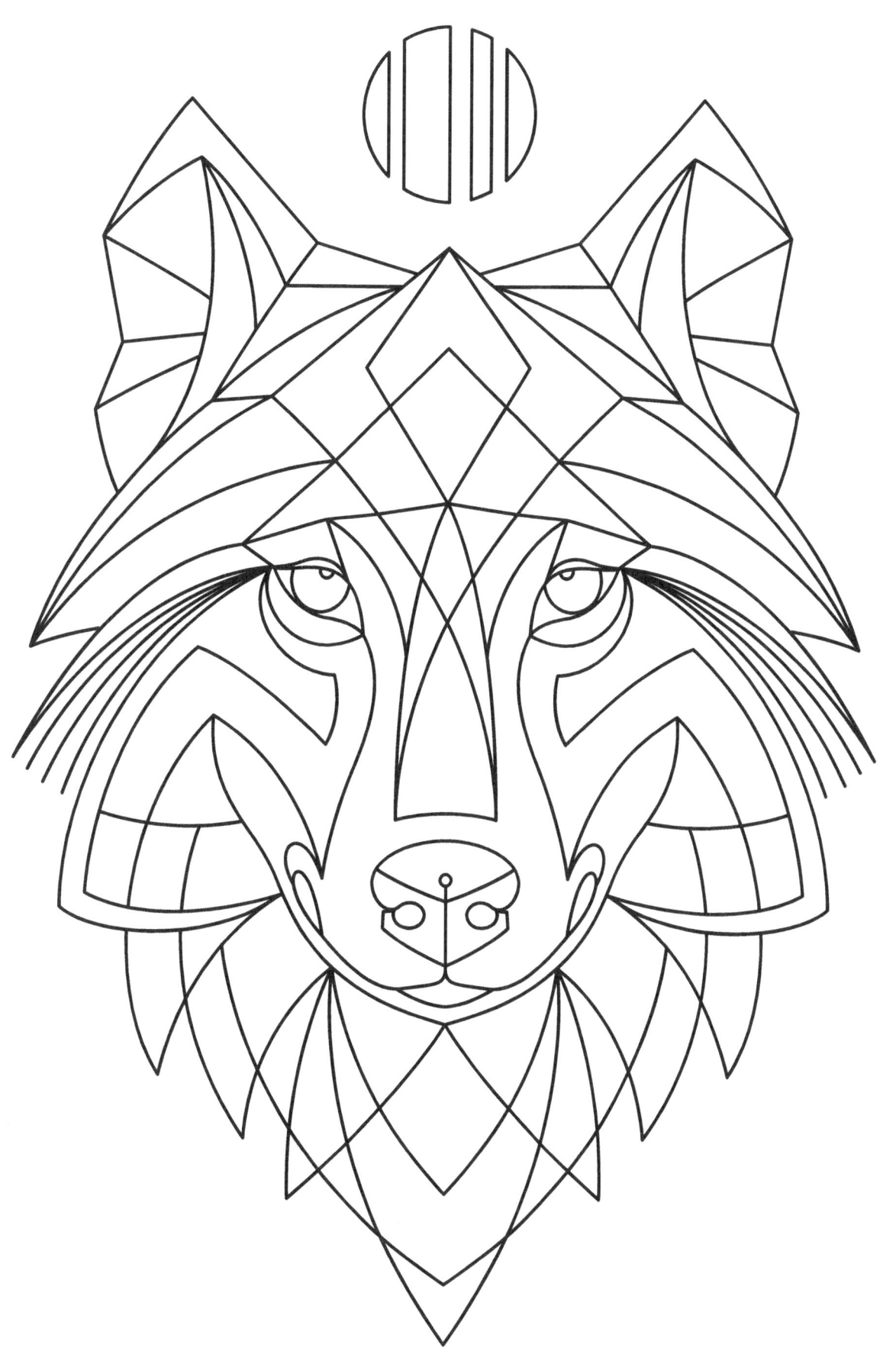

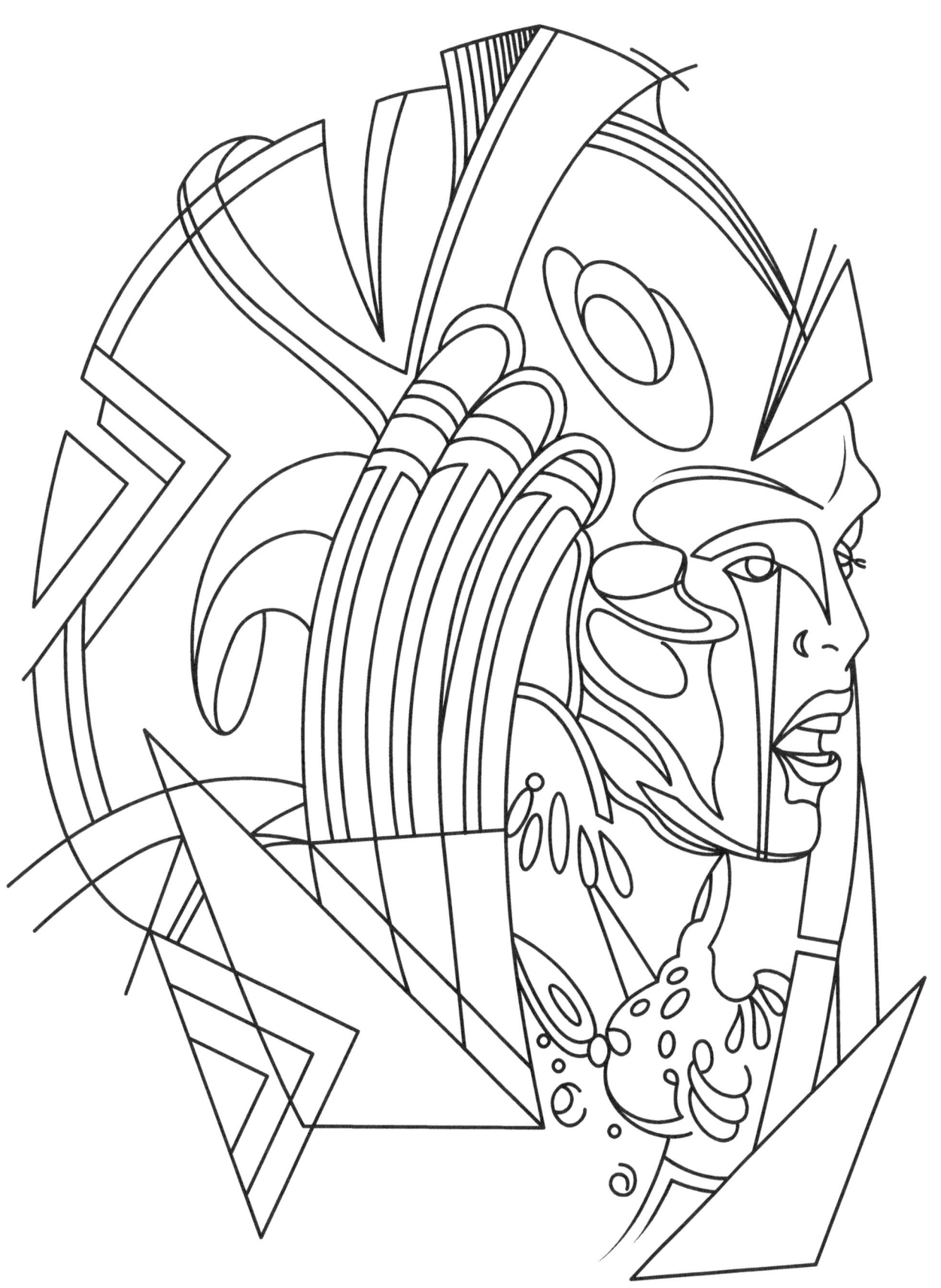

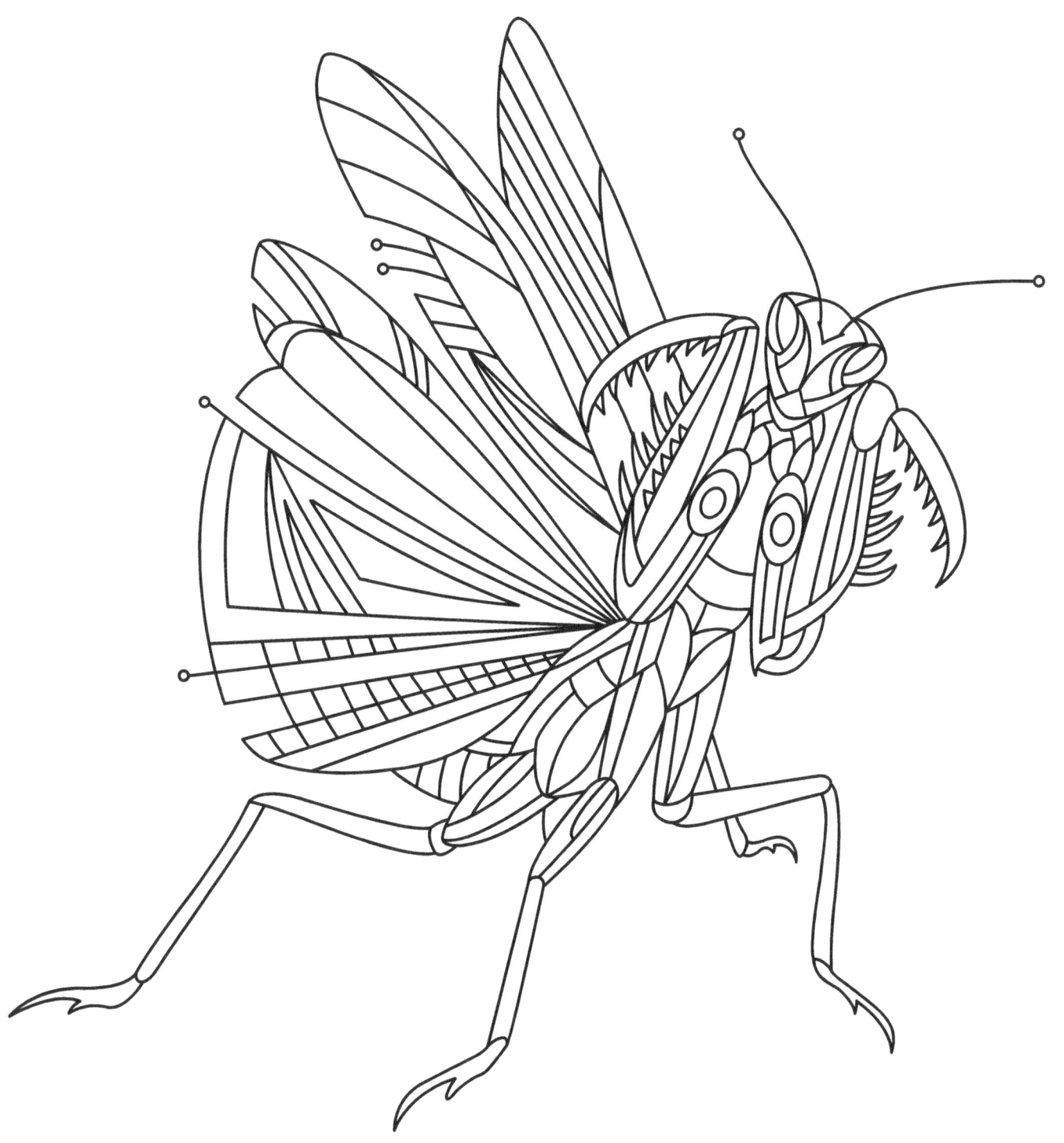

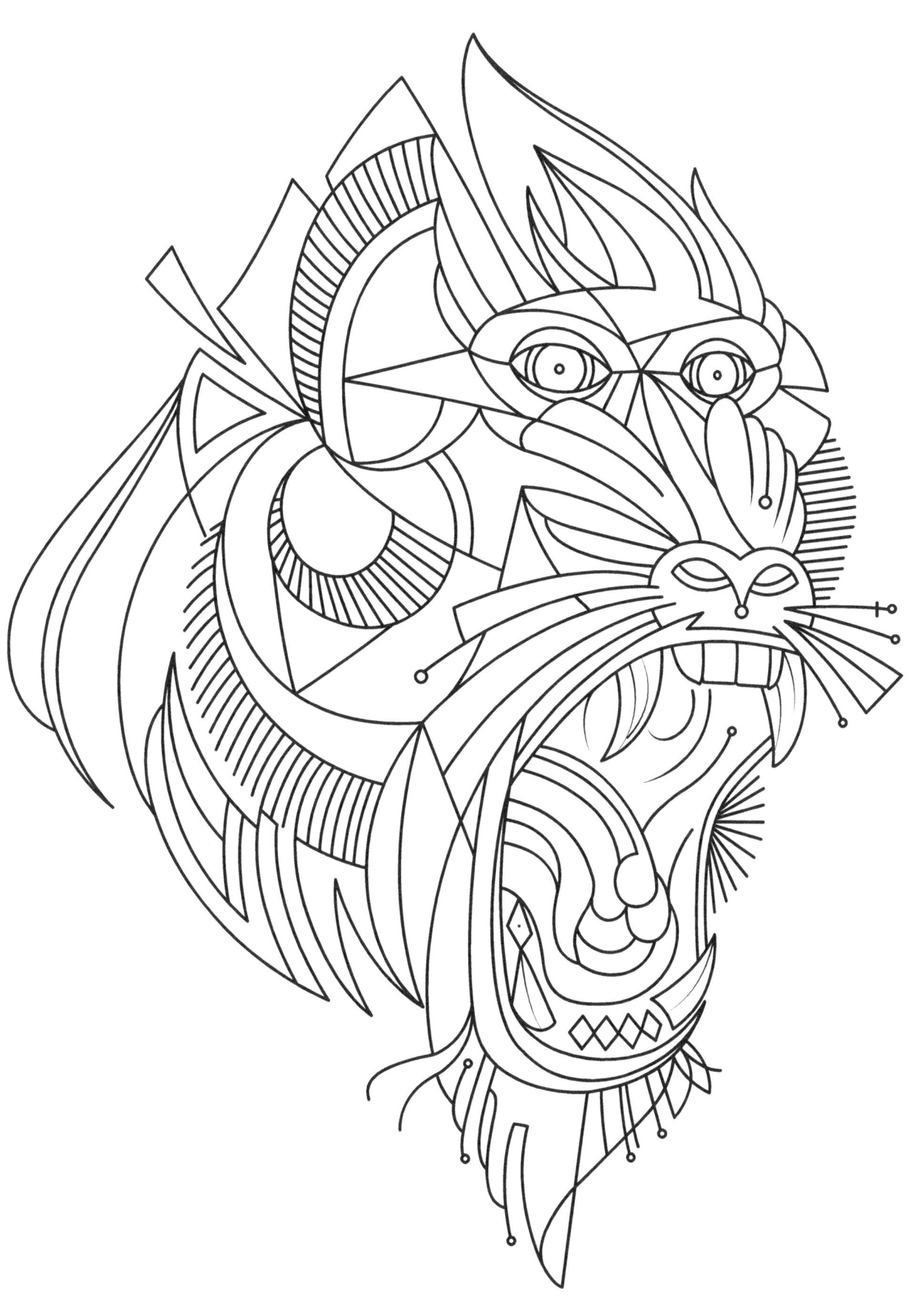

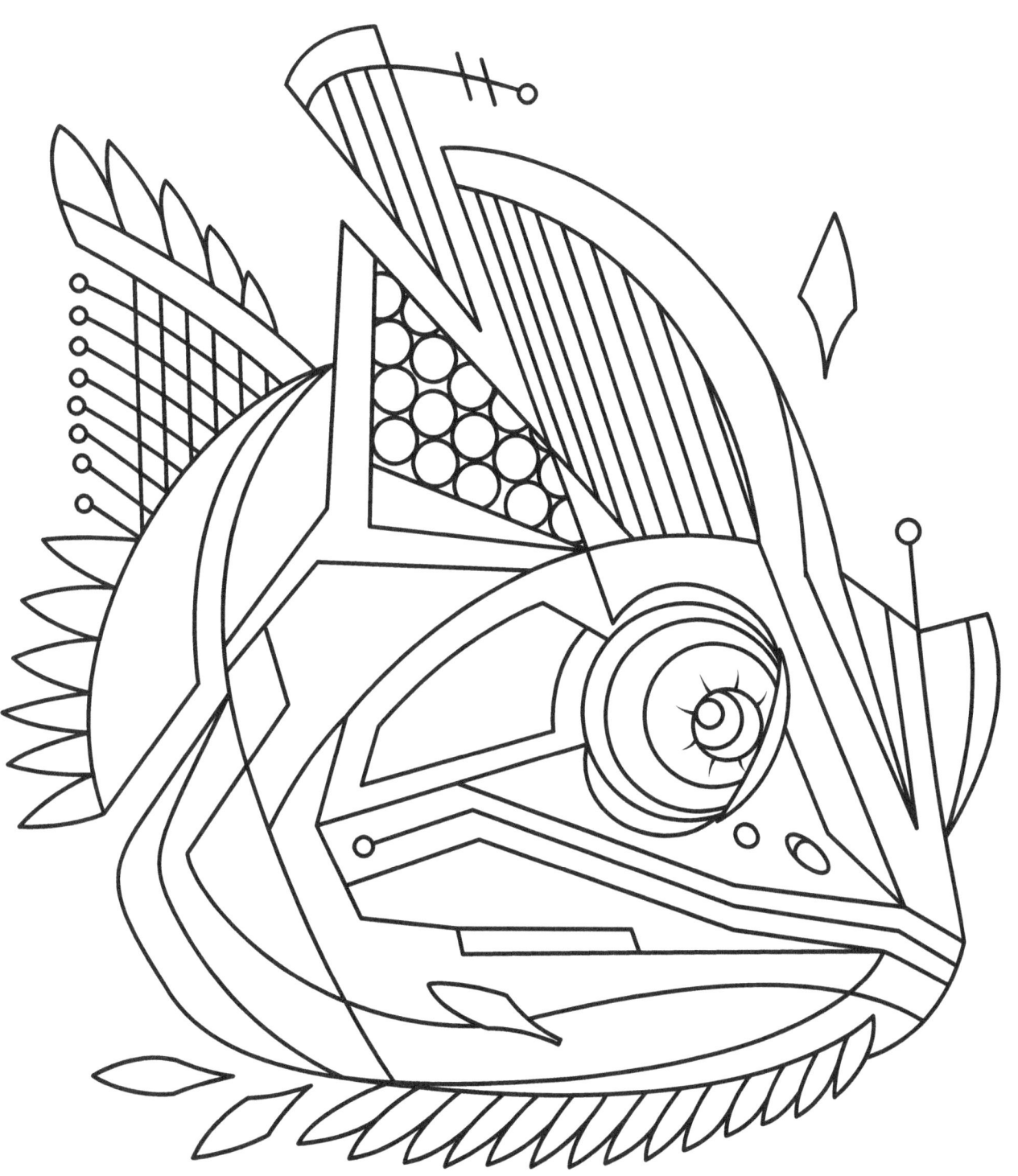

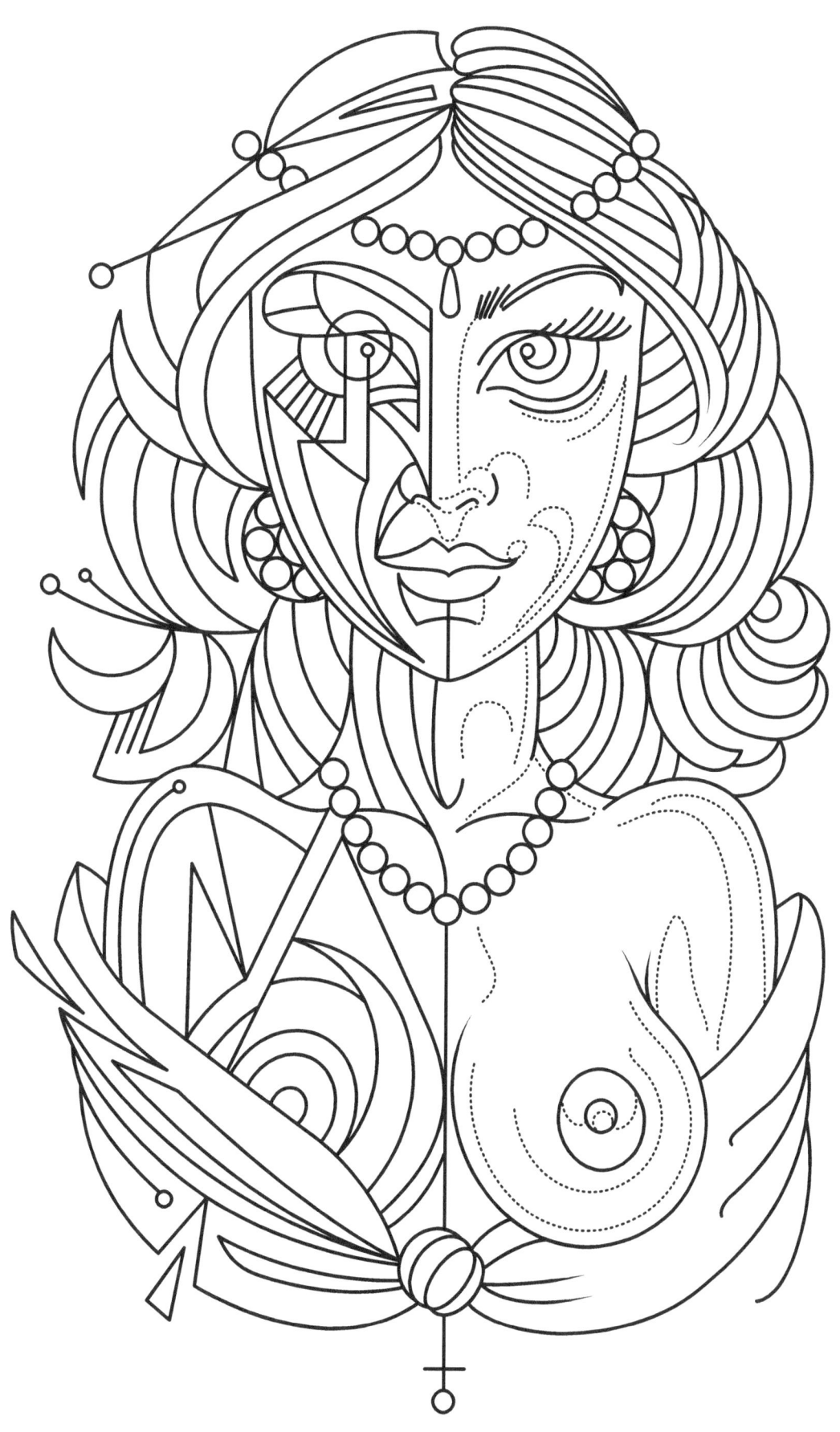

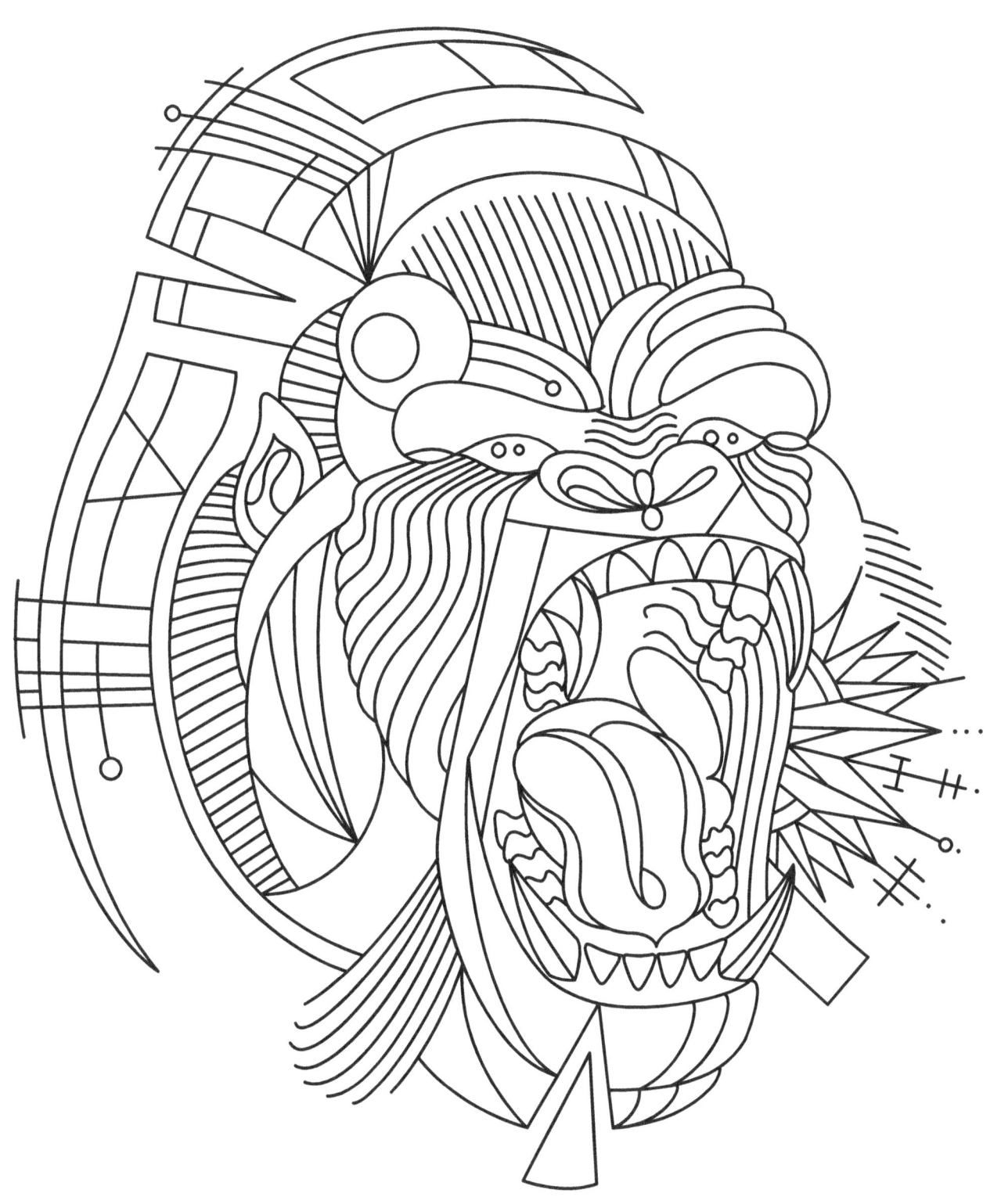

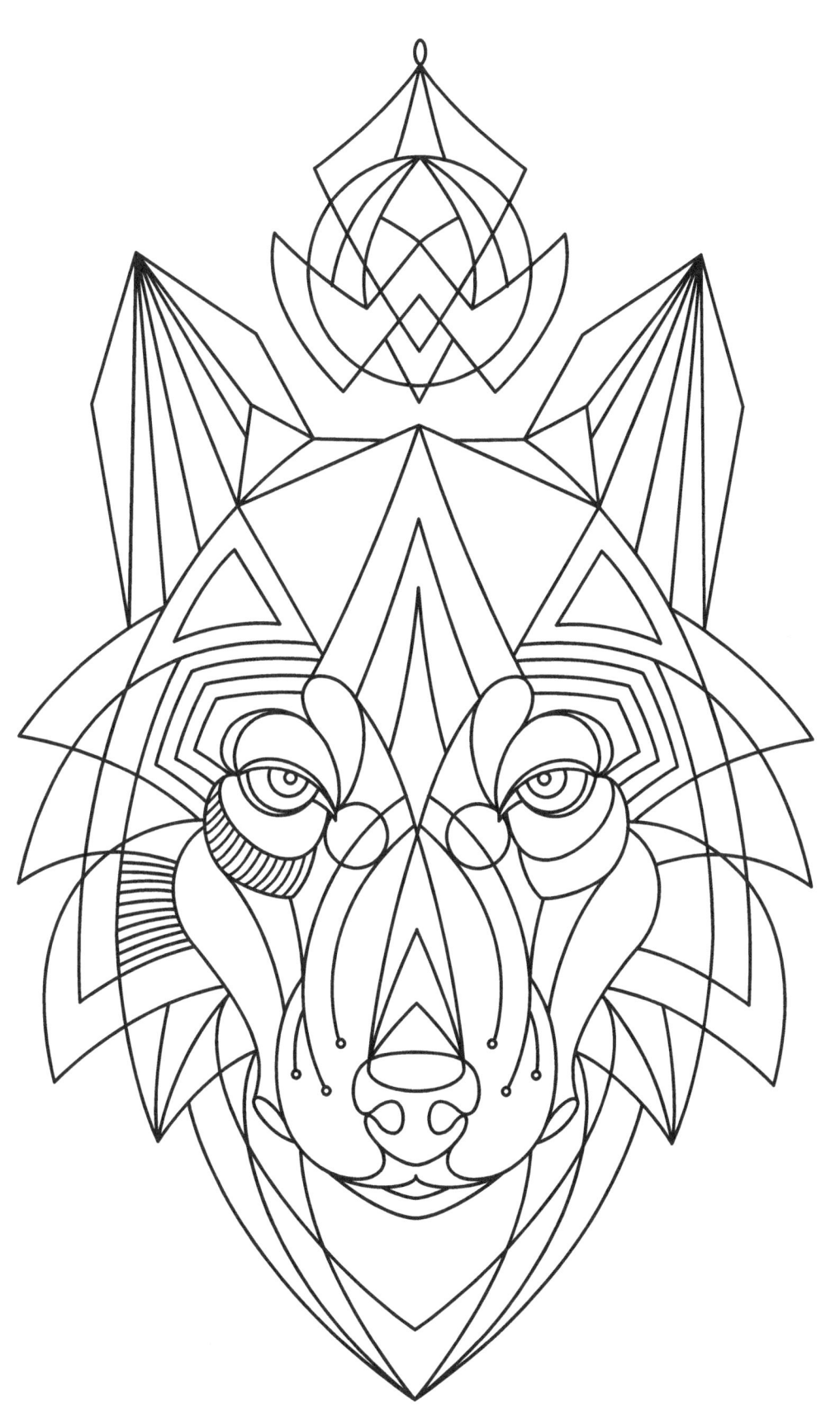

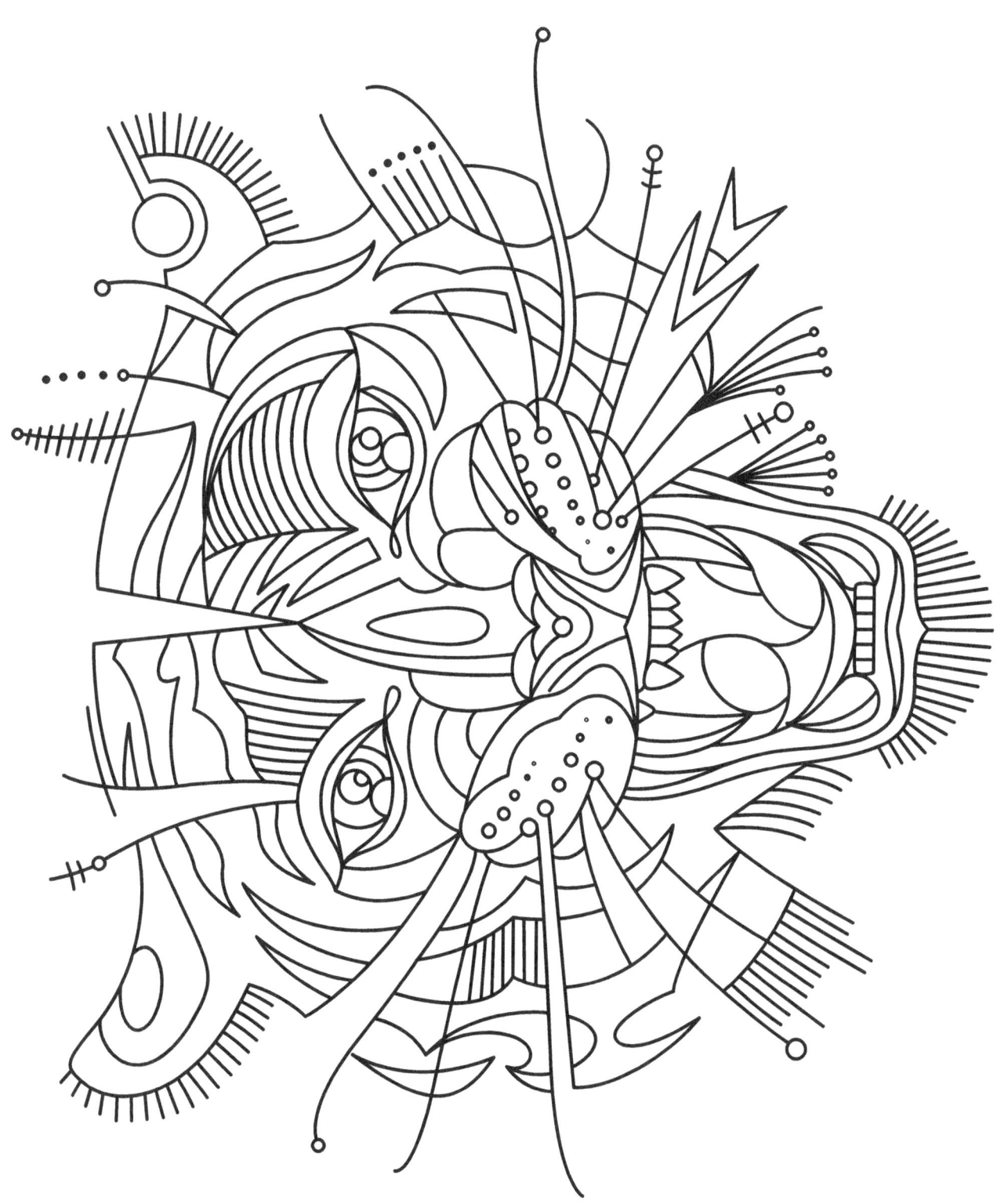

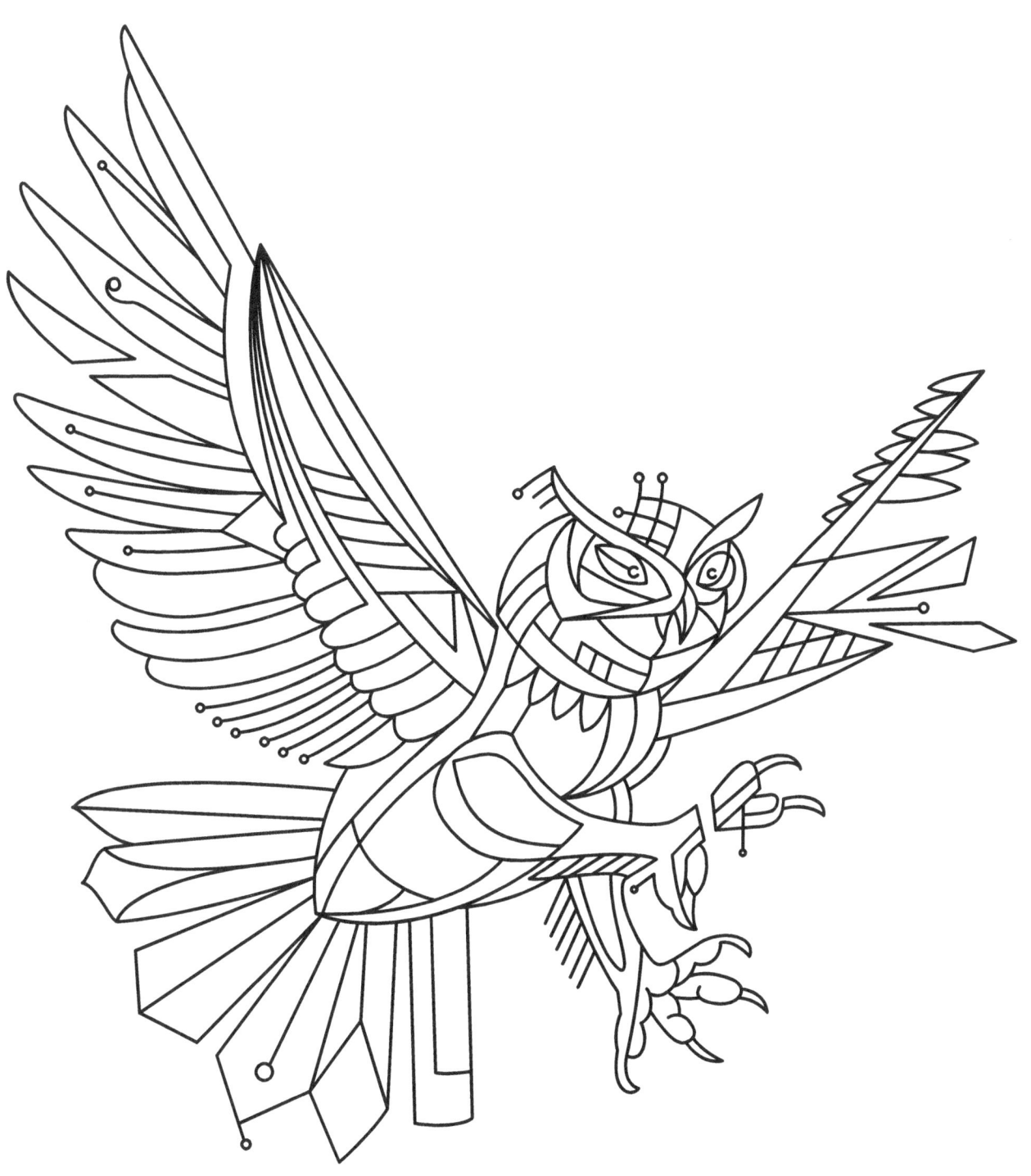

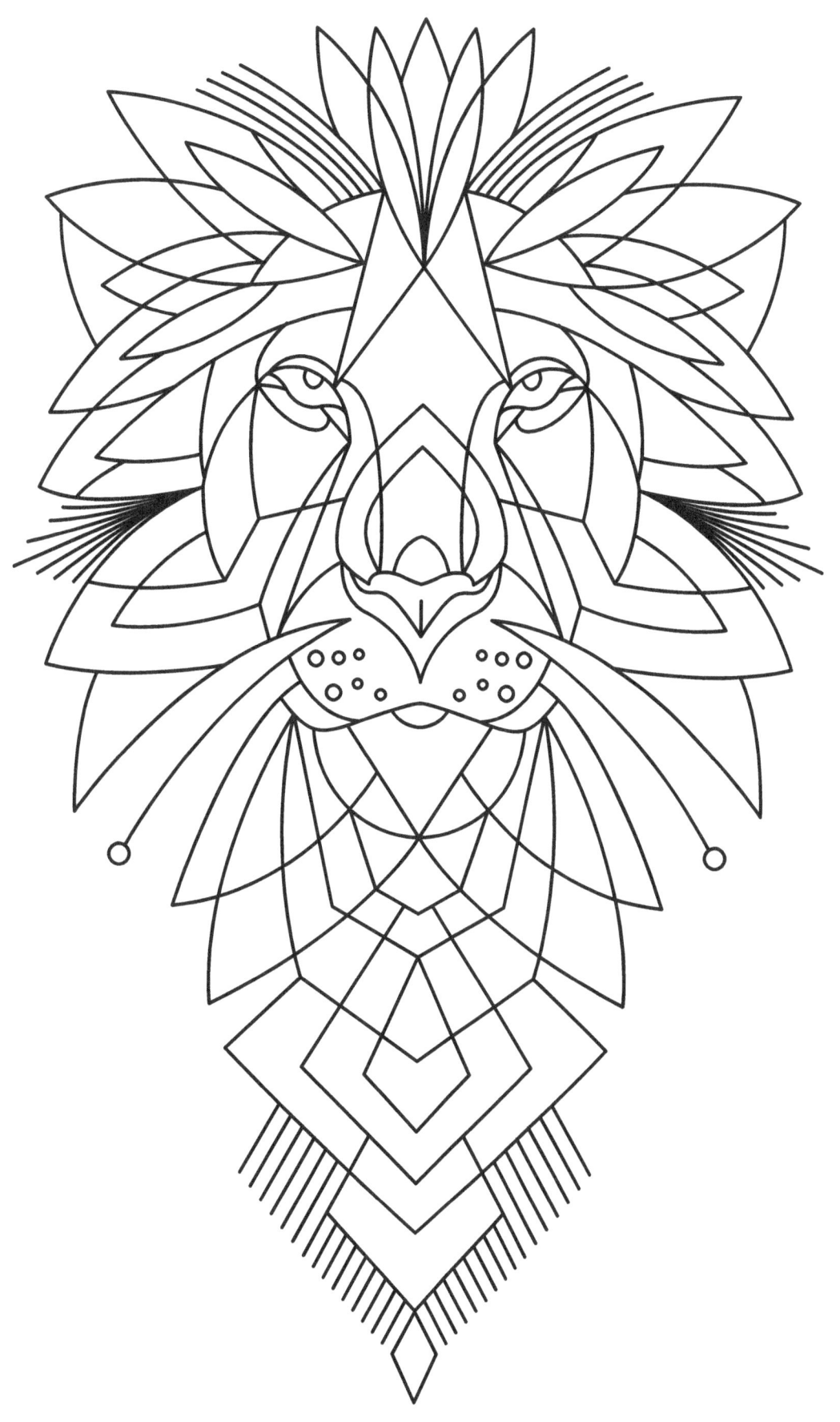

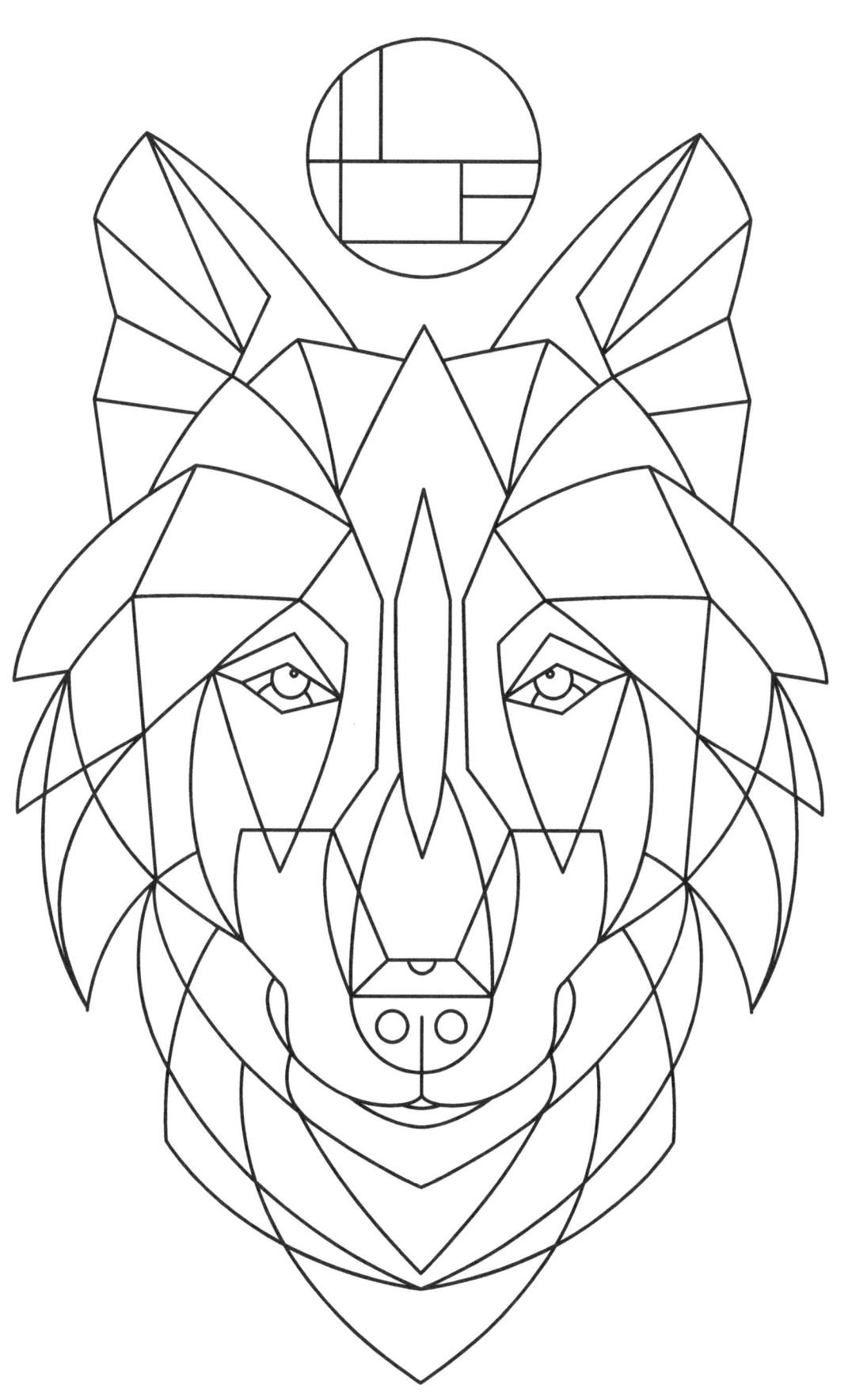

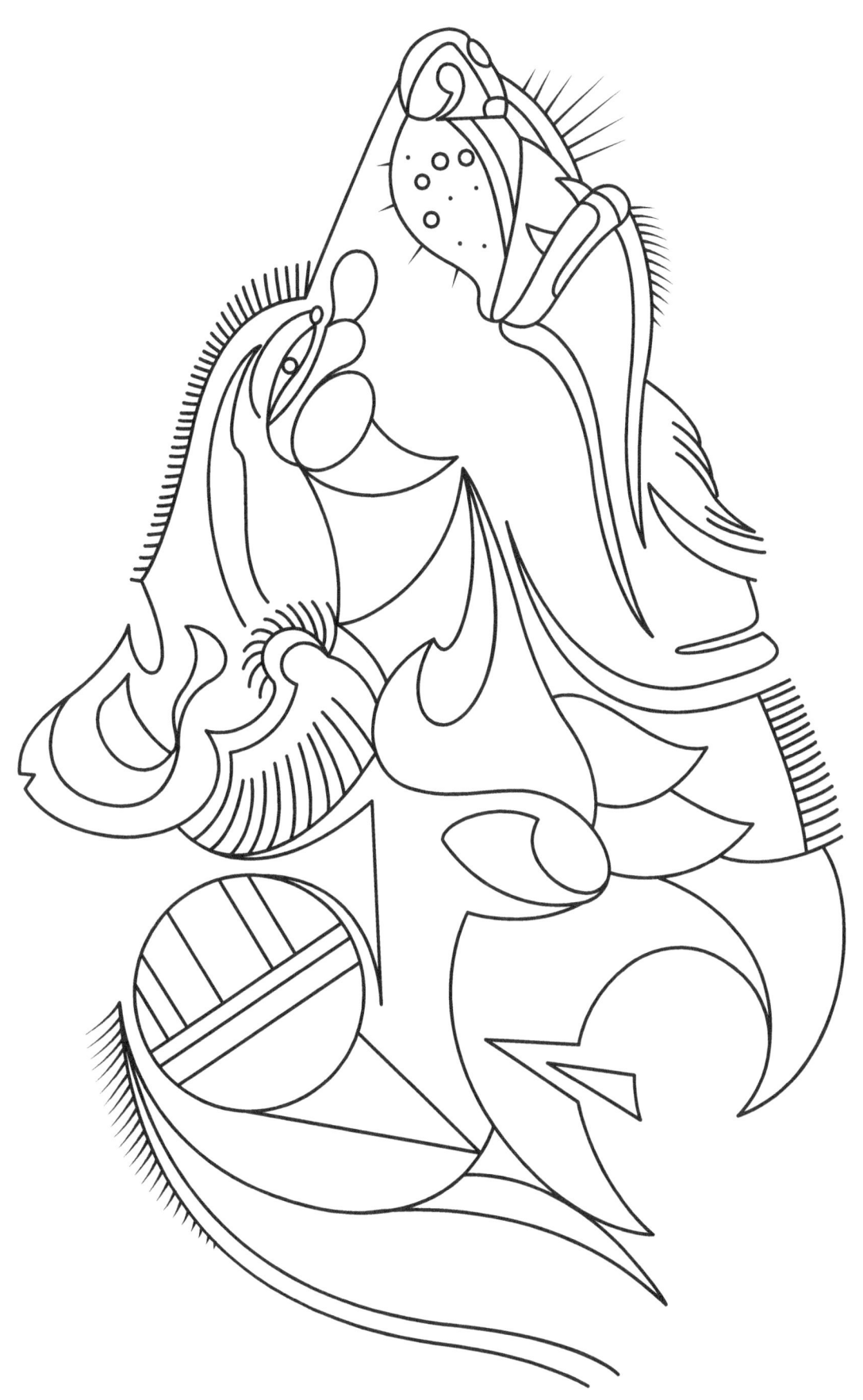

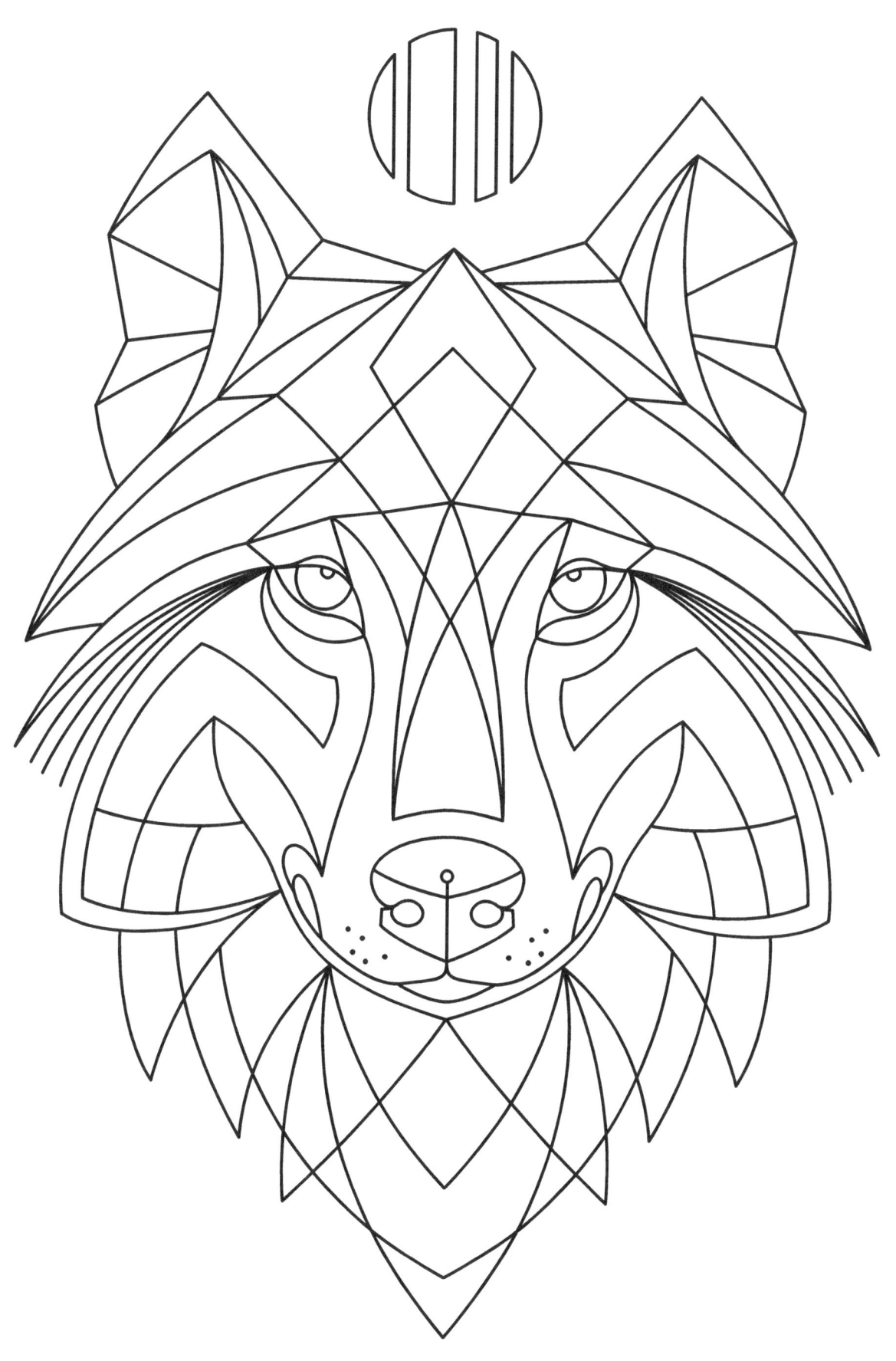

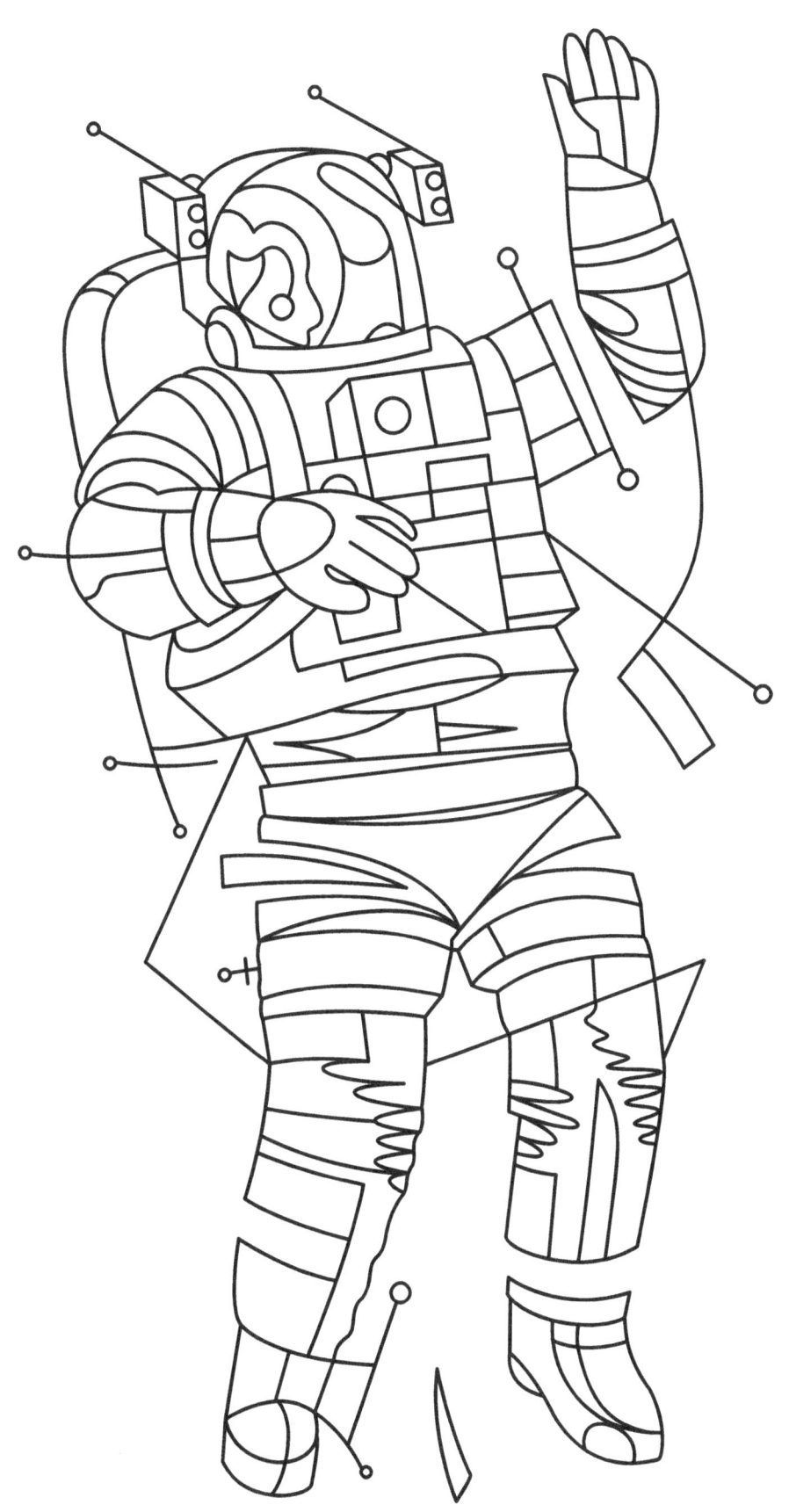

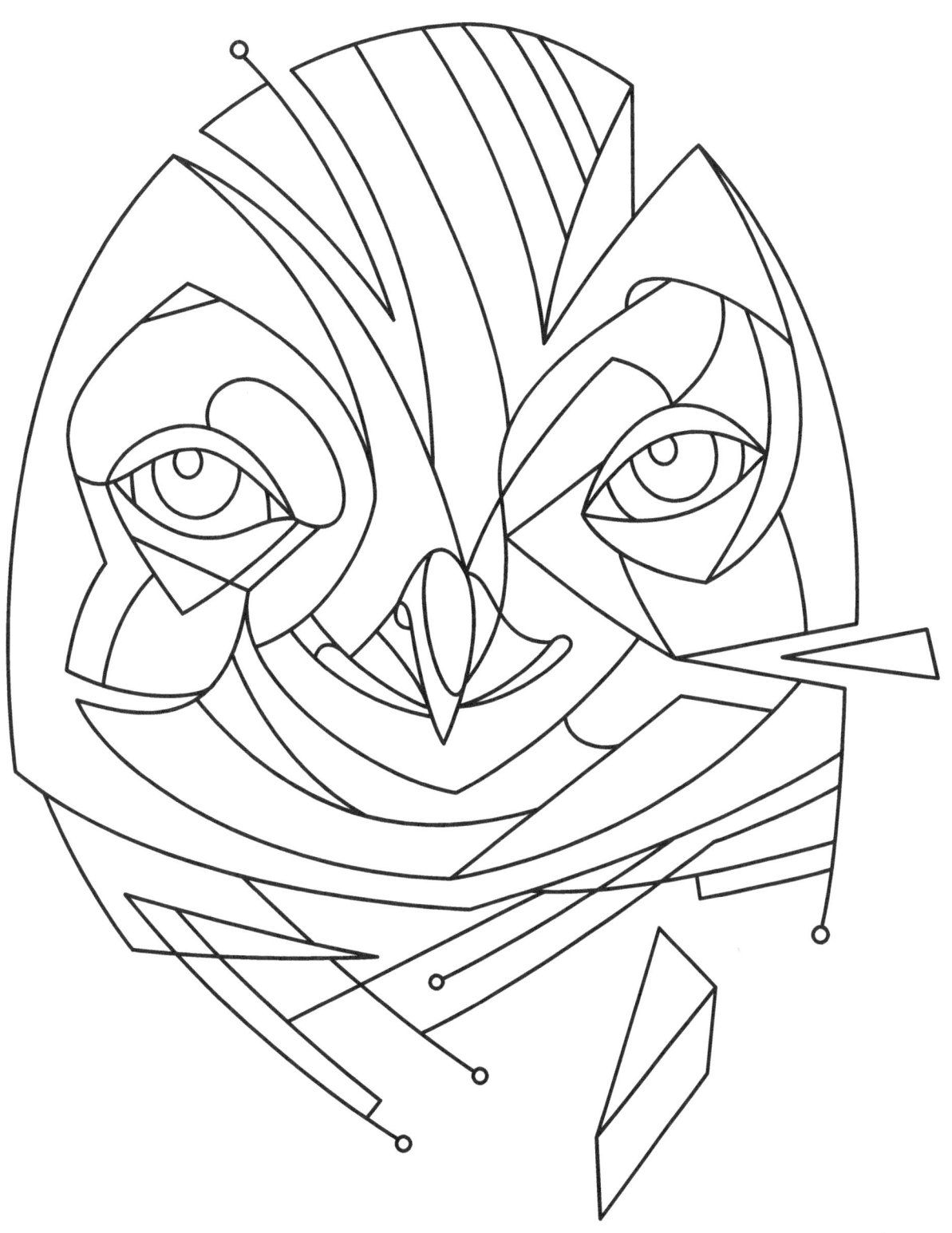

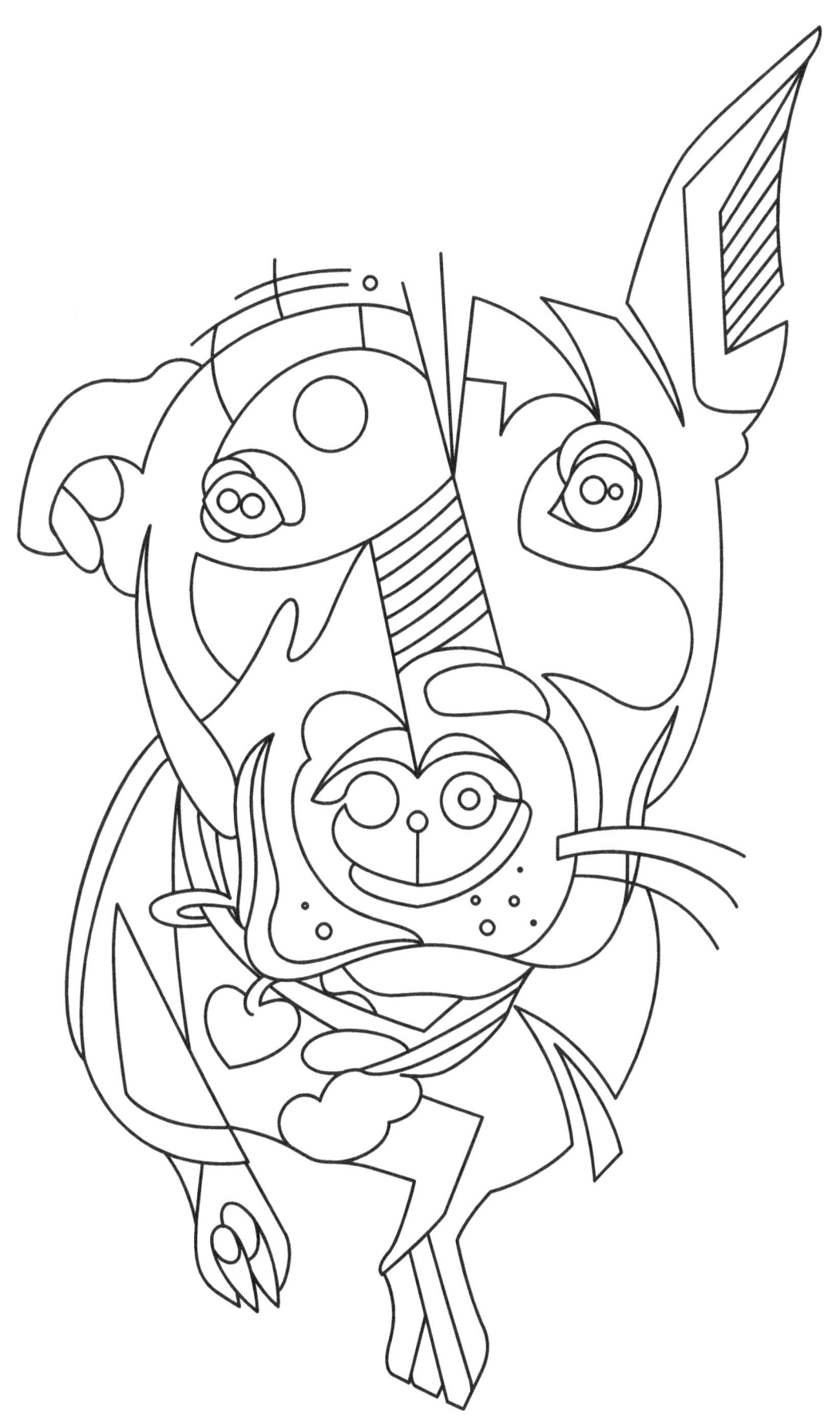

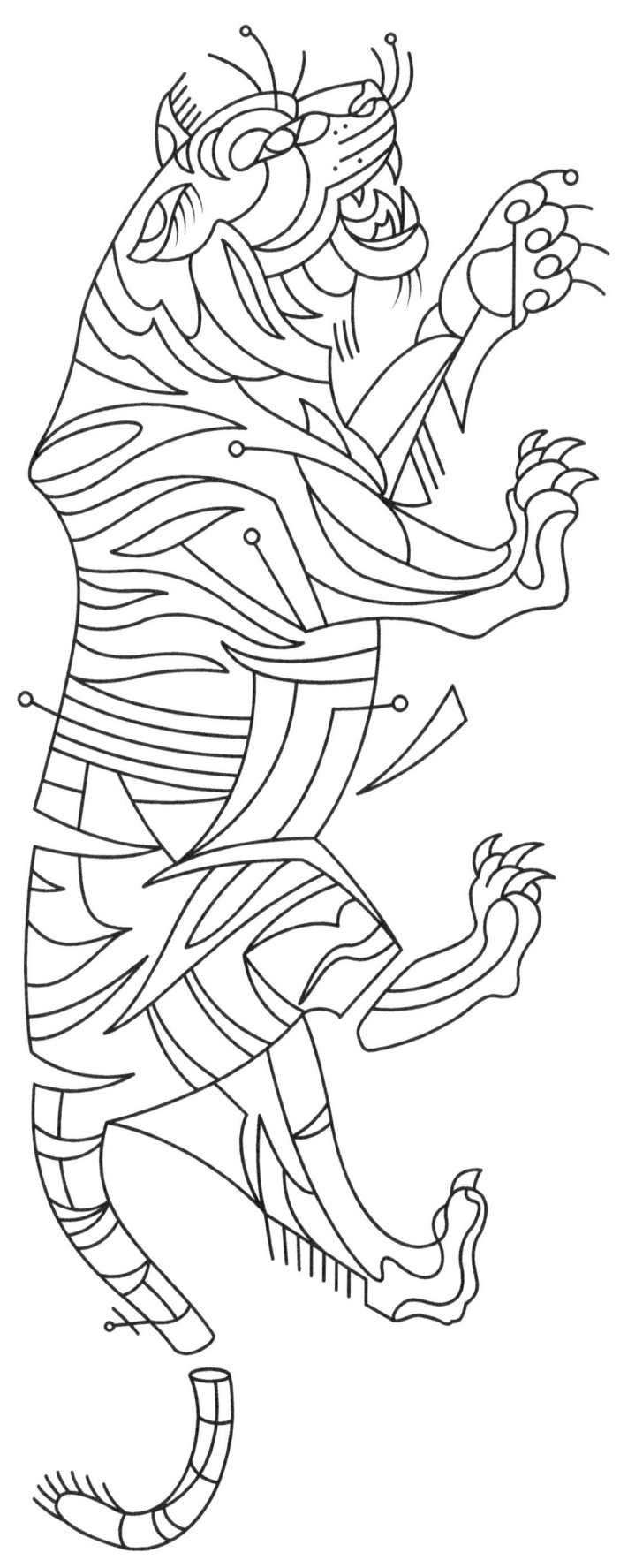

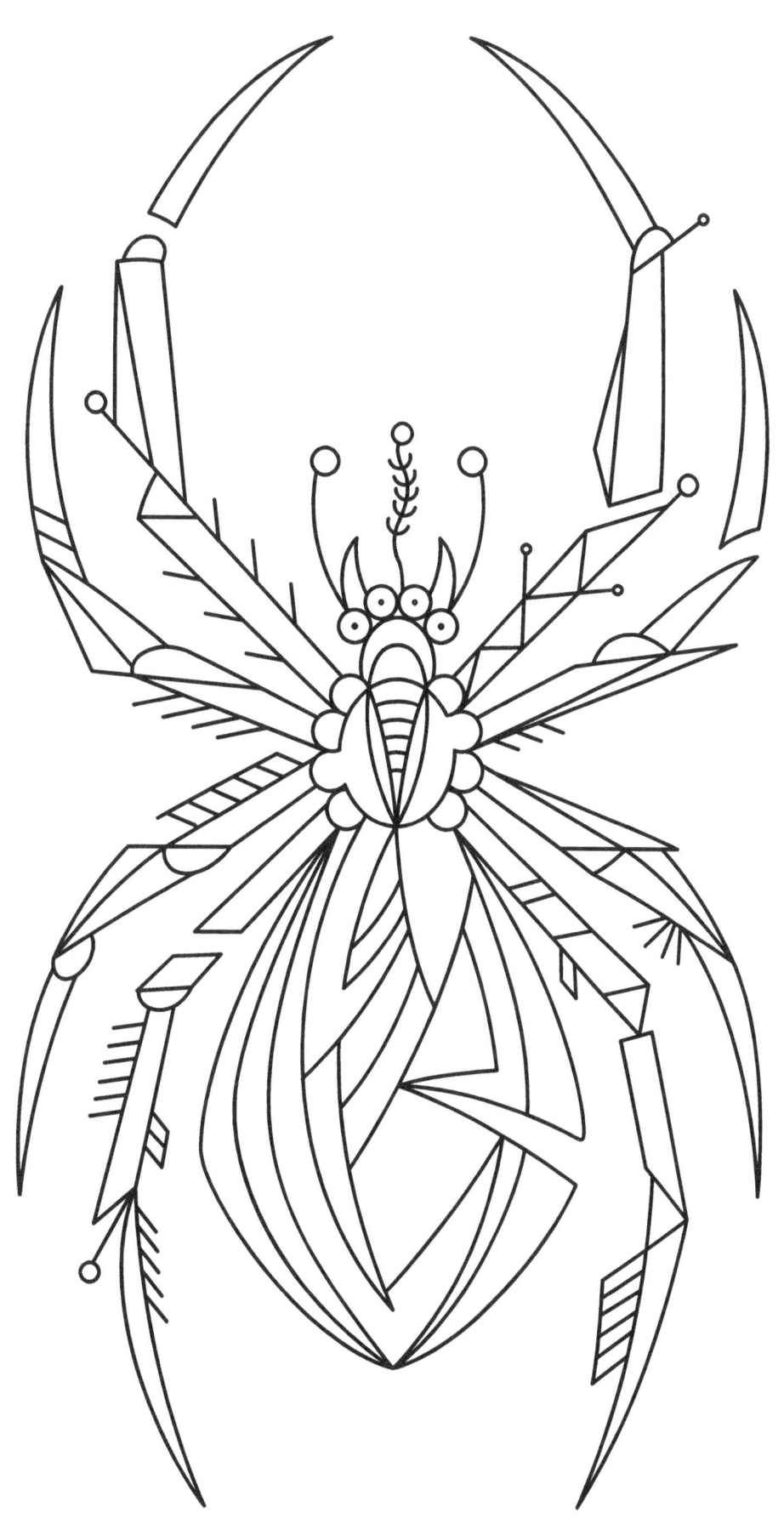

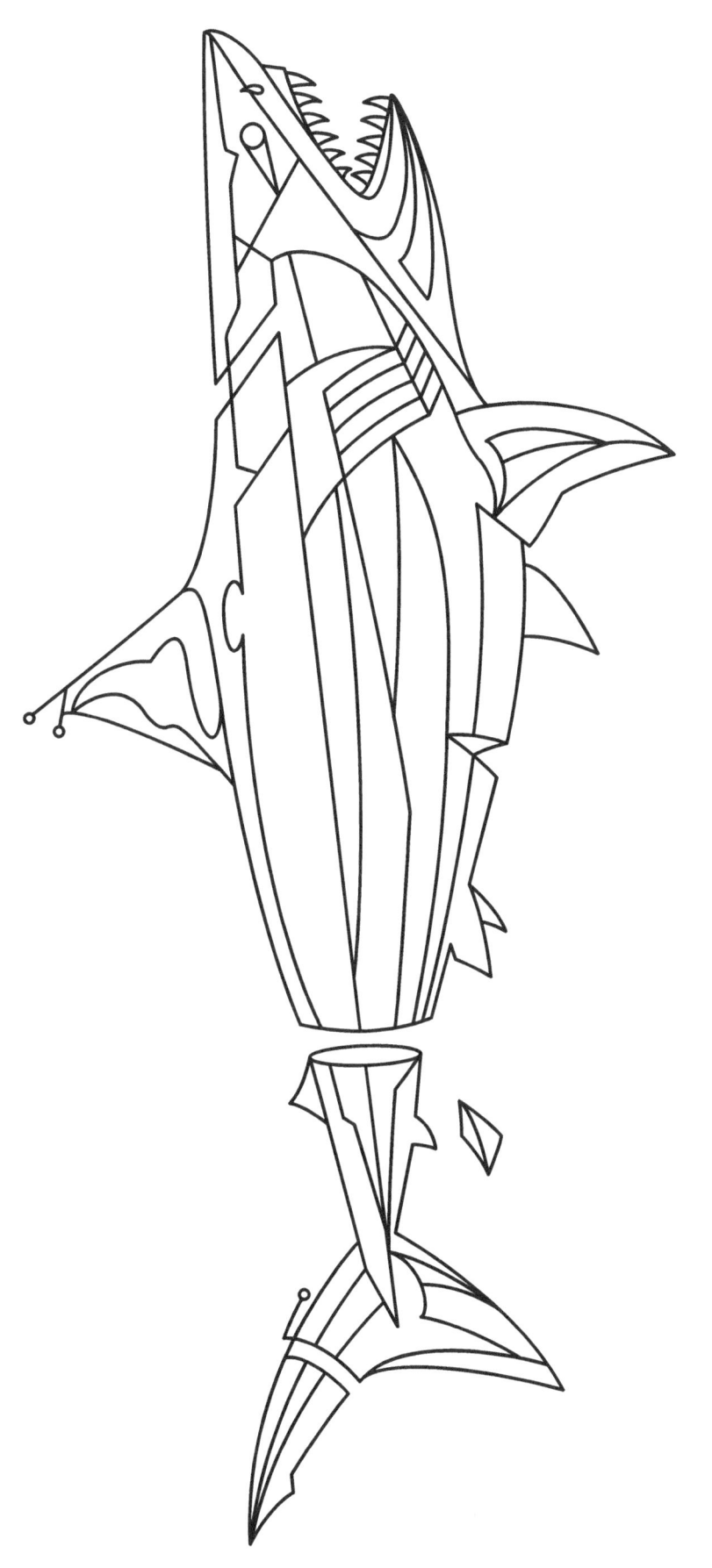

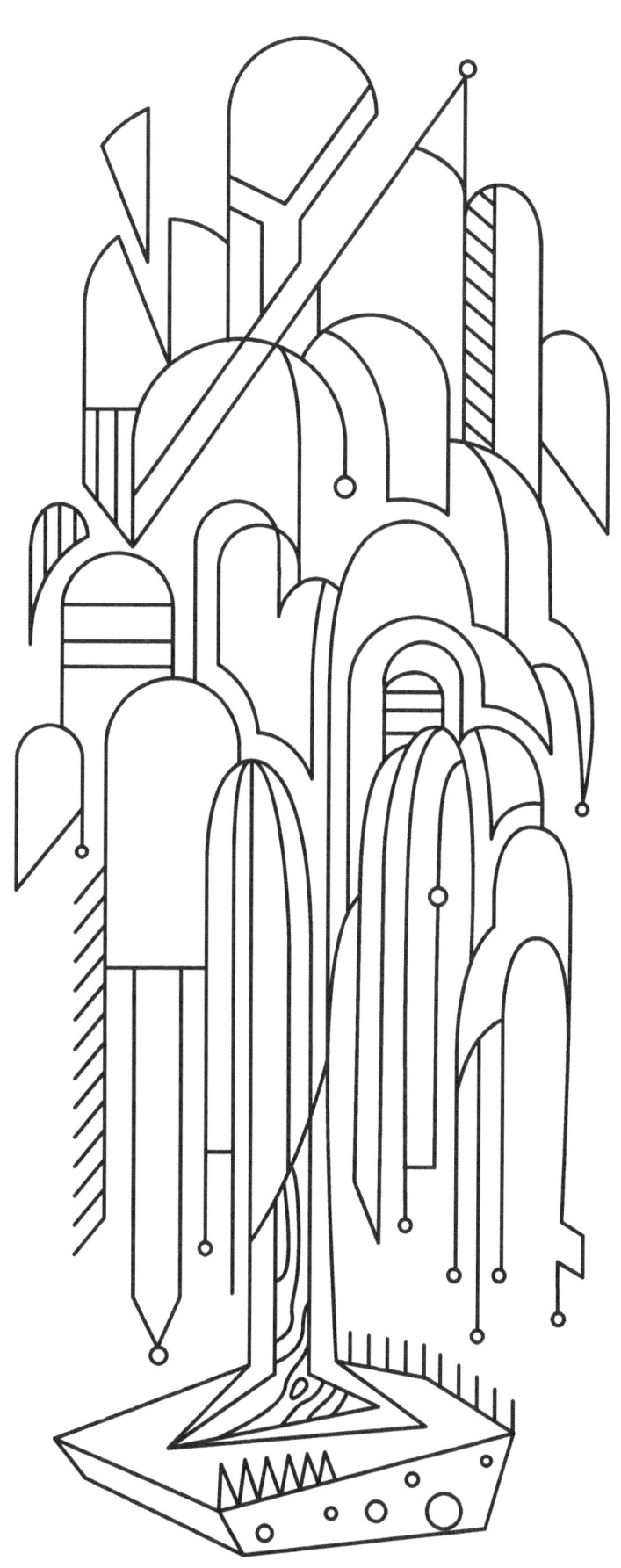

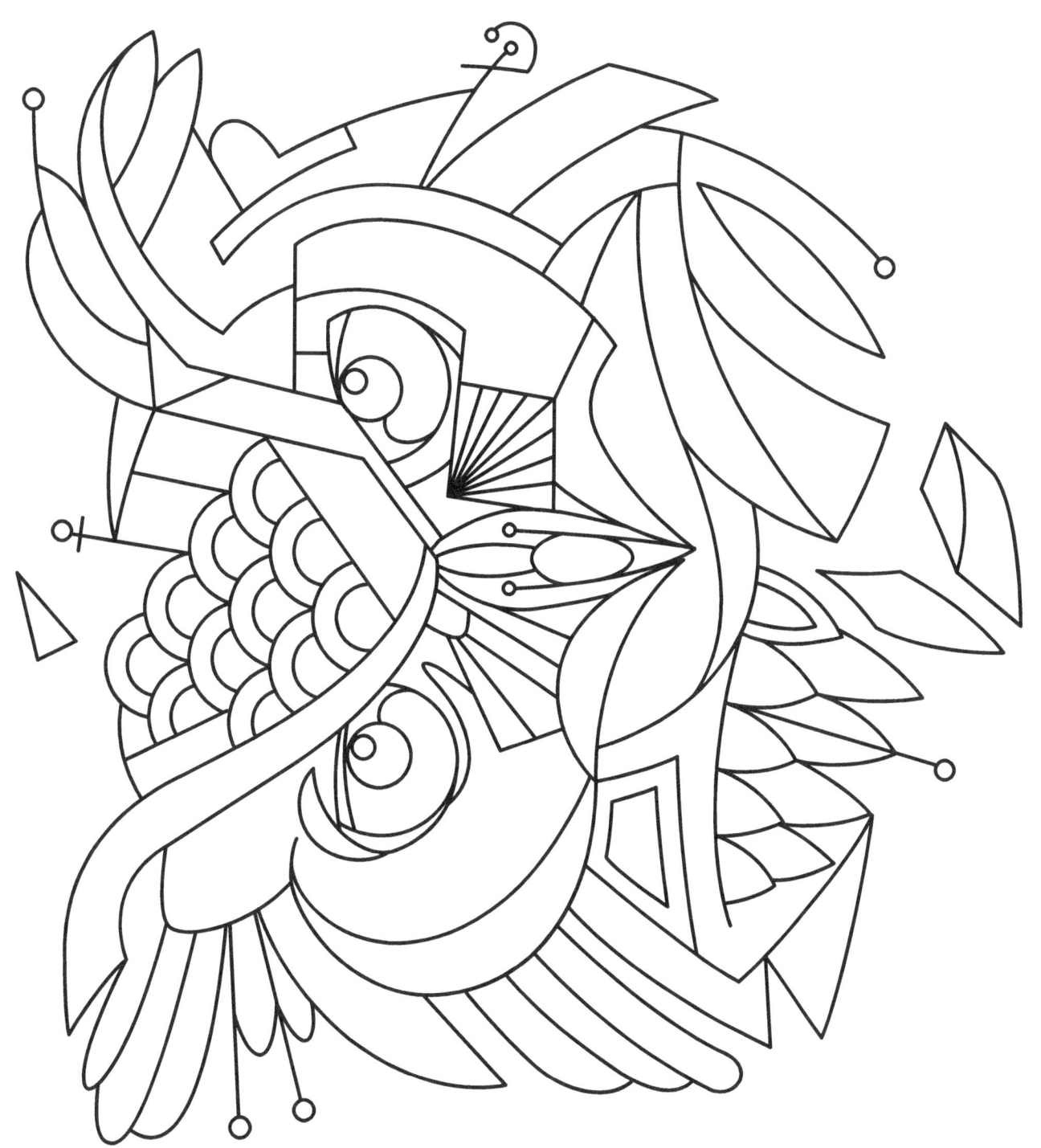

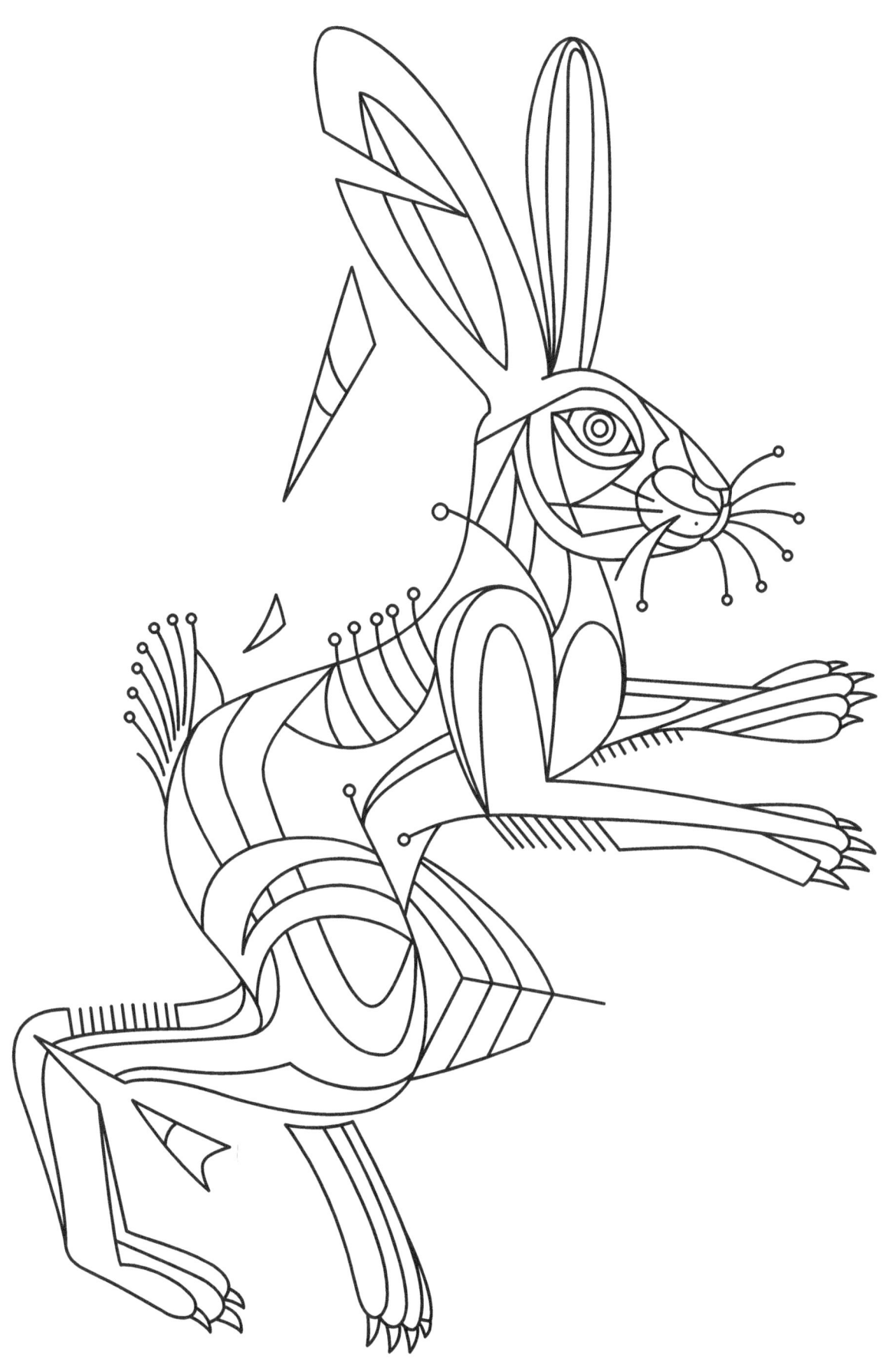

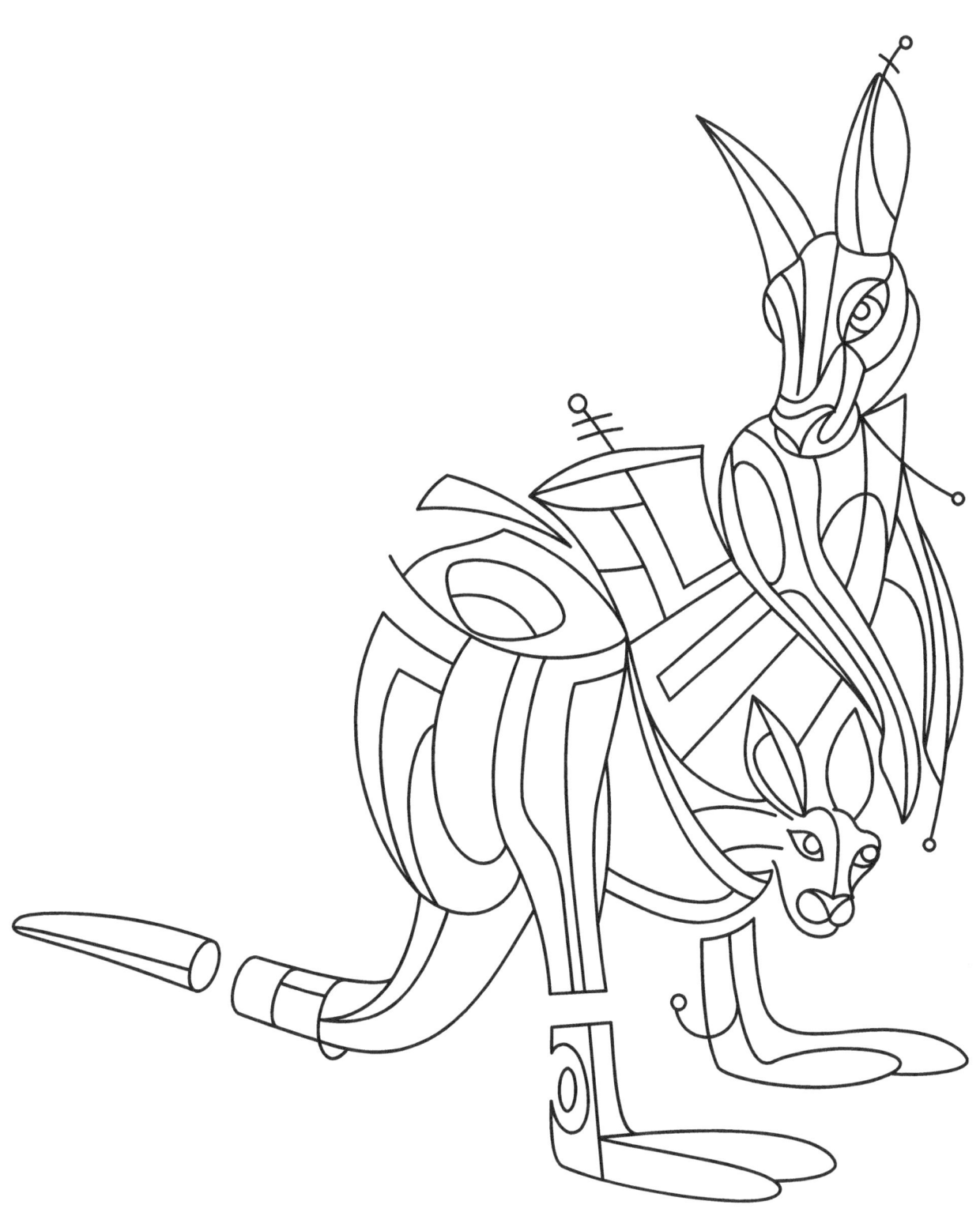

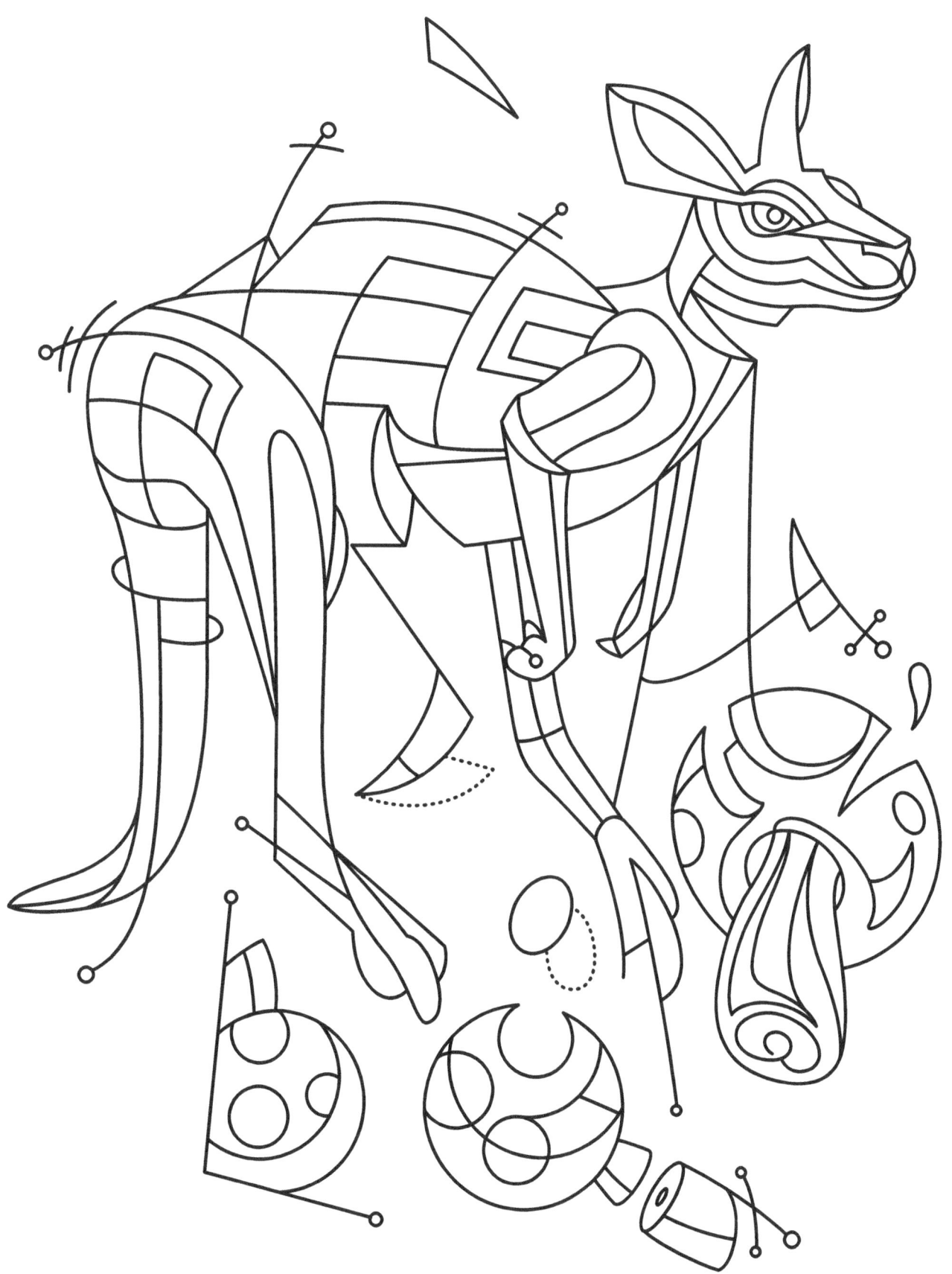

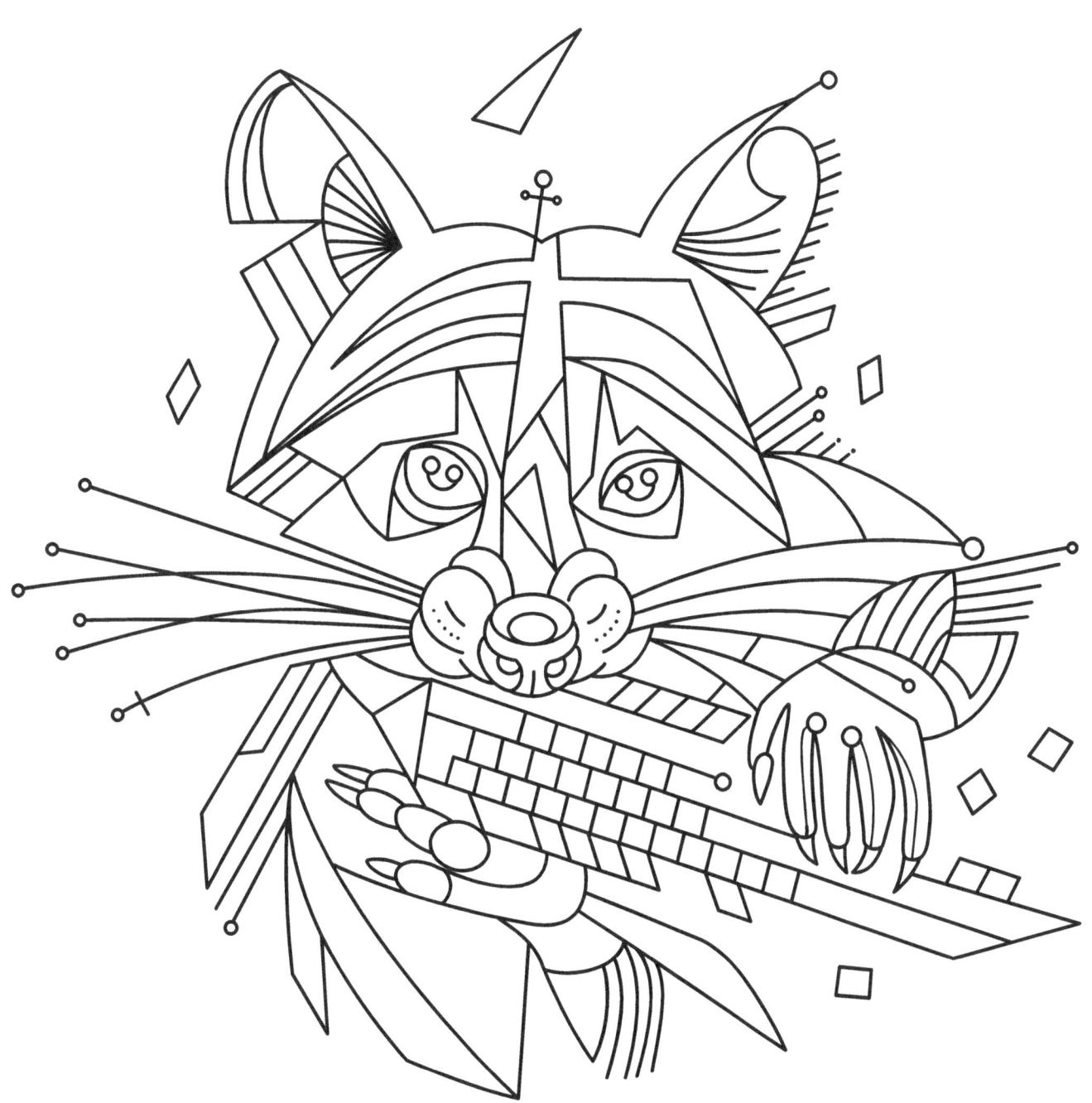

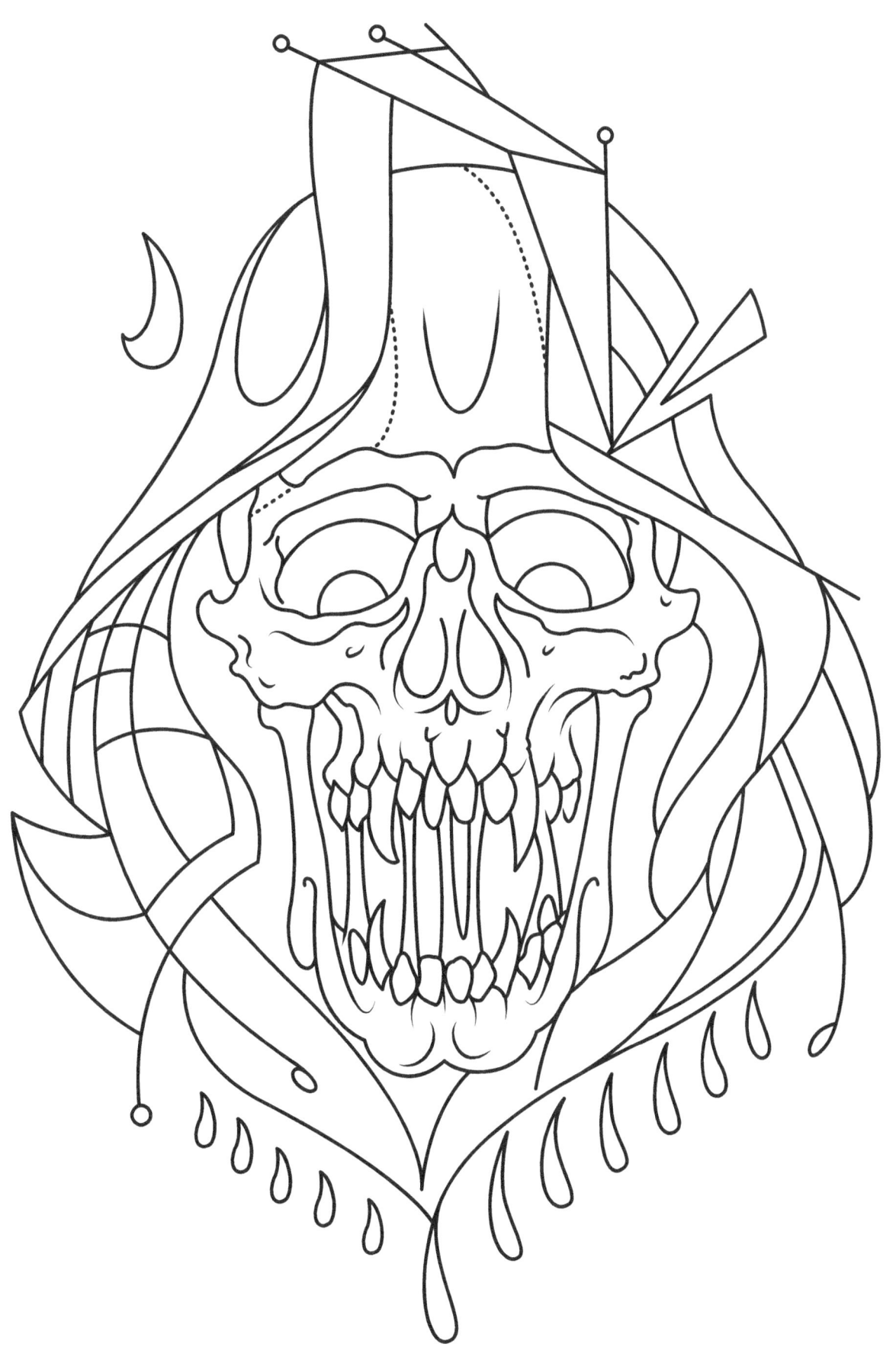

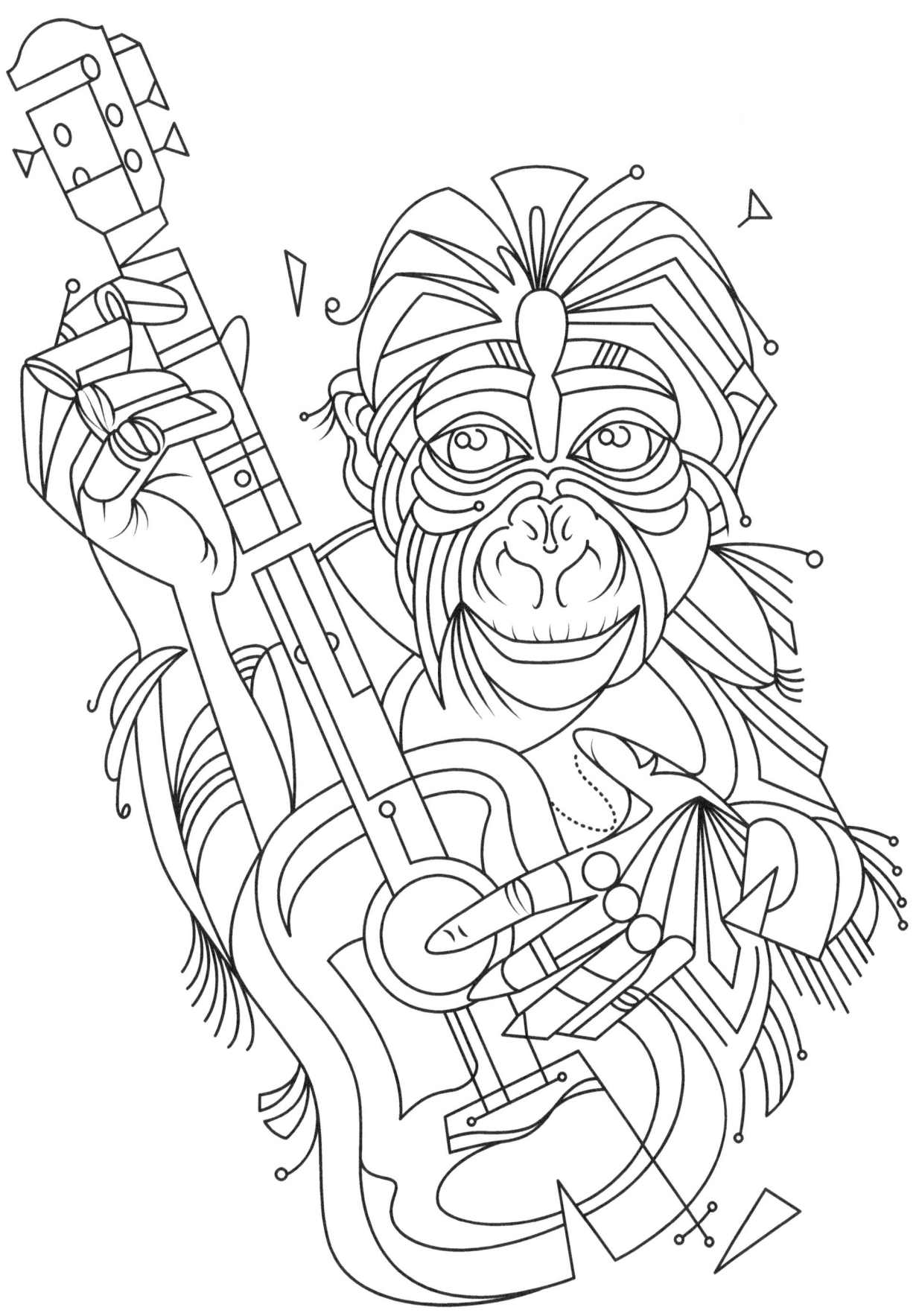

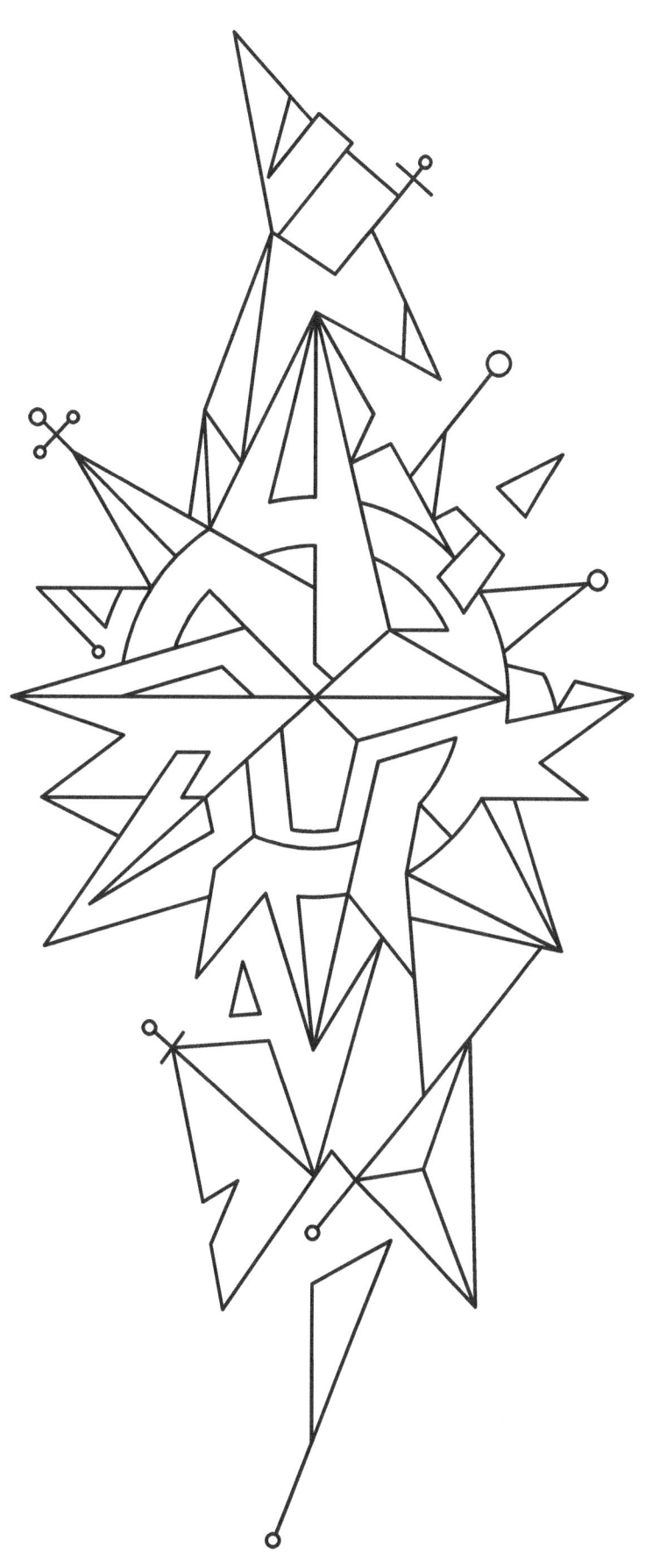

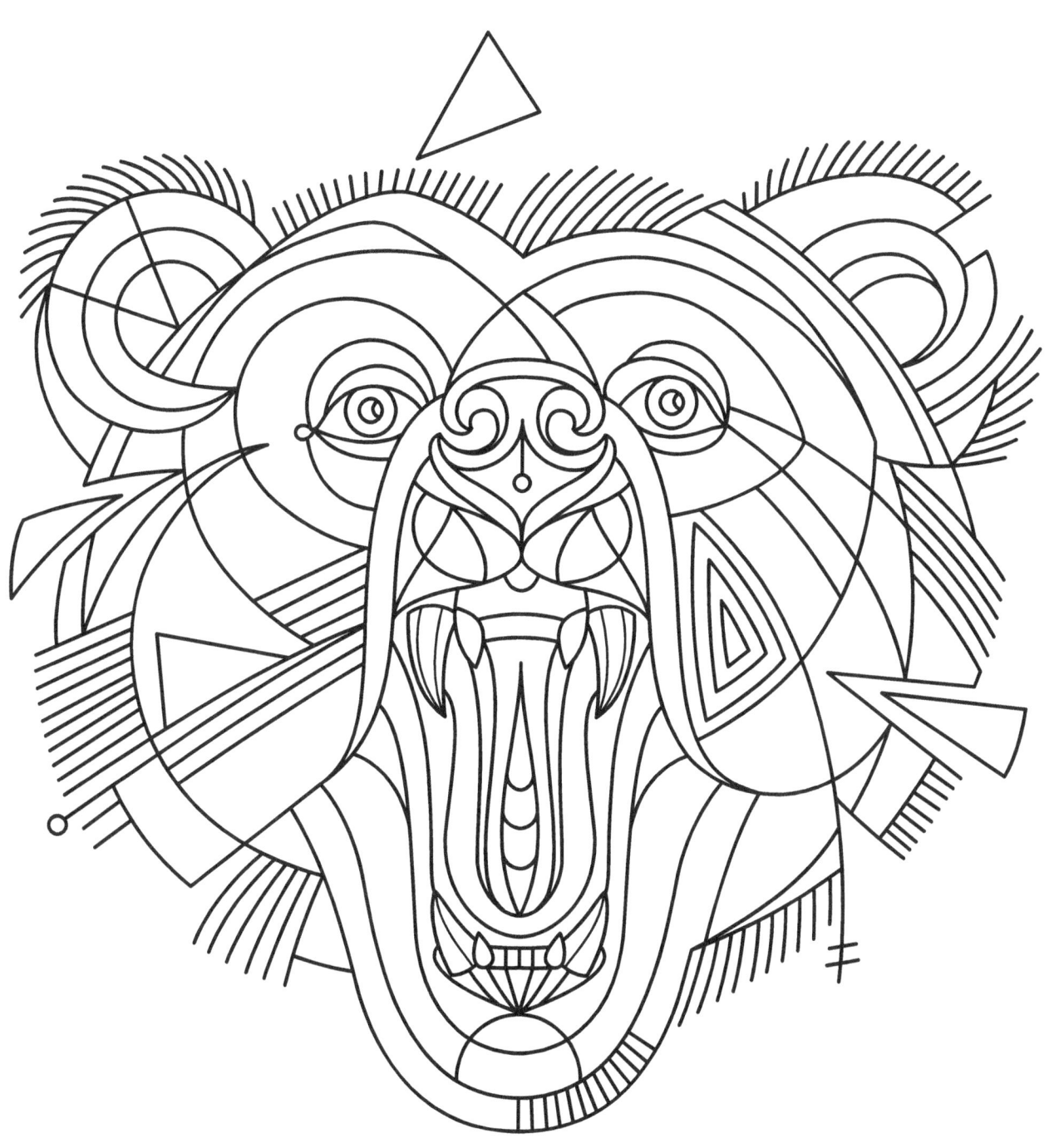

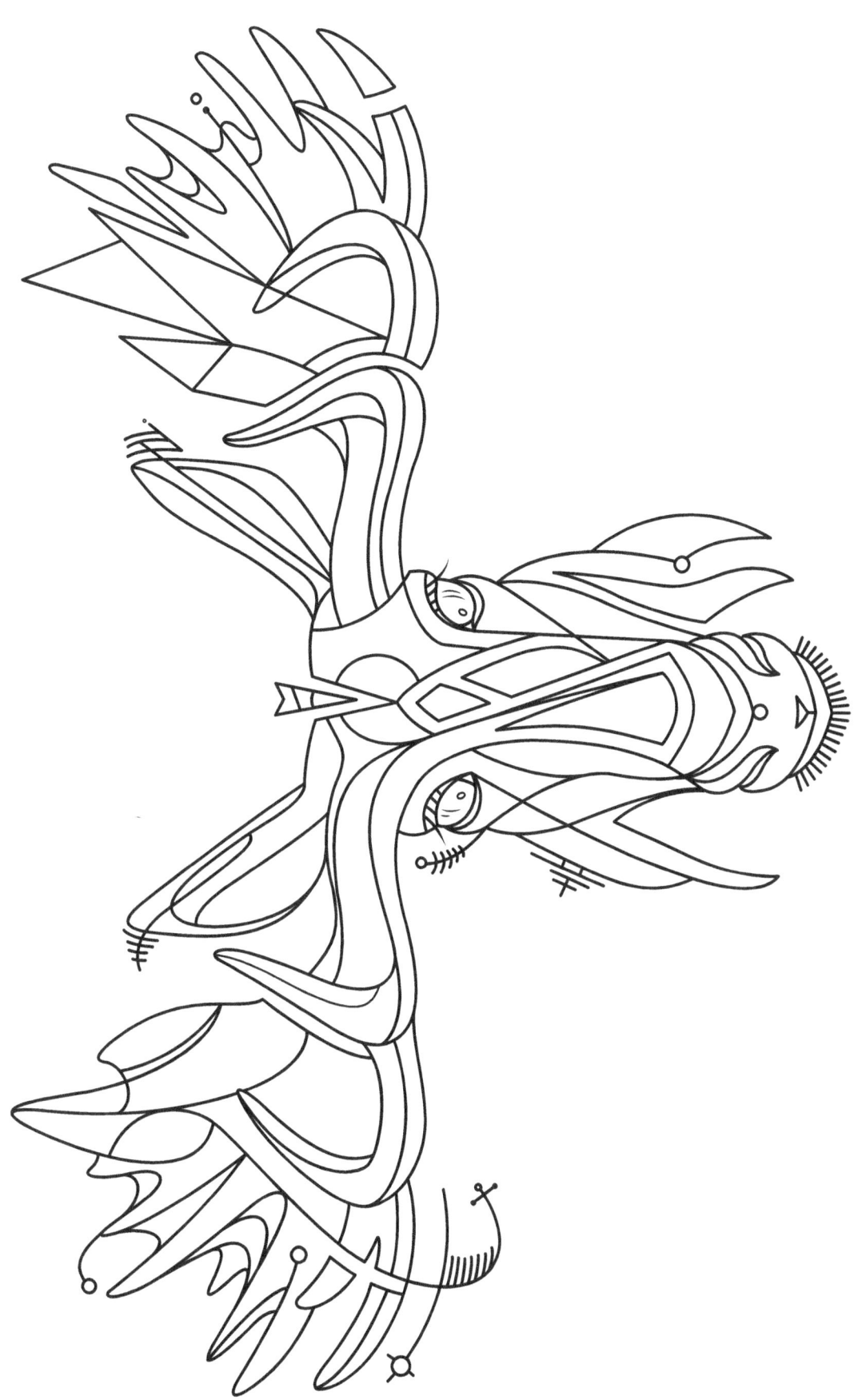

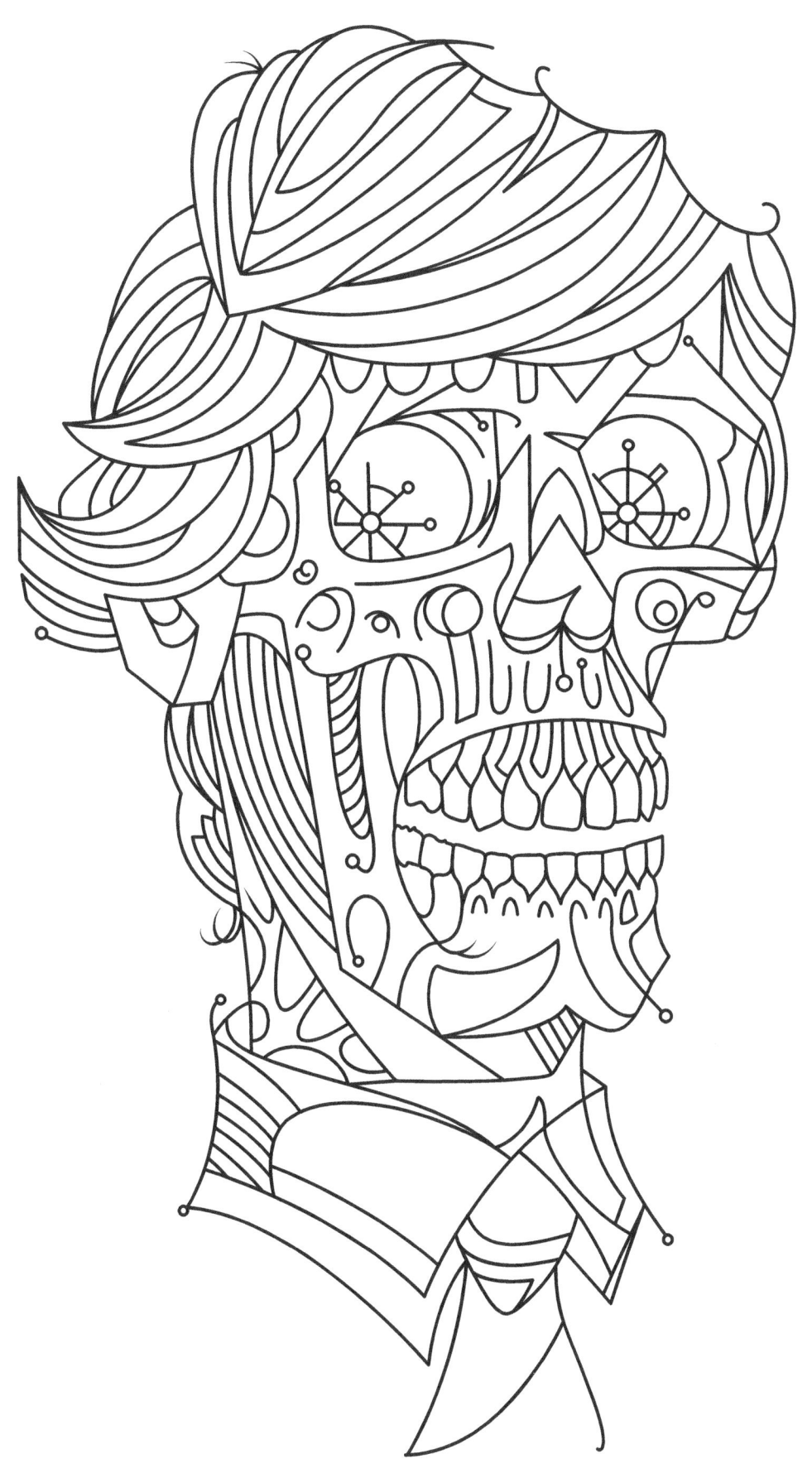

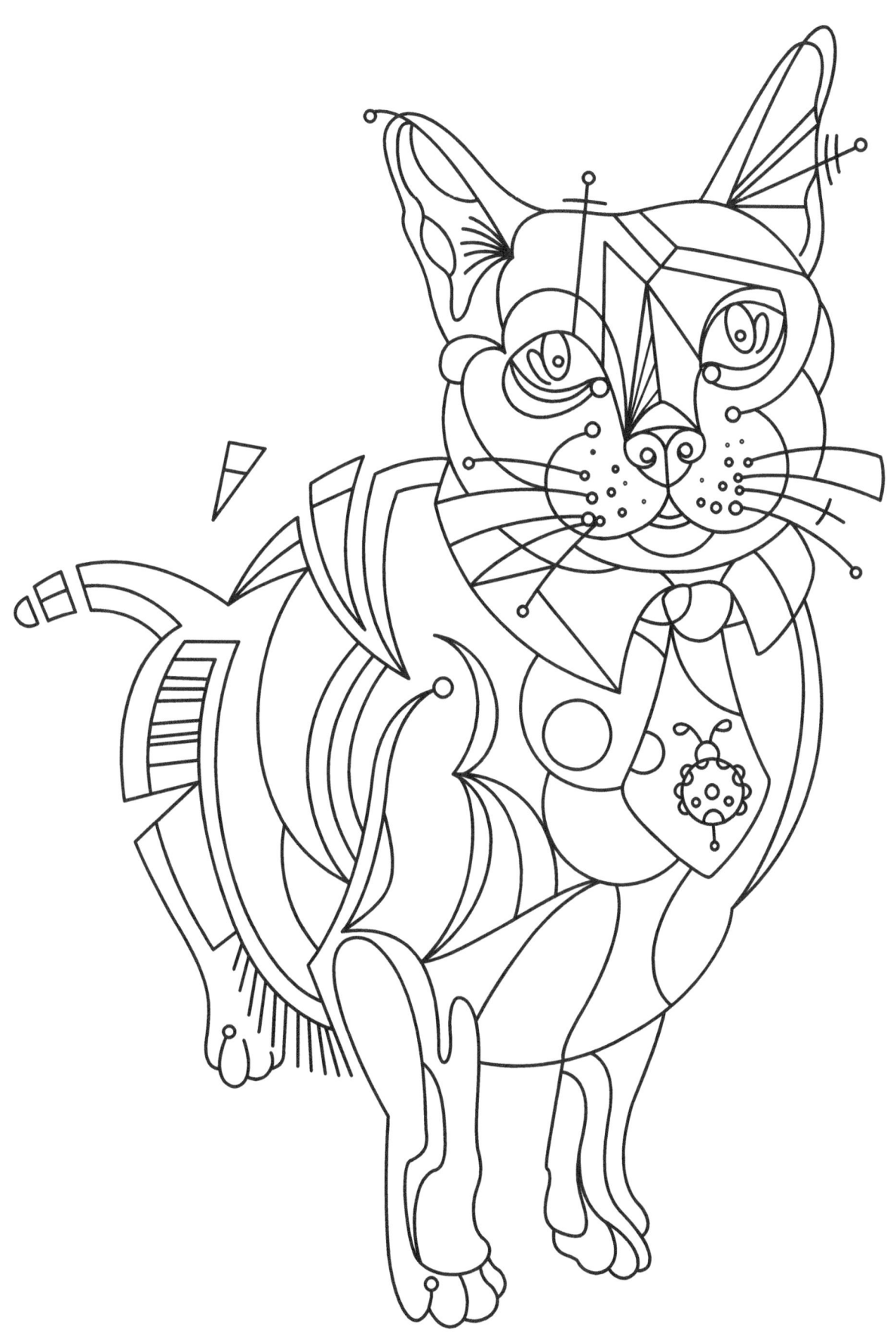

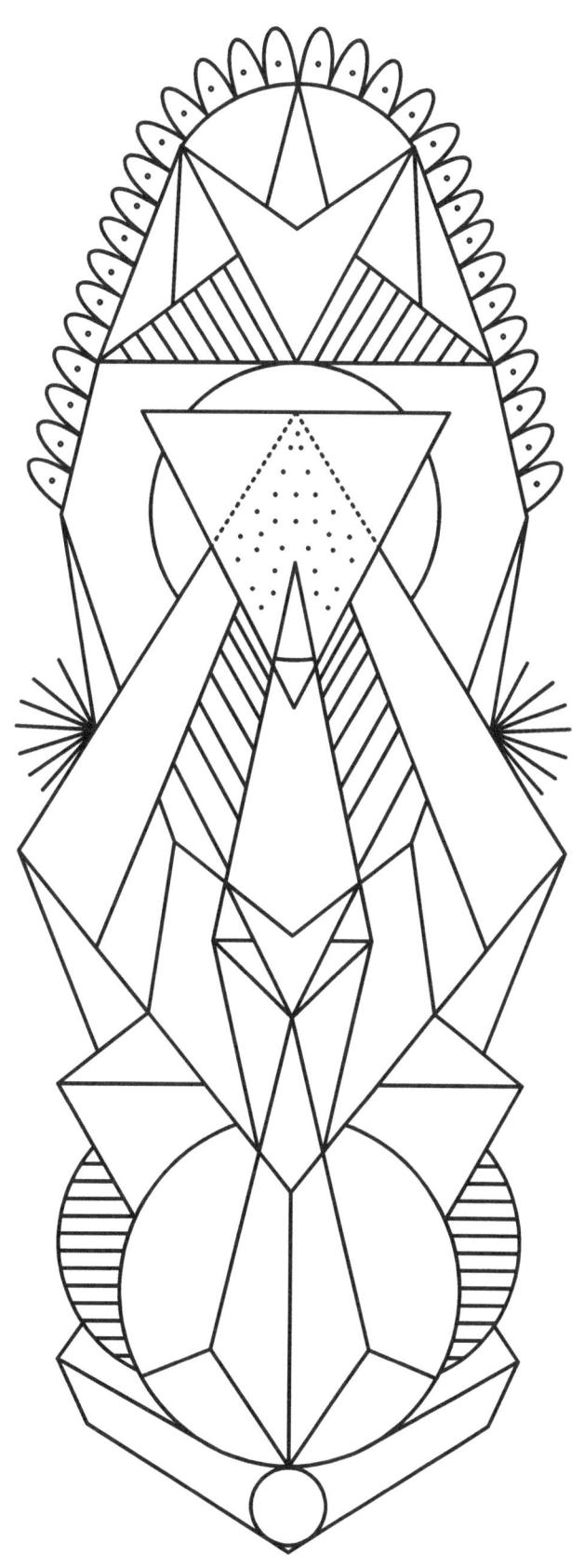

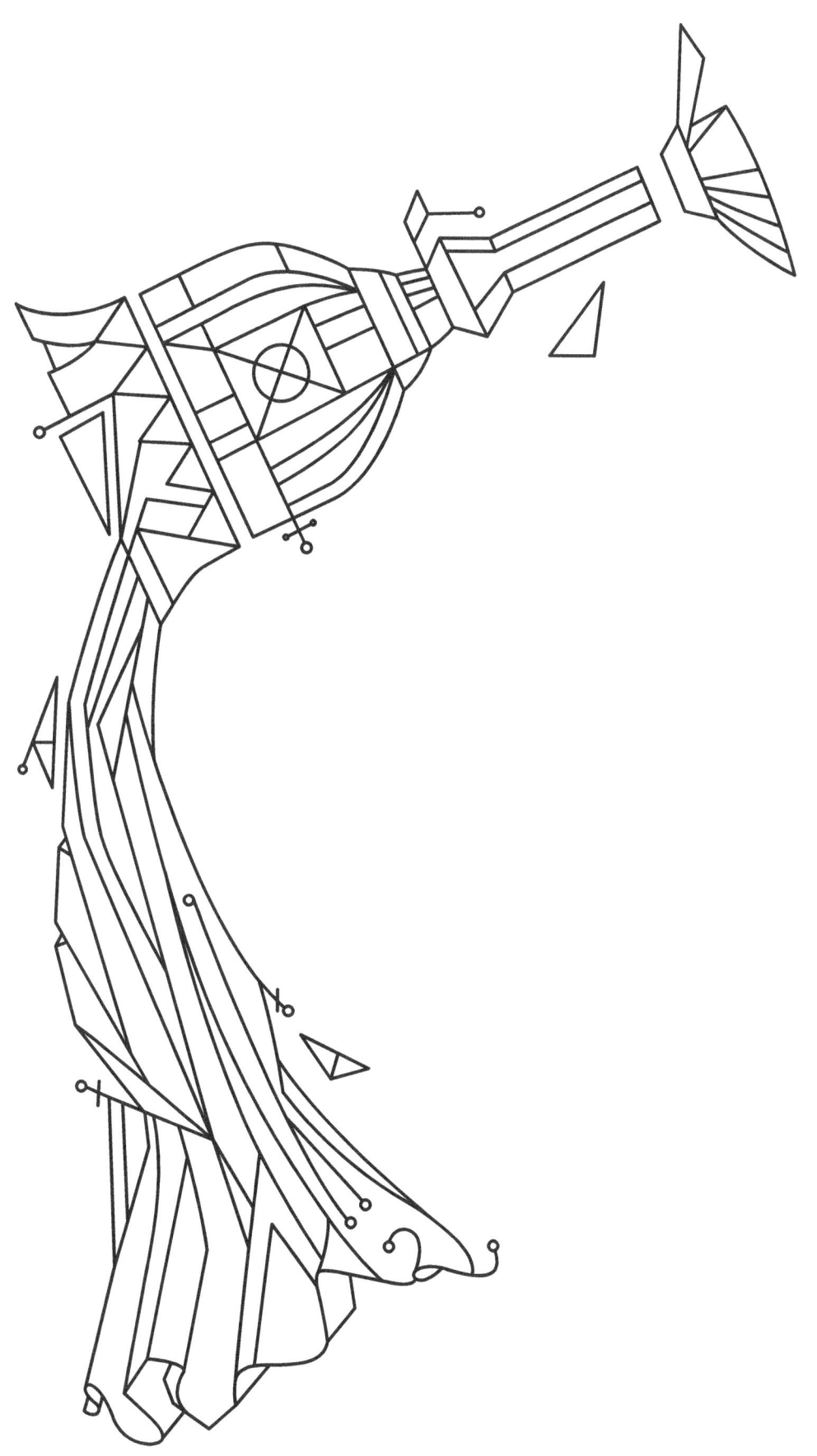

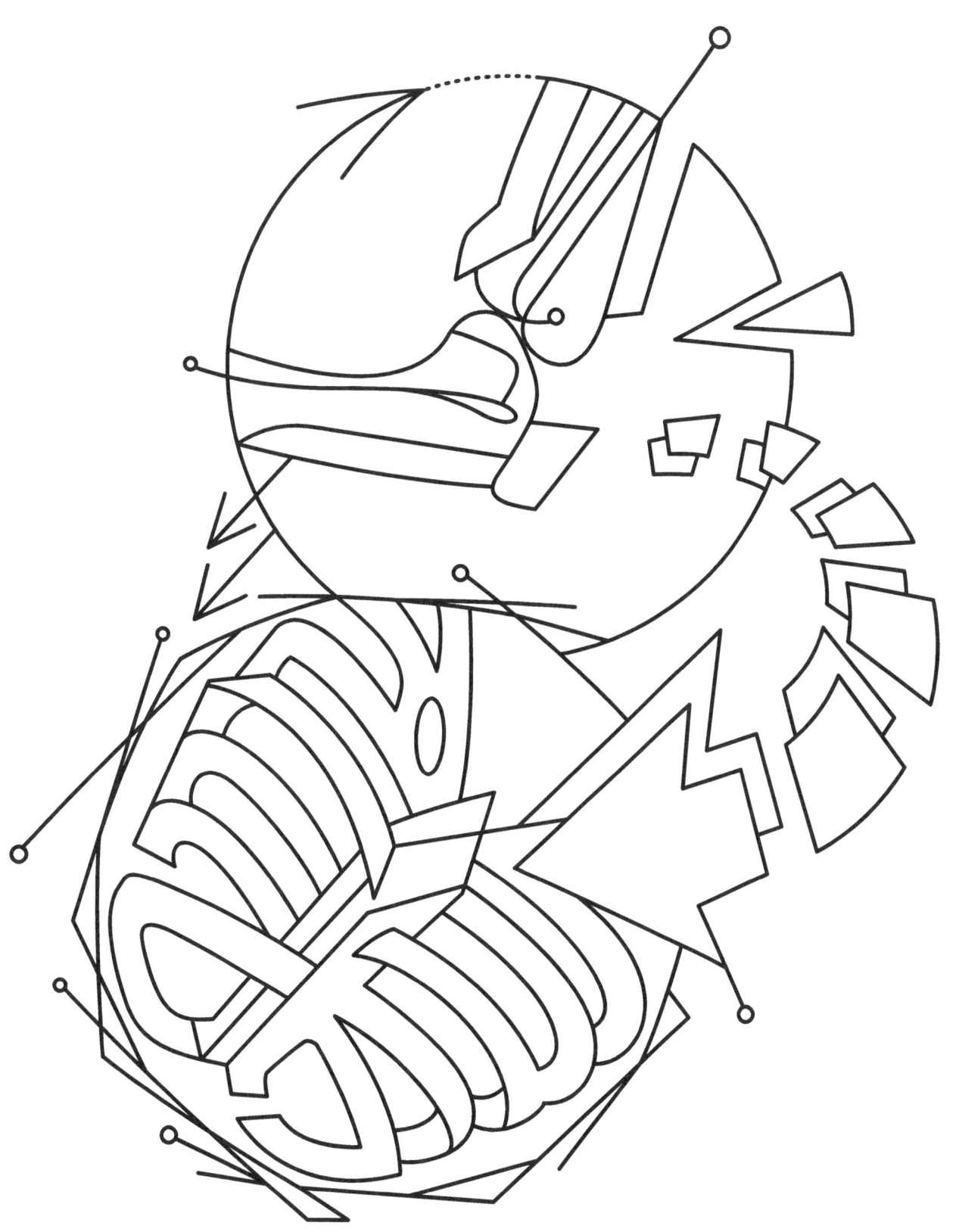

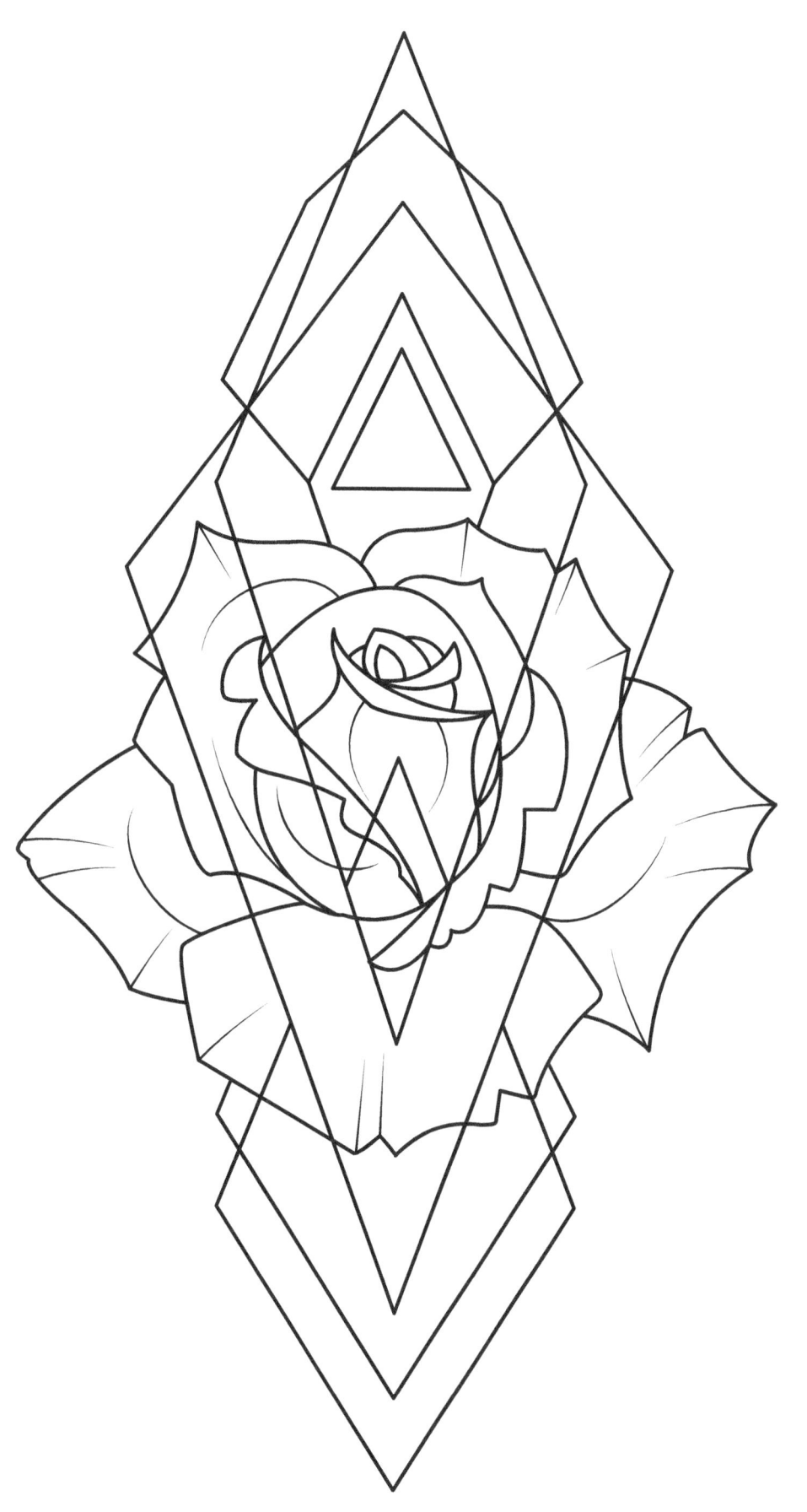

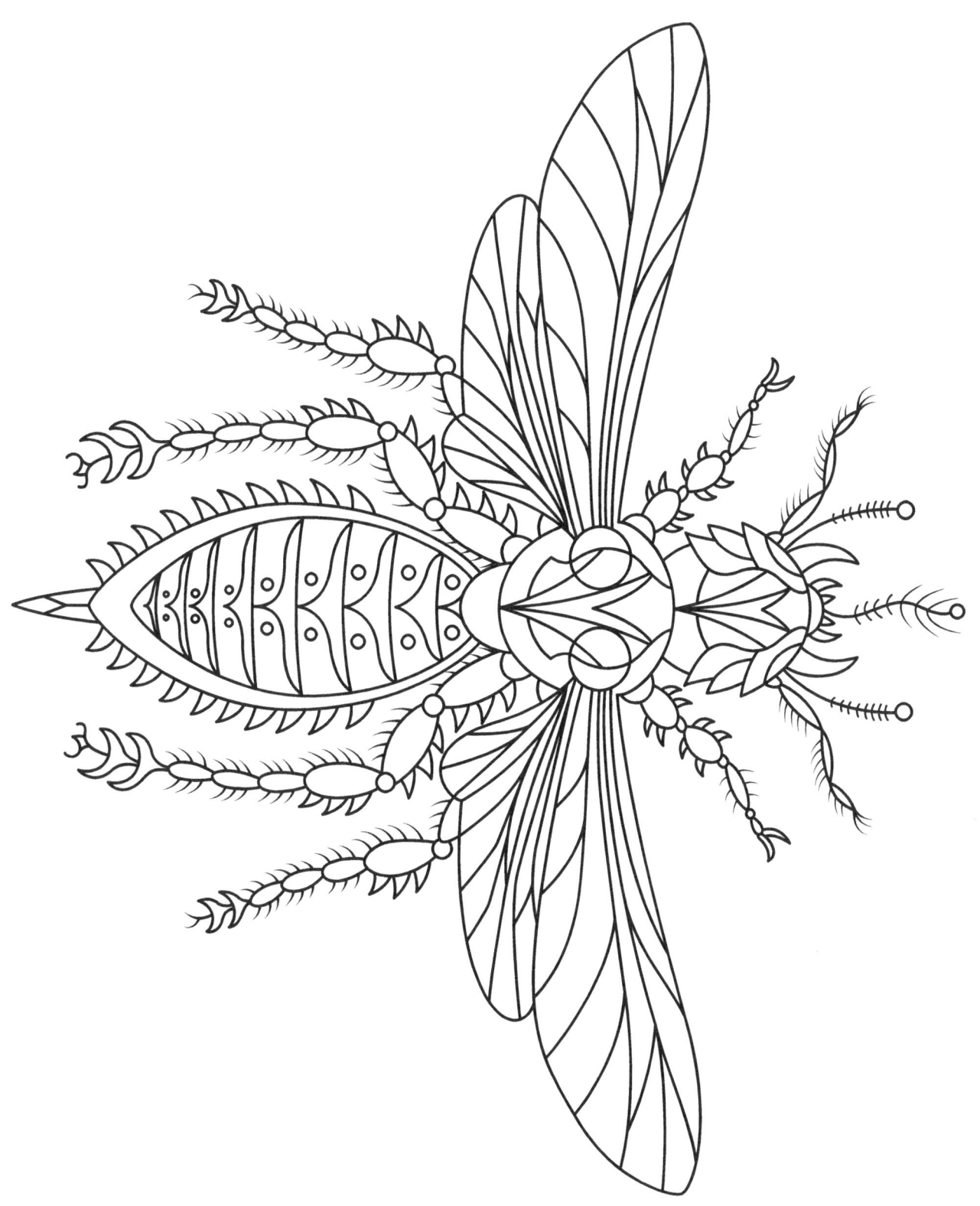

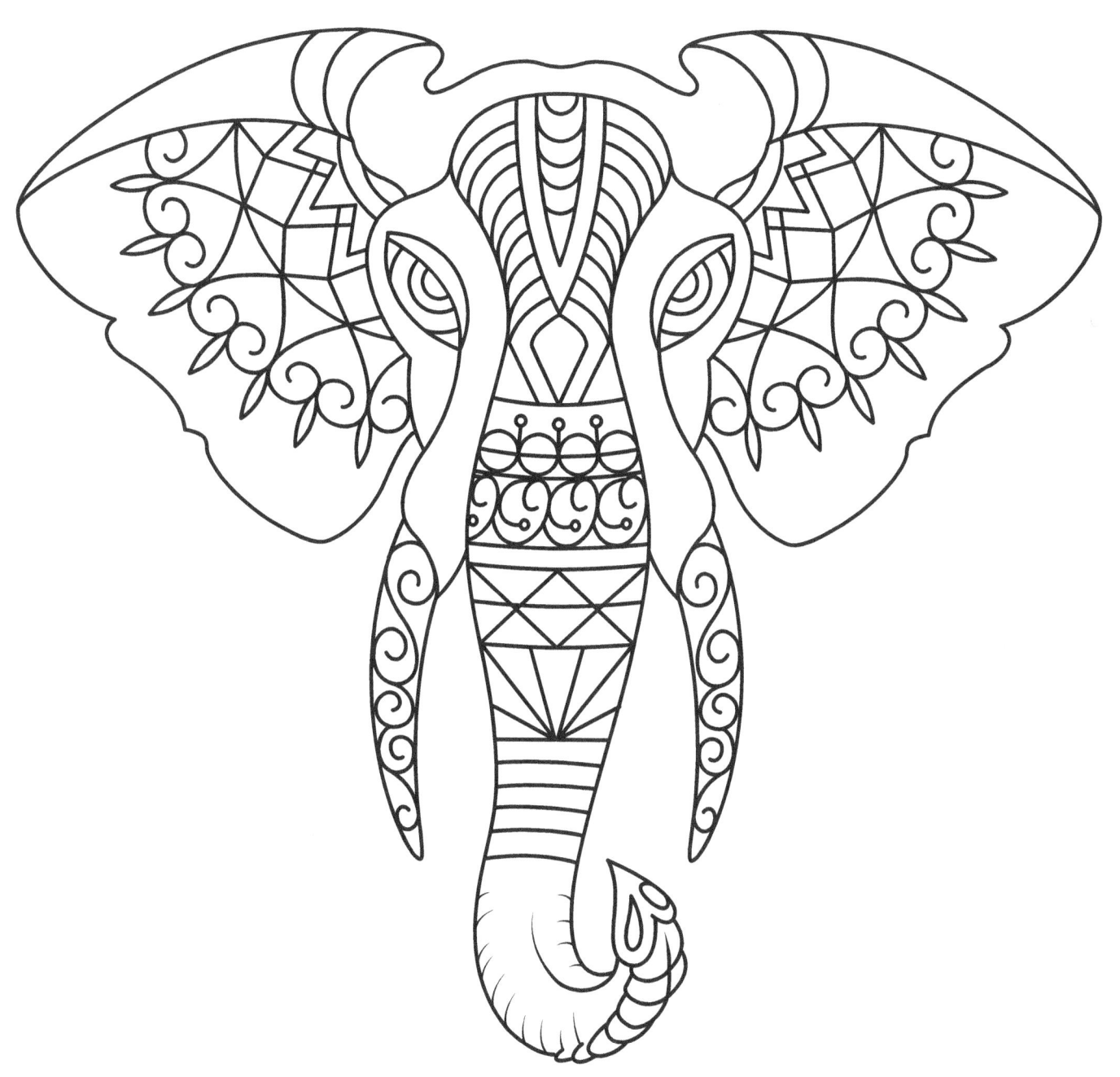

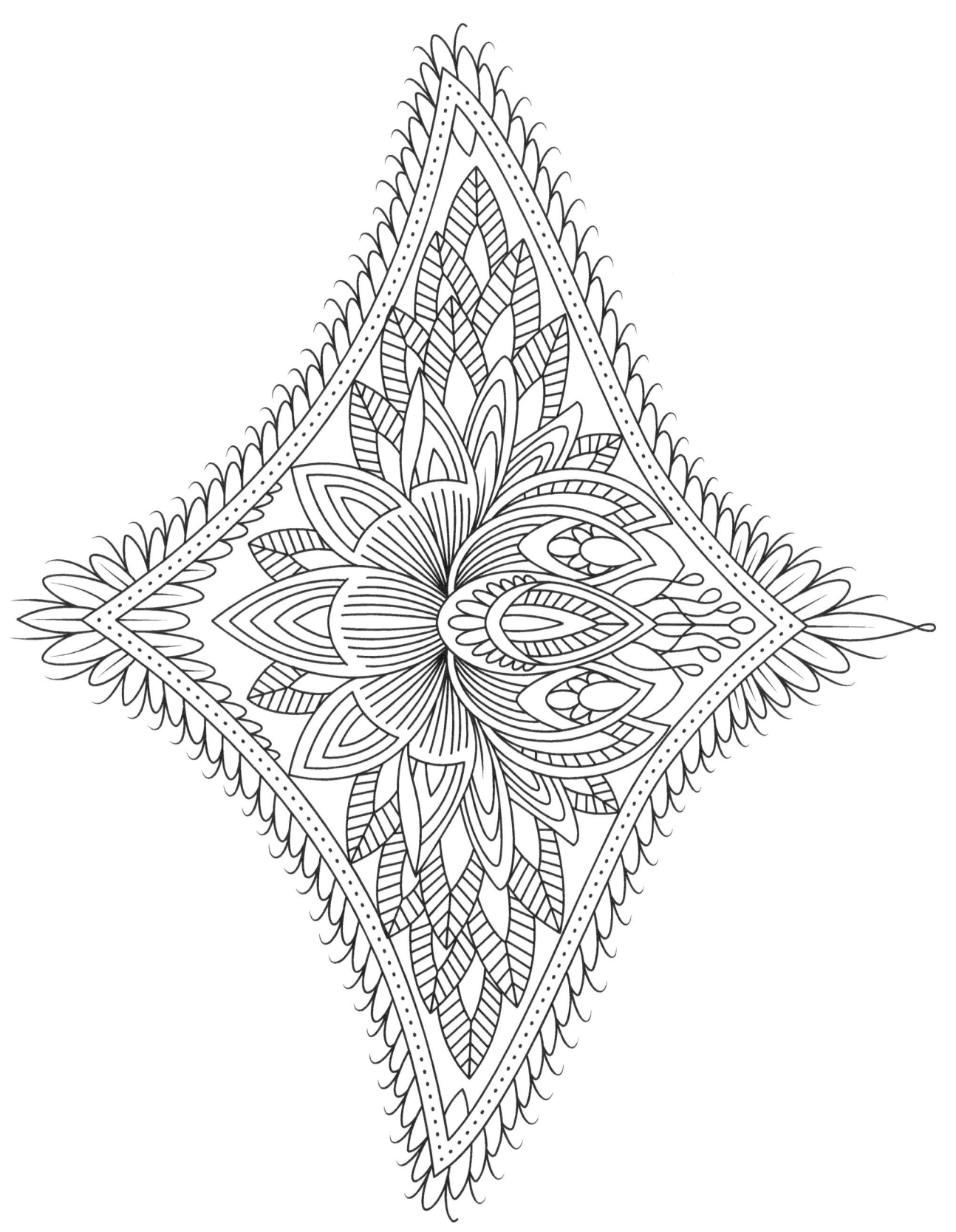

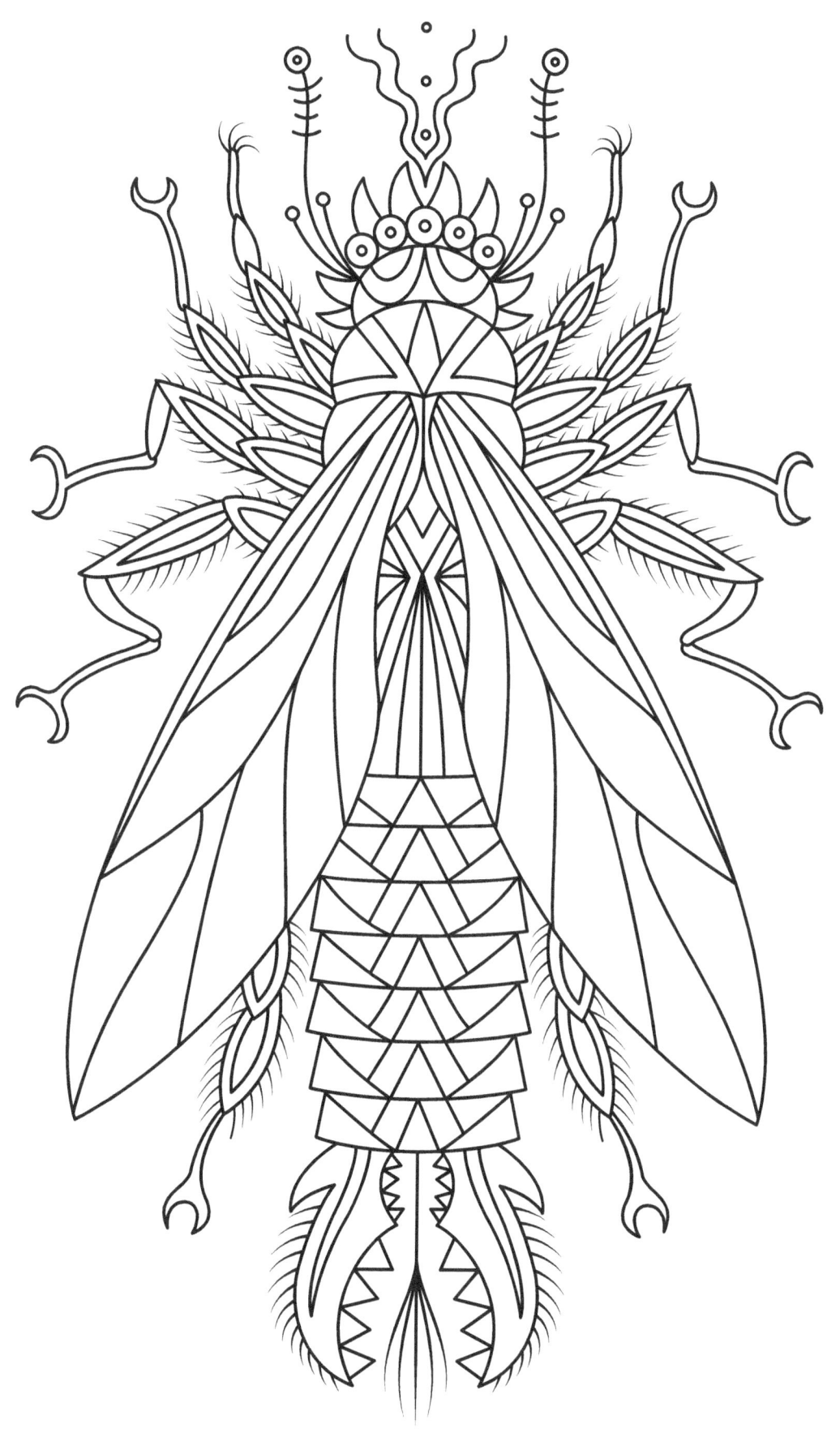

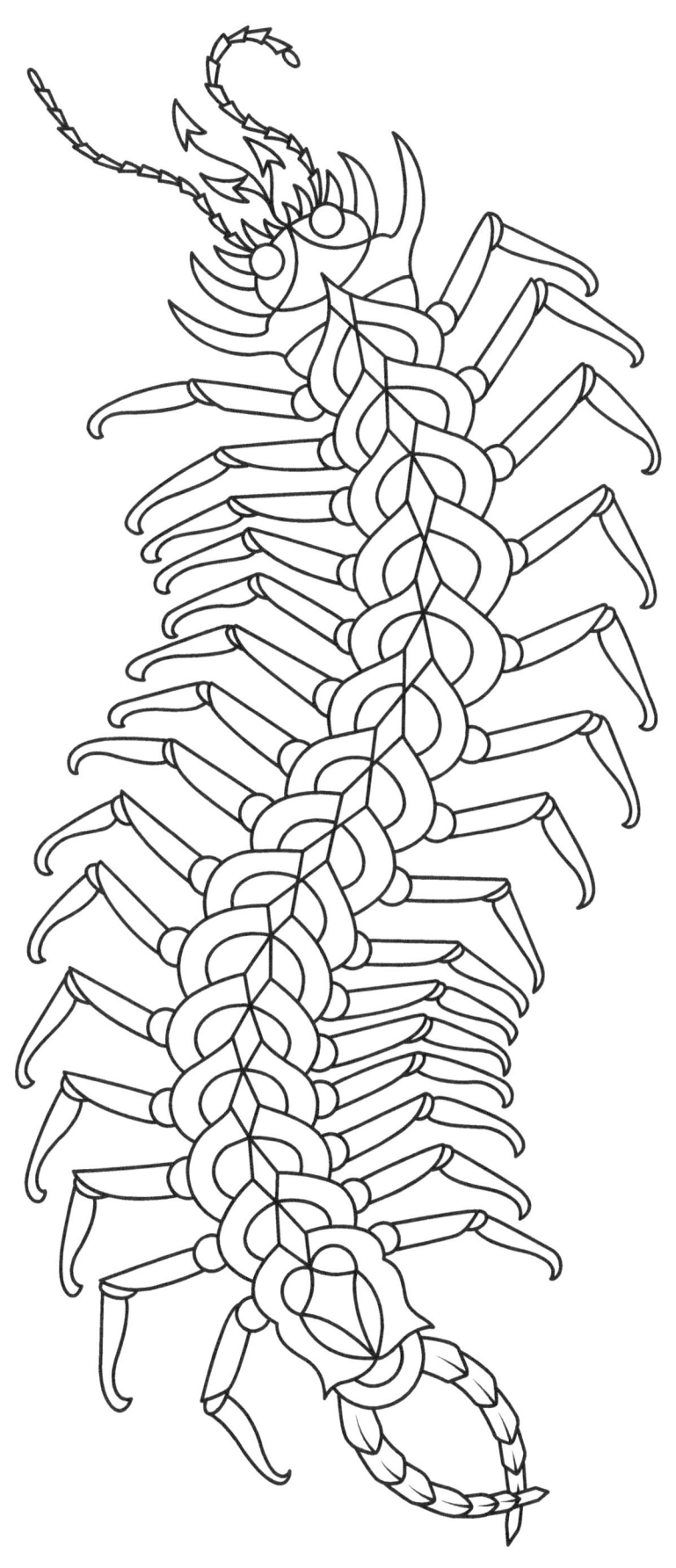

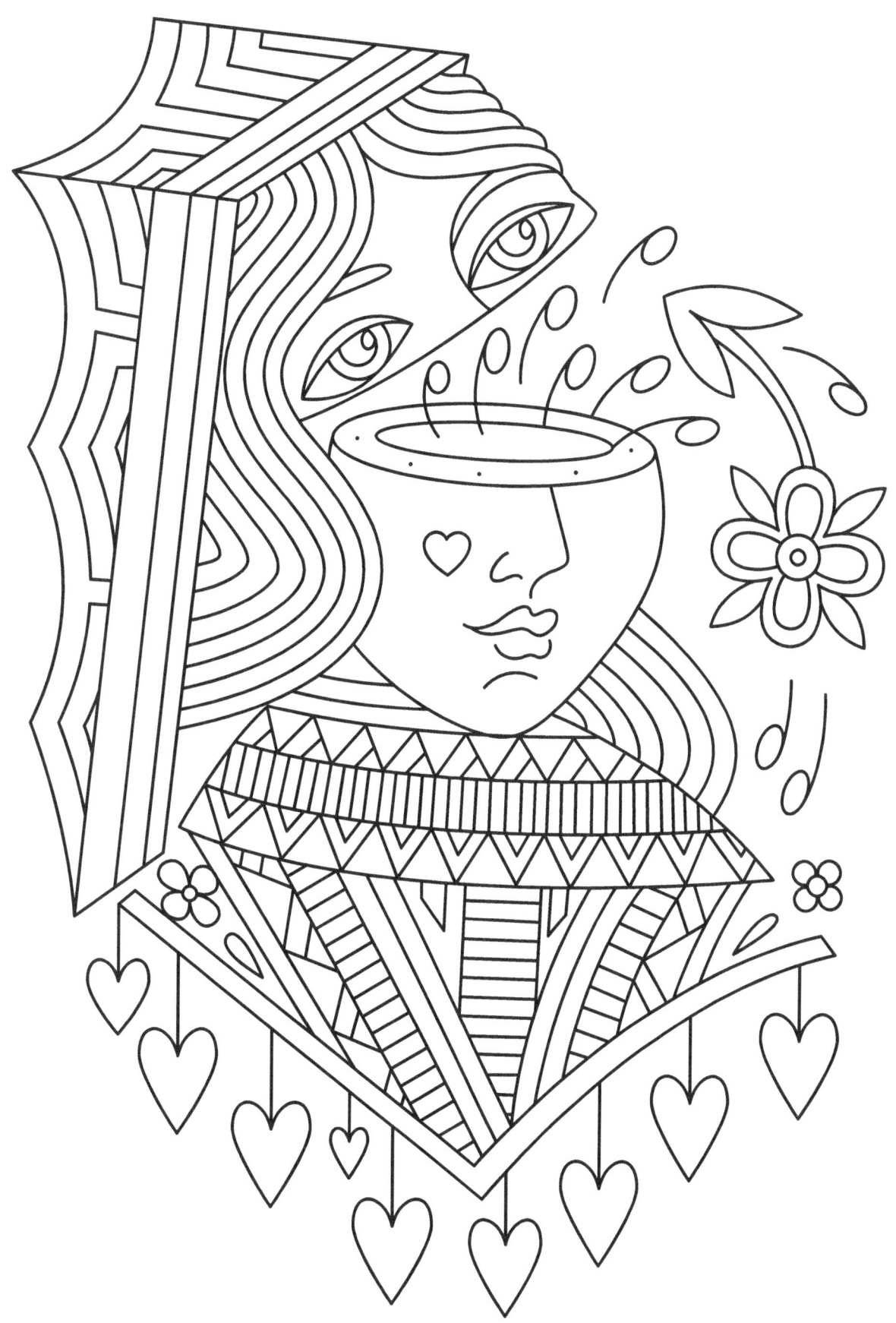

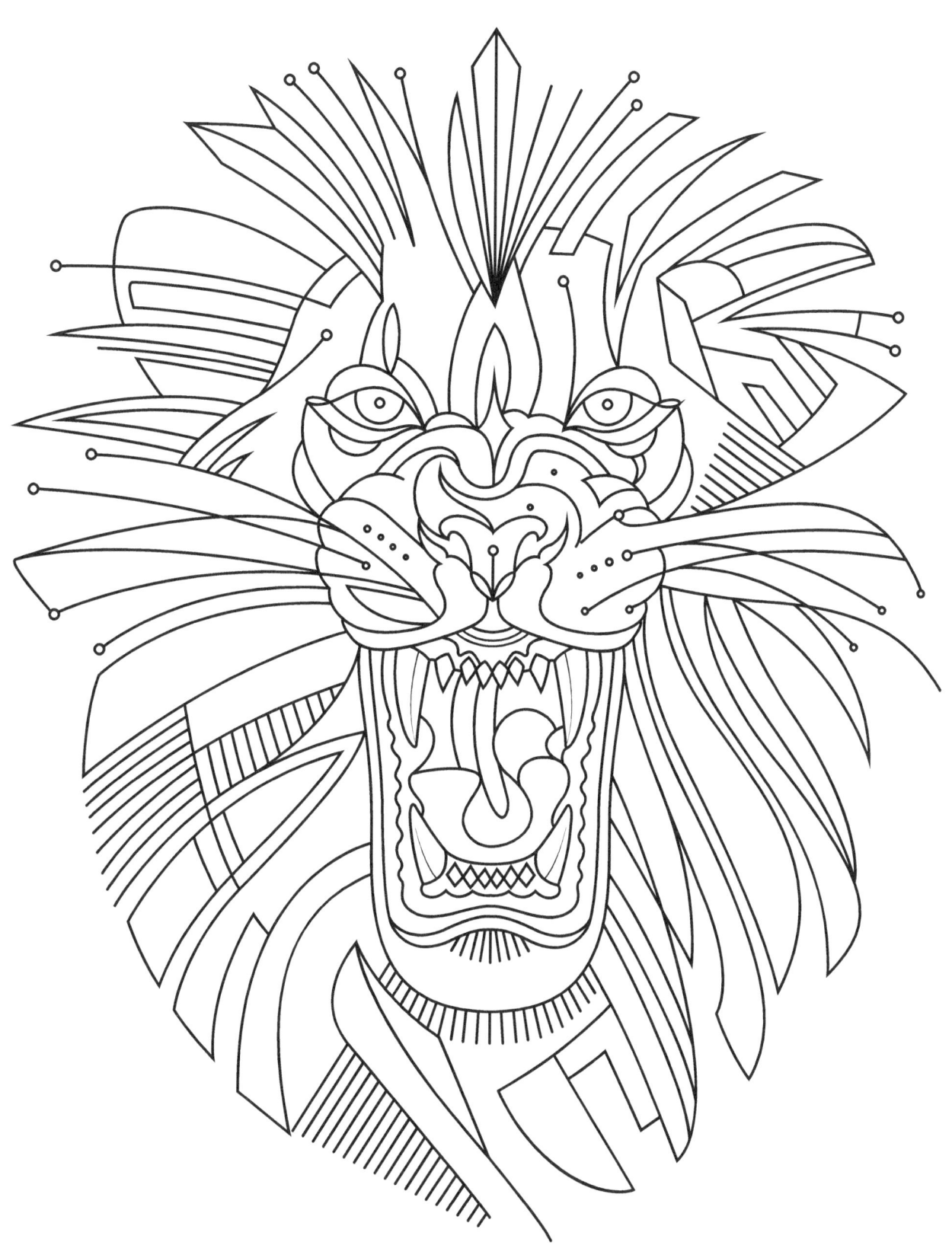

www.ingramcontent.com/pod-product-compliance
Lightning Source LLC
Chambersburg PA
CBHW081017240526
45471CB00017B/3188